How to Be Your Own Bodyguard

SELF DEFENSE FOR MEN AND WOMEN FROM A LIFETIME OF PROTECTING CLIENTS IN HOSTILE ENVIRONMENTS

Nicholas Hughes

Warriors Krav Maga / Lake Norman, North Carolina

Nicholas Hughes/Warriors Krav Maga
105 Parr Dr., Unit C
Huntersville, NC 28078, USA
www.H2BG.com

Publisher's Note: This is a work of fiction. Names, characters, places, and incidents are a product of the author's imagination. Locales and public names are sometimes used for atmospheric purposes. Any resemblance to actual people, living or dead, or to businesses, companies, events, institutions, or locales is completely coincidental.

The information in this book is distributed "as is" and sans warranty. The author shall have no liability with regards to information contained within and nothing in the book constitutes a legal opinion. The author also has no control over, nor assumes any responsibility for websites or other resources referenced within.

While the author believes everything within is accurate, questions regarding specific self-defense situations, legal liability and/or interpretation of federal, state or local laws and ordnance should be addressed by an attorney.

This book has been written for informational purposes only and in no way should be used as a substitute for instruction by competent professionals. The author is providing the reader with the information contained within so they have the knowledge and can choose, at their own risk, to act upon it.

Book Layout © 2016 BookDesignTemplates.com

How To Be Your Own Bodyguard/ Nicholas Hughes. – 2nd ed.
Print Edition ISBN 978-0985856519

To All The Crazy Bastards Throughout History Who Fought For What They Believed In & Lived To Pass Their Knowledge On. Also, To All Of My Instructors & All Of My Students, Wherever They May Be.

While The Will To Survive Is Instinctive,
The Ability Is Learned.

Unknown

Contents

READ THIS FIRST

This book is self-published. I thought long and hard about going the traditional route and seeking out a publisher, but after finding out just how long it would take from writing the manuscript to seeing it on a bookshelf, I decided to do it on my own.

That of course means it hasn't been professionally proof read so please forgive me for any grammatical errors and/or typos. They are absolutely all mine. I know they irk some readers, but I am emboldened by hearing back from someone who attended a speech by the founder of Zappos, who had written a book sans proof reader, who said what's important was the message.

There's also a famous quote by General George S. Patton that states *"A good plan violently executed now, is better than a perfect plan next week."*

I will, however, make you this promise…if I sell a slew of copies I will absolutely hire a proof reader and re-release it with all the necessary corrections. Fair enough?

PS: To all the people, myself included, who've bitched about the typos in electronic books they've downloaded on their Kindles etc., I have noticed in several print versions of books that the typos aren't there, but the typos still appear in the Kindle version. I think it's due to the formatting process when Smashwords is trying (heroically) to take an original document and make it work on all the different electronic platforms out there.

BONUSES

If you'd like to stay up to date on the latest tips and tricks and anything that's relevant consider joining our facebook page under "How To Be Your Own Bodyguard."

This group of likeminded people will be able to stay in touch, contribute and be aware of any training events and so on as they become available as well as getting advanced notice of the new books on hard skills that are in the draft stage at time of writing.

You'll also be able to ask me any questions pertaining to anything you read within.

THE APP

After you've read this book you're going to realize that's an awful lot of information to try and retain. Don't worry, I've got you covered.

Download our app on your I-Phone or Android – it's under How To Be Your Own Bodyguard or I-Bodyguard. Now, all the important stuff is laid out like bullet points in handy checklists. No memorization necessary. How cool is that?

There's both a free version and a professional one. I highly recommend the latter because yes, I make some money, but more importantly it comes with extra stuff and no annoying advertisements.

One advantage of the pro version, for example, is the emergency numbers for every service in every country in the world. (Too many Americans think everywhere you go it's 911. It's not) We'll list the numbers for police, fire and medic as well as tell you whether they speak English or not.

By the way, the pro version costs less than lunch at a fast food restaurant so don't be a cheap bastard.

INTRODUCTION

Professional bodyguards do everything in their power to avoid getting in a situation that would require the use of force or violence to get out of. Hollywood aside, they rarely run road blocks, ram other cars, get in shoot outs, and physically assault bad guys. If they did, they wouldn't be in the business for very long. Their whole job revolves around making their client's trip hassle free by the judicious use of the strategies of avoidance and awareness; awareness of how bad guys operate, the particular threat they're up against, and the best way to avoid both. It is proactive and not reactive by nature.

Most self-defense books and training on the other hand begin, for the most part, with the premise that you're already under attack and this is how you fight your way out. Wouldn't it make more sense to steal a page from the bodyguard's playbook and not get into trouble in the first place? That is what this book is about. Until now that type of training has been largely unavailable for members of the public for obvious reasons...unless they wanted to pay thousands of dollars and go to one of the schools for close personal protection specialists. It's also a lot less exciting than learning how to dispatch bad guys with a couple of simple moves.

As good as the avoidance and awareness skill set is, that doesn't mean for one minute that you can ignore what I call the hard skills; i.e. the techniques of sophisticated violence designed to stop the enemy in his tracks. Any professional bodyguard is going to be trained in unarmed combat, weapons, and high speed offensive and defensive driving for such times as when the avoidance and awareness aren't enough. You are going to learn some of that in this book as well, but if you into practice the soft skills, and MORE IMPORTANTLY, put them into practice on a daily basis, the chances of you ever needing the hard skills will be greatly diminished.

Just so we're all on the same page during the reading of this book, I call the hard skills on their own "self-defense." The broader field that encompasses both the hard skills and the soft skills of avoidance and awareness, home, vehicle, and travel security, i.e. "self-protection." In the former you are actively engaged in defending yourself against an attack, whereas in the latter you are setting up protective measures to try and dissuade the enemy from ever gaining a foothold in the first place.

That's my own description by the way, so don't be surprised if you're talking to someone about self-protection and they assume you mean self-defense. I've always thought the two should be better clarified, otherwise we end up like the business world where so many people assume marketing and advertising are one and the same.

To that end, this book will be divided into three parts. Part one is the preamble which is a slew of knowledge and information that you should be aware of that will help your overall game plan. Part II is what we call "Soft Skills". These are the techniques of avoidance and awareness as used by the pros in the industry. Part III is devoted to a quick look at "Hard Skills," or physical fighting measures that you can use in the event you didn't use your soft skills enough and find yourself stuck in a physical altercation. We'll delve into the hard skills in much more detail in the next book.

Please don't be tempted to skim over the preamble and get into the soft and hard skills portion of the text. Take it from me; there is a load of very important information that you're going to need to be able to process both the soft and the hard skills. I'll also be making references to various bits of information in the preamble that will leave you scratching your head if you haven't read the relevant section.

1

SELF PROTECTION
VERSUS
SELF DEFENSE

For many people the terms self-protection and self-defense are one and the same. Some would argue that it's just semantics, but self-protection, in my view, is a broader term encompassing every aspect of looking after oneself such as personal hygiene, wearing a seat belt when driving, protecting yourself from identity theft, as well as learning to fight for yourself. Self-defense on the other hand is only concerned with the physical techniques of fighting, or, what we in the trade call hard skills.

It never made much sense to me to see guys buying guns and going to the range with the excuse that it was for self-defense when the same guy is 100 pounds overweight, smoking two packets of cigarettes a day and eating a diet of fried food, pizzas and beer. He's going to die from a self-inflicted heart attack or stroke before he ever ends up needing his gun for self-defense. My argument is that if they understood the concept of self-protection as opposed to self-defense they'd make moves to remedy that.

If you learn and master the soft skills, chances are very good that you will never have need of the hard. Soft skills help us deal with the first three steps of the human predator's plan to choose you as a victim, (More on that later), and they even help to some degree to deal with the fourth element. Hard skills on the other hand only deal with the fourth and final step in a criminal's plan of action.

So, what are the soft skills and hard skills exactly? Well, we're going to go into them in some detail later in the book but soft skills deal with lowering your profile; learning what to say, and more importantly, what NOT to say during a potential altercation; tips and tricks of avoidance and awareness; dealing with the legal ramifications of fighting; the psychological effects after a violent incident; understanding criminals and how they think, and so on. Hard skills on the other hand will deal with both armed and unarmed combat.

As an example of self-protection, and avoidance and awareness I'll take you through an actual story from my days as a bodyguard[1] which illustrates the avoidance skills and then I'll take you through a fight in London that illustrates the need for the hard.

Fun In Texas: At the time I was responsible for protecting the members of a famous band during a tour of the United States. On the night in question the crowd got completely out of hand. Unlike the reception we faced in almost every other city in which we'd played, the crowd here, made up largely of itinerant workers from what I could see, thought they'd express their rapture by hurling stuff at the band members. I was in my usual position on the side of the stage where I was the last line of defense. The guys in the pit, hired locals, were supposed to deal with fans being crushed, feinting and any attempts to get on stage to dance or touch the band members. Assuming an overzealous fan got over the pit, through the security and on to the stage, I would then intervene and throw them out to security guards waiting in the wings.

---

[1] The professionals in the industry detest the term "bodyguard". They prefer executive protection specialist or close personal protection specialist. I use the term because more laymen are aware of it and its implications.

With the lights set up the way they were, and shining directly in our faces, it was nearly impossible to see anything coming at us from in the crowd until it was too late. Something eventually got through and hit the lead singer in the head, cutting him above the eye. He immediately left the stage while the other band members, unaware of his plight, continued to play on. Seconds later, another band member got hit and he too left the stage leaving one guitarist, the drummer, and the keyboardist playing on and doing their best to keep the increasingly antsy crowd entertained.

I ran back to see what was going on and found the lead singer bleeding like a stuck pig, the tour manager on the phone trying to rouse our bus driver, and the other band member holding ice to a lump on his head the size of an egg.

The road manager and I made the decision to leave the venue. The lead singer was adamant he wasn't going back out on stage, and given there was a sellout crowd of over 10,000 fans who would, in all likelihood, riot and want their money back once they discovered the headliners weren't going to perform, the decision was a relatively easy one.

The hard part was figuring out a way to get the rest of the band members and roadies out of there without alerting the crowd that we were leaving and getting the bus driver up and present.[2]

Eventually it was decided to have the tour manager drive the bus to the hotel for the driver so he took off to fire it up and get it near the back door while I informed the promoter of our plans. Naturally he wasn't happy, as he knew full well he was about to have upwards of 10,000 angry fans to deal with, and the probability of refunding ticket money. I reminded him that if his security had been any good in the first place, none of this would

---

[2] The bus drivers typically go to a hotel and take sleeping pills to get some uninterrupted sleep before having to drive 500 plus miles through the night to the next town. Our guy Bill had dropped the band off for sound check hours earlier and wasn't due to get up for another 3 hours to include the after show party and subsequent partying.

be happening. Like a lot of promoters looking to save money he'd cut corners by hiring amateurs who were more intent on watching the show than watching the crowd which is what they should have been doing.

I managed to grab the drummer, the base guitarist and keyboard player off the stage and we made it onto the bus and out of there before the place imploded. A cop in the parking lot informed us that the place was about to take a trip to hell in the proverbial hand basket. He said the crowd would be hunting us and advised us not to stop till we hit the next town. En route to the hotel to get our driver I noticed a convoy of police vehicles, sirens and lights blaring, heading at full speed to the venue from whence we'd come. I spent the next couple of hours riding shot gun – literally –making sure no one could identify the band's bus and vent their spleen on us while we got out of Dodge.

London: I hesitate to mention the next story because people – mostly those with no concept of fighting – don't believe it could possibly be true. Having said that I can assure readers that it is, and I'll even mention the name and number of the police constable present who witnessed the entire brawl from start to finish.[3]

On this particular night I was standing outside Camden Town tube station in London with my French girlfriend while waiting for the bus. Normally I'd walk the three miles to home but she was wearing four inch heels and walking that distance, in those, wasn't going to be comfortable.

While waiting for the bus, two scruffy looking sods came weaving down the road tipping over trash cans and rummaging through dumpsters etc., clearly looking for something. Eventually they found an old broom handle which they tried to insert in the hasp of a padlock that was affixed to a door of a nearby building. While one worked on the lock (and kept

---

[3] The officer in question was one Constable Ridley and his Metropolitan badge number was #666. His nickname, he told me later at the station, was "The Beast" due to his unusual badge number and small stature. At the time, he worked out of the Kentish Town Police Station.

watching his wooden piece of dowel splinter to the obviously stronger metal of the lock hasp) his colleague was launching kicks at the door.

For readers who aren't familiar with the vagaries of UK law there is a term called "squatter's rights". What that means is that if you happen upon an unoccupied dwelling and move in, it now becomes yours. It doesn't matter if the real owners have only gone out to a restaurant for the night, or to the beach for a vacation, you now own the property until such times as the case can be brought to court and heard. What typically happens at that point is that the "squatters", about to lose their ever so humble abode, will destroy the place and vandalize everything they can lay their hands on before moving on to another dwelling.

The law in question says that you can't break in to achieve your aim which is supposed to protect the legitimate owner who would have locked up before leaving. However, if you can't prove they broke in, all the squatter must do is claim the door was wide open when he happened upon it.

Our clowns at the bus stop were obviously looking for a squat and hoping, by breaking in to the building, they'd find digs for the night. Given that it wasn't my business and that I had my girlfriend in tow, I decided not to become involved other than letting the police know at my earliest possible convenience. (Awareness and Avoidance at this point) Another chap at the bus stop, an older guy, had different plans though and asked them what in hell they thought they were doing.

They replied, as thugs often do, by telling him to *"shut the fuck up"* and began moving towards him with fists raised and threats of violence. I stepped in at this point and said something along the lines of *"if you bother him, you'll also bother me."* They then re-directed their attention towards me and began closing in. One was reaching for something in his pocket as he got close, so in keeping with the principle of "attack is always the best defense", I shoved him backwards. His mate moved in at speed now and drew his hand back to punch me so I dropped him with a hook punch to the jaw, knocking him out as I did so.

5

His mate started ranting that I was going to come undone because he was coming back with all his mates. Anyone who has done security will tell you the really bad guys never forewarn you they're coming and that they'd rather turn up unannounced and just drill you from behind. I'd heard literally thousands of such threats over the years as a bouncer that never panned out so I wasn't overly concerned. I began explaining this to my girlfriend when she pointed down the road to the tube's entrance from where a horde of ne'er do wells was approaching. She asked me if that was an example of them not coming back as threatened and I could only shake my head at one of the rare exceptions to the rule.

Running away, as some so-called experts advocate, wasn't an option here. My girlfriend had on a tight skirt, four inch heels, and was toting bags from shopping. We had no idea if, given the time for her to toss her shoes and the shopping, we'd be faster than them which could have meant fighting them while exhausted from our failed efforts to run. Finally, where were we going to run to? Home was three miles away and any attempt to duck down a side street could have put us in a blind alley with nowhere to go.

Realizing that avoidance wasn't an option I ordered my girlfriend to move away from me, and told her, if asked by them, to say she had nothing to do with me. This group was clearly the sort who would have no qualms about bashing and/or sexually assaulting a girl during the melee, so I moved out into the middle of the street to lure them away from the people at the bus stop.

I honestly thought at the time, seeing the numbers, (Constable Ridley would later say he counted twenty-one whereas my initial guess to him at statement time was eighteen) and, noting they were armed with bottles and lumps of wood, that I was about to perform my swan song and exit the planet. I knew, given my line of work, i.e. bouncing, bodyguarding, and being in the military at the sharp end, that such a demise was always possible and remembered thinking this was it. There's a lot of truth to the old saying *"He who lives by the sword, dies by the sword."*

I didn't waste time with the old advice about challenging the leader to a one on one fight man to man. Whoever wrote that nonsense all those years ago has clearly never been in a fight with multiple opponents who hunt in packs. If they had any honor, which is what you're supposed to be using as leverage against them, by challenging them to a man to man duel in front of their followers, they wouldn't be out in a pack to begin with. (And I found out later this group of yobs had been "politely" mugging young girls in the tube station forecourt only moments before, which is why the police constable was down there in the first place.)

The fight began and I can still remember snippets of it. I dropped the closest one first who was holding a weapon figuring I'd take at least one of them with me. He'd drawn a lump of 2x4 back behind his head to swing when I hit him with a dropping elbow strike through his cheekbone. (Later at the station, while I was giving a statement, I found out from the doctor summonsed to check on the injured criminals that this guy had a fractured cheekbone, broken nose, broken teeth, broken jaw, and concussion from my elbow shot). The rest bum rushed me and I remember looping my hands into one's pile of dread locks and reefing knees into the miscreant's head till he eventually fell away and I was left holding two bits of his scalp with dreads still attached. The others were actually getting in each other's way given there were so many of them, which is often the case in uncoordinated gang assaults, and I was able to hit bad guys at will. They, on the other hand, had to be careful where they were swinging because, if I ducked, there was a very real possibility they'd hit their mates.

The fight raged on for about three minutes in total. I remember kicking one in the side of the head (he was standing at the time and swinging a bottle at me) right as an old woman drove through our midst who yelled out *"why don't you leave him alone you big bully."* Funny stuff. I dropped another one who was screaming at his girlfriend to finish her bottle of booze so he could use the bottle on me and that was when the sirens could be heard and the remainder fled.

By the time the police arrived there were three that needed ambulance transport, about eight in various stages of unconsciousness and the

7

walking wounded had fled into the tube station leaving a blood trail which we attempted to follow. Unfortunately, that particular station has multiple lines running through it and the police dogs with us couldn't go down the escalators as the pads on their feet would get stuck. We had to use the spiral staircase instead to get to the bottom. By the time we got down there they had jumped one of the plethora of trains running through Camden and disappeared.

At that point I finally got a chance to talk to the constable who'd witnessed the entire event. He had been called following complaints from women tube travelers who'd been "mugged" by the gang. What they did, to avoid making it look like an act of violence, would be to stand in a large group around a lone female and ask for a hand out and intimidate the victim into handing over some money. The women would usually comply rather than risk enraging the group and the constable explained later it was referred to as a "polite mugging."

The constable was doing what he'd been trained to do i.e. be a good witness until back up could arrive when he saw their mass exodus and followed them out to watch the fight. He apologized to me later for not stepping in to help but explained that standard operating procedure was for a lone officer to not enter a gang fray as more often than not both sides would unite against the common enemy. I told him I understood perfectly and was just glad that he'd witnessed it as I didn't want to be the one receiving the assault charge.

During our conversation, the businessman from the bus stop turned up and told the constable that I had been the victim and Ridley again explained that he'd seen the entire thing.

My girlfriend and I were transported to the Kentish Town police station to give statements and were plied with cups of tea and biscuits while doing so. This is when we discovered the police were having a hard time coming up with something to charge them with as I didn't have any injuries apart from a bruise on one leg from a 2x4 falling on it. They were trying for affray but didn't think they could make it stick. (In a follow up months later I found out they charged them with common assault which is not a felony. They had given false names because in the UK one isn't required to carry photo ID. So, in effect, apart from the beating they got at my hands, they got off scot free.

In the first incident, physically fighting more than ten thousand people, and thus endangering my charges, was out of the question. The soft skills of avoidance and awareness were key here and that is what I put into practice. In the second instance, a clear-cut example of self-defense, I fought my way clear. Also, note that I wouldn't have survived either incident without the type of training and techniques you're going to learn in this book. (Do keep in mind that this book is primarily devoted to the soft skills, and while I'll go over some of the hard skills very briefly, they will be addressed in far more detail in the series of Warrior Krav Maga books to follow soon.)

2

STUFF YOU NEED TO KNOW

R ight. Let's tackle this first because it's a bunch of information that's technically not soft skills per se but it is stuff you need to know and it will help you immensely when it comes to learning and understanding the field of human combat. If we just charge on ahead with a collection of both soft skills and hard, I will have failed miserably in preparing you for fighting off human predators. This is one of the reasons the average black belt will lose to the average street fighter. At the risk of generalizing, simply put, the average martial artist learns a collection of techniques pertaining to his respective art. The fact that he knows them, the fact that he's mastered them, in no way prepares him to use them in a real fight.

To make matters worse they take those techniques and they spend years and years polishing them but don't use them the way they were intended. Imagine buying a box of tools and all day long all you do is take them out, clean them, sharpen them, polish them and put them away without ever building anything with them. Welcome to the world of most traditional martial arts schools.

Read on then and learn some of the stuff that will massively increase your understanding of the field of human conflict as it pertains to self-defense.

3

TACTICS, TECHNIQUES AND MINDSET

A nyone who's been in the martial arts for very long will tell you that it seems that a new martial art arrives on scene every couple of years and becomes the talk of the town. We began with Judo, and every movie had a "Tomoe Nage" or sacrifice throw (the one where the good guy falls on his back, puts his foot in the bad guy's belly and flips him over the top) or a "Judo" chop. Bruce Lee burst on to the screen next and put Kung Fu on the map. After that came Karate, then the Hapkido of Billy Jack. Things quieted down for a while then Tae Kwan Do took the US by storm. Ninjutsu came next with a spate of movies, courses, and books. After that it was Steven Seagal and his own unique blend of Aikido, then it was Brazilian Jujutsu, the Israeli martial art of Krav Maga and finally, mixed martial arts where we find ourselves today.

The question that intrigued me was why people seemed to flit from system to system instead of staying where they were? It would seem they weren't finding the answers to their questions in their respective styles. I talked with hundreds of them and a lot still didn't seem confident that they could prevail in the street which is a challenge that should be addressed by any competent school.

As I thought more about it I realized I needed to discover what was missing. I boiled down winning a fight to three essential ingredients. You must have techniques, you must have tactics and you must have the correct mindset. (And in warfare you typically must have equipment).

The story I use to illustrate the difference between the three elements is the following; imagine police officers being summonsed to an armed robbery in progress. The first officer on scene is a good technician – which means in this instance he's a good shot – this guy can shoot the proverbial fly off the pig's back at 400 yards in the dark. Arriving on scene he exits his police cruiser and is immediately gunned down because he decided to stand in the middle of the parking lot without cover.

The 2nd officer, also a good technician, has undertaken a tactics course and knows that if he's to stand a chance in a shootout he must get behind something solid enough to stop incoming rounds. He promptly exits his cruiser and takes cover behind the engine block and wheels. He draws his pistol, lines up a bad guy in his sights but finds he can't bring himself to pull the trigger. It's the first time he's been engaged in combat with anything other than a paper target that didn't shoot back and discovers, in this instance, that he doesn't have the internal fortitude or willingness to pull the trigger and kill another human being.

This might seem crazy to a layman but it happened to a SWAT officer that I'm personally aware of in a major Metropolitan city. They were called in to a barricaded suspect who was shooting from his house at police officers attempting to serve a warrant for his being part of a car theft ring. After negotiations failed, and he narrowly missed shooting yet another officer, the order was given by the unit commander to take the suspect out. Nothing happened. Again the command was given and again nothing happened. The unit commander gave up and gave the job to the backup sniper and she took the shot, narrowly missing the subject's head. He laughed but the commander in charge recovered nicely by telling the suspect that he had ordered them to miss on purpose to show him how serious he was, at which point the suspect surrendered.

During a subsequent debrief they asked the first sniper why he hadn't taken the shot when so ordered. His answer floored everyone in the room *"How can you expect me to play God and take the life of another human.*

I have to face fellow parishioners in church this Sunday…how would I explain it to them?" I'm not going to go into whether the sniper should have been charged, whether he should have been made to reimburse the department in question for all the money to train him, and why he still works the streets carrying a gun he's demonstrated that he's not willing to use, because that's not germane to our story. What is important is that it illustrates that mindset is a critical part of any fight.

Now, let's return to our fictitious armed robbery in progress. The third officer to arrive on scene has no problem with mindset. He's gung-ho with a capital G and wants to rid the world of bad guys as fast as he can. He's also taken part in a tactics course and takes appropriate cover. Unfortunately for all concerned his technique is poor and he can't hit the target. He shoots his own foot, his partner, the lights of his car, a nearby old lady at a bus stop, and some pigeons on the roof.

The fourth officer arrives. He is a good shot, knows tactics and has the correct mindset. He immediately takes cover, draws his weapon, engages the enemy and kills them. In all the other cases the officers in question were missing one of the vital ingredients to win the fight. Only the one with the technical ability to hit what he's aiming at, the tactical knowledge to take cover, and the correct mindset that enabled him to drop the hammer on another person could prevail.

Let's go back to the martial arts now. Very few schools make a conscious effort to teach all three of these, and those that do, almost always teach it in the context of sport. Despite their arguments that sport martial art techniques will work in the real world of a street fight, the techniques, tactics and mindset are completely different.

Let's analyze that for a second. The techniques in a sporting event are 'safe' techniques. Even the so called "no holds barred Ultimate Fighting Championship" had a list of techniques that were illegal. Eye gouging, biting, kicking with shoes, small joint attacks, fish hooks, et al, are all banned. In regular tournament karate the list is even longer, no kicking below the belt, no hitting a man when he's down, no joint techniques, no throws, no head butts, knees, or elbows, etc. The techniques that I use, on

15

the other hand, generally begin with everything on the outlawed list of the sporting event and go from there. I want my students focusing on things such as eye gouging, biting, throat punching, kicking the knees, groin strikes, pulling the hair and so on. So, we can safely say the techniques in the street are going to be different than the techniques we focus on in a ring.

What about tactics? I'm going to list two that I've seen used at tournaments all over the world that are fairly effective depending on the caliber and honesty of the judges. The first is to feign injury and have the other side disqualified for excessive contact. You see it all the time. Fighter A charges in, fighter B barely tags him with what should be the winning shot, when "A" collapses on the ground writhing in pain and putting on an Oscar winning performance. The judges confer and "B" is disqualified and "A" gets up to take home the medal or trophy. Can you imagine trying that as tactic in a street fight? Some sweaty biker decides to rearrange your face, and after the first blow, you collapse and try and have him disqualified? Good luck with that.

Another effective tournament strategy is getting one point ahead and staying there. Typically, in tournaments there is a time limit. Every time you score a technique you get awarded a point (sometimes only a half point if the technique is deemed sloppy). Whoever has the most points at the end of the clock is declared the winner. What usually happens is fighter "A" gets a sloppy punch in and is awarded a half point with a minute to go. Every time the referee declares continue our "hero' backpedals out of the fighting area as fast as he can. Every time he steps out of bounds the referee blows his whistle and both fighters are returned to the middle to begin again. If our "champion" can stay out of the ring long enough the buzzer will ring and he'll be declared the winner by virtue of his half point lead.

Again, try and use that one in a bar fight and see where it gets you. You're going to halfheartedly hit someone, be awarded a point (by who) and then jump out of the bar and have the fight restarted until the clock runs out? It's not going to happen, is it?

How about street tactics that have proved effective? One is to hit the enemy when he's not looking. Human predators constantly ambush their victims either by distracting them – *"hey buddy, got a light?"* – or finding a victim who's task fixated and not paying attention. They might, in a bar fight, apologize, wait till you've turned your back and then brain you with a bar stool. While that's an effective street fighting tactic, can you imagine trying it in the sporting world? Imagine waiting to fight Oscar de la Hoya. You bash him over the head from behind in the dressing room with a baseball bat before the fight and then declare yourself the winner?

The 2nd tactic for street combat is ganging up on someone. This is the whole concept of gangs in fact. Most gang members are too afraid to be out on their own so they hunt in packs. It's remarkably effective and is even taught in our military academies. Readers might remember "Stormin Norman" Schwarzkopf in Desert Storm One refusing to give the "go" command until he had five guys on the ground for every one of the opposition. Can you imagine trying this in a sporting match? Can you imagine turning up to fight Mike Tyson in the ring and bringing thirty of your friends with you! You'd probably win – depending on who your friends were – but you couldn't get away with it.

Finally, we come to mindset. This one is easy. With the referee ensuring both sides abide by the rules, doctors present to administer aid in the event of injuries, a padded floor, protective gear etc., the mindset in a sporting event is pretty much *"If I don't win, I don't go home with the trophy."* In the street, with weapons, the element of surprise, disparity in the size and weight of the adversaries, no rules, etc. The mindset should be *"If I don't win, I may NEVER go home."* Big difference.

Another example of mindset I'm fond of using is the following. Almost every mate of mine in the military is willing to go out and play with paint ball guns in the wood. How many people who play paint ball though would be willing to engage in the same game if the bullets were real?

One final example, and I apologize if it seems like I'm belaboring the point, but mindset is clearly the most important of the three aspects we're discussing.

On a forum that I was on a discussion came up about Kelly McCann – one of the most prominent Combatives instructors in the world – who had upset the sporting crowd by putting out a DVD on how best to deal with them in a fight. (Given the popularity of MMA now, it's becoming increasingly more likely that, if you fight some youngster, he will have had some training in MMA just as they had the rudiments of boxing down in the old days).

One of the MMA kids who was mad at McCann said this…

"a "seasoned" (read truly skilled) MMA practitioner can ONLY be countered by

1. Luck;

2. Equal or greater skill;

3. A massive size/strength/injury disparity." Quote unquote.

Notice with his sporting mindset he omitted that his MMA fighter could also be defeated by the following;

- A guy with a gun
- A guy with a knife
- A group of guys
- A group of guys with weapons
- Impact Weapons
- A pre-emptive strike
- A sucker punch
- Being ambushed
- Rolling around on the floor trying to put a submission hold on while a mob uses your head as a football.

The whiner in question's training in the ring had clearly left him unprepared for the type of violence he'd be likely to run into outside the ring. This is a classic illustration of the dangers of a sporting mindset.

4

JEFF COOPER'S COLOR CODES

Play along for this exercise and imagine you're sitting at home enjoying your favorite television show. You're completely relaxed and everything is as it should be in your world. At some point you hear a noise out of the ordinary…nothing loud and not too ominous but enough to make you sit up and take notice. You're about to dismiss it, it's probably the cat you think, and go back to your show when you hear it again and you notice the cat is under the coffee table. It's louder this time and you identify it as someone trying to get through the back door. Adrenalin begins to pour through your system; you grab a golf club and go to confront whoever it is. Suddenly, the door bursts open and two men are standing there with masks on, holding screwdrivers, and the fight is on. You manage to hit one and drive him to the floor but he's hanging on to your leg and trying to plunge his screwdriver into it. The other one grabs a knife from the knife block on the kitchen bench and runs back towards you screaming he's going to kill you. You wind back the golf club and bring it down full force on top of his head and kill him. His mate quits when he realizes you're serious and curls up in a ball nursing his injuries. You call the police and sit back to await their arrival.

The reason I tell you that story is to help you identify the various frames of mind you typically go through in a fight with another person. Initially you're completely relaxed. Upon hearing the first out of the ordinary noise you go into a state of relaxed alertness...more a sense of curiosity i.e. *"what was that?"* Once you realize something isn't right you go to the next level, that of heightened alert. It's still not serious because it could be a wild animal or your spouse trying to get in because they lost their key. Upon realizing it's the enemy and combat is imminent you go to another level again, i.e. full on engaged in combat, and finally, realizing you're going to have to take someone's life in defense of your own, you go into mortal, life or death combat mode.

Jeff Cooper, a former Marine Lt. Col. (now deceased) is considered by many to be the father of modern combat hand gunning in the US. It was he who codified these states of mind and assigned them colors in a bid to help people understand conditions of readiness to take life. While his system is not about situational awareness levels per se (it was Claude Werner who pointed this out in his excellent "Tactical Professor" blog) it can be easily adapted as such. If you don't like the idea of using colors you could use the military's DEFCON (Defense Readiness Condition) system as an alternative.

White or Defcon 5

The first level, white, is relaxed, unaware, and unprepared (the bulk of the human population on a daily basis). It's the state you were in while watching your television show in the above story. If you survive a criminal assault while in this phase it is only due to the ineptitude of your attacker(s) and has nothing to do with your skill level or ability. These are typically the victims who tell the police after an attack *"my God, he came out of nowhere."* The reality is you were so relaxed your senses were dulled to the point where the predator could get close enough to launch his attack without you perceiving it.

Yellow or Defcon 4

The second level, yellow, is the state of relaxed alertness. This is an acceptance that *"while I hope nothing happens to me today I am ready if it does."* This is the sort of mind-set you got in the above story when you heard the noise while watching the TV. It's the same reason you put on a seat belt when you get in the car to drive somewhere. You're not expecting to get into an accident but you're prepared if you do.

As an illustration of this mind-set, one of my students, Donna, is the owner of a prestigious jewelry store specializing in customized baubles, and as such, is often driving from client meetings to the store wearing some serious bling. On the day in question she was gassing her car and noticed two sketchy looking guys checking her out from the door of the station. She looked around checking to see if they were interested in something or someone else but noticed there were no other cars around. At this point they zipped up their hoodies (it was 97 degrees that day) and split up to flank her. Recognizing an impending attack she dropped the nozzle where it was and took off in her car not even bothering to replace the gas cap (this later caused her check engine light to come on which had to be addressed at the dealership). After thanking me for the training she pointed out that, prior to attending our school, she would have been task fixated on pumping the gas, would not have noticed them, and almost certainly have been a victim of a violent robbery or carjacking.

Orange or Defcon 3

Orange comes next and is a "specific alert." This is the level you went to upon realizing it wasn't the cat at the door but possibly an intruder intent on doing you harm. It also might be the mind-set you get into when someone has just cut you off in traffic and is getting out of their car and storming towards yours. It is the *"I may have to fight this person"* mind-set. It's the level you should drop in to momentarily when a stranger encroaches in your personal space.

Red or Defcon 2

The fourth color in the code is that of red and this is the color we symbolize with the fight being on. For Mr. Cooper, concerned only with gun fighting, his code stopped here. As a former Marine and a man concerned with teaching the civilian population how to survive gun battles it is understandable that it would do so. You are either engaged in a gun fight trying to kill the opposition before they kill you, or you are not. For us however, dealing with people that may not have the right to go armed, or someone who may not have access to their weapon when attacked, I think it incumbent upon us to add another level to the mix and that is:

Black or Defcon 1

The fifth color black is used in mortal combat and is the frame of mind one would have to be in to take another person's life if necessary to protect yourself, or another innocent third party, from death or serious injury. I sincerely hope you never have to go to that level. A lot of people don't deal with it well, and assuming you do, the legal ramifications, both civil and criminal, are enough to cause some people to think not defending themselves at all is the better option.

One of the major goals of this book is to help you realize that you should never again be in condition white or DEFCON 5 no matter how seemingly innocent the surroundings. Human predators go out of their way to find victims in that frame of mind because they know, from experience, that getting close enough to them to launch an attack is easier in that state of mind than any other, except perhaps asleep. Even if you're in a state of relaxed alertness i.e. condition yellow, good (for want of a better word) human predators will use dialogue and dress to put you at ease so they can successfully launch their attack. The phrase that applies to this technique is "lulling you into a false sense of security."

It's equally important to teach everyone the very real dangers associated with maintaining too high an alert level at all times. This constant being on edge is often experienced by soldiers who never get out of condition red for days on end and they end up with either burn-out or post-traumatic stress syndrome.

Now might be a good time to deal with the issue of being accused of being paranoid if people discover that you are constantly switched on. Paranoia deals with fear not preparedness. If you were truly paranoid you'd stay at home and hide under your bed. If you're guilty of being paranoid simply because you maintain a state of relaxed alertness then so is everyone who puts on a seatbelt when they drive a car. They're not afraid of getting in an accident because if they were the simple solution would be to not own a car. They are simply practicing relaxed alertness by buckling up, admitting that while slim there is always a chance of an accident, and therefore being prepared for it. It's too late to put the seat belt on when you realize you're about to rear end another vehicle at forty-five miles per hour. You put it on in advance "just in case."

The other criticism I've heard of maintaining a state of relaxed alertness is *"why would you want to live your life that way?"* What way is that exactly? Being ready in case a human predator tries to attack me for my money, my dignity, or my life? Here's the funny part. After a while that state of mind will become second nature to you and you won't have to even think about it. Secondly, the behaviors that you adopt as a result, don't take any longer than doing it the old way. Let's use our seat belt analogy again. How much longer does it take to climb into your car and buckle your seat belt than not buckling it? Two seconds. What difference does that two seconds make to your existence should someone have a heart attack behind the wheel, cross two lanes of traffic and hit you head on at thirty-five miles per hour?

Let me give you a more concrete example. One I do personally all the time is to sit in a restaurant, or any public venue, so I can see who comes in the door. One of the biggest massacres in this country was in a McDonald's restaurant in Texas back in 1984 when James Oliver Huberty, a forty-one-year-old former welder, walked in to the San Ysidro McDonalds armed to the teeth and completely intent on killing everyone inside. Huberty used an Uzi, a shotgun and a handgun to kill twenty-one victims and injure fifteen more people before being shot by a SWAT sniper from a nearby roof top. If you'd been inside and able to see the door, and seen someone approaching with weapons, that may have given you sufficient advance knowledge to either leave the premises or draw your own weapon and get ready to engage them. If, on the other hand, your back was to the door the first thing you'd have known about it is was when you were either shot in the back of the head or ordered onto the ground to be killed execution style.

How much longer does it take to sit in a seat where you can see the door versus the one where you can't? About two seconds again. Two seconds is not a long time and the potential return on that tiny investment of time is absolutely huge. For men, go into the stall of a public restroom as opposed to standing at the urinal. Two seconds. Put on boots or lace up shoes as opposed to flip flops. Two seconds. Take your weapon with you versus leave it at home. Two seconds. By now you should be getting the idea. Being prepared takes very little extra time compared to not being prepared, but the payoff is vast.

5

THE CRIMINAL'S PLAN

Per statistics the average rapist has raped seventeen victims before he's caught. During that time he's had a chance to plan his attacks and test and hone that plan in the real world, making it even tougher to catch him as time goes by. Assuming he does get caught – and many don't despite the best efforts of law enforcement – he now gets to attend "college" with fellow inmates at the local prison and discuss ways to not make the same mistake that led to his being caught in the first place. You think I'm kidding but rapists are now being caught who are using condoms and bleach etc., to thwart DNA testing which are lessons they've learned from watching crime shows such as CSI and listening to the evidence as it's being presented in court.

Whether their attempts are effective is out with the jury – no pun intended – but the point is they're not stupid and they do learn from their mistakes.

Most victims on the other hand have no plan at all. The only thing they'll say when asked about their plan is *"well, I just hope it never happens to me."* Hope should never be part of a self-protection plan. Ask yourself this question. Would you vote for a President who, upon being asked what his plan for national defense was, replied with *"well I just hope we never get attacked."* Sounds ridiculous right? But right now, millions of people are protecting themselves exactly that way.

S.I.V.A.

To understand how human predators hunt we're going to take a moment to study their counterparts in the animal kingdom. Predators go to the watering hole typically because they know that's where the game will be plentiful. Next, they isolate their victim by spooking the herd and causing the prey to be left alone, either due to the fact that it is feeble, lame, or very young. Once it's isolated they roar and they attack.

Human predators typically operate in much the same way when attacking their victim. If you take a moment to understand how, that will help you formulate a plan for not getting caught in the net. Imagine if you were a fish and someone shared with you how fisherman baited their hooks. What would be the likelihood of you falling for the lure? Almost non-existent, right? That's why it's important to understand the following sections.

Using and understanding the acronym S.I.V.A. will help you understand the process that most attacks follow. Before we do that, however, I want to explain there is another step in the process before we get to the S of "S.I.V.A." and that is "Intent." I don't include it in the attack plan simply because it's not one we can

Rapists Using Condoms

In 80 sexual assault cases submitted to the forensic laboratory of the Las Vegas Metropolitan Police Dept. between Sept & Dec of 93, 19 victims reported that one or several of the assailants had worn a condom during the assault.

Eight additional victims believed their assailant might have used a condom.

Terry L. Cook,

Criminalist, Forensic Laboratory

Las Vegas Metropolitan Police Dept.

have any control over. If some miscreant was dropped on his head too much as a child, wasn't hugged enough, is using drugs and opting to prey on his fellow humans, neither you, nor I, can control that. That's best left to the sociologists, shrinks, government, and educators to try and figure out why. We on the other hand can have some impact on the other four steps of S.I.V.A. which is why we begin with the S.

Selection

First, (after the bad guy intends to go out and commit a crime), he will SELECT his victim based on whatever criteria appeals to him. A rapist, for example, may like petite blond girls, a mugger may look for well-heeled out of shape business men, whereas a con man may look for the elderly. They usually make that selection from wherever there is a wide choice. The rapist may target a mall or universities as there are large amounts of potential victims present in both locations while the mugger would be more likely to hit crowds found at street fairs or tourist traps. The reasons are fairly obvious. Tourists have money and cameras etc., and they are far less likely to return in the rare case of a criminal trial to testify due to expenses. Who's going to pay a couple of thousand dollars for a plane ticket to go back to some third world country to testify over a $500 camera that was covered by insurance anyway?

Isolation

Whichever criminal type and whatever his or her choice of crime may be, their next move is obvious, and that is "isolation" from the safety of the herd. They may do this by prowling deserted areas and waiting for their victim to walk into their trap, or they may follow the victim from the mall to the parking lot. They don't have to spook the herd like their animal counterparts because typically the victim will isolate him or herself.

Victim has isolated herself

Verbal

Once they've isolated their victim, the next step is called the "interview". This is the verbal component of the attack and equivalent to the roar of the beast of prey as he attacks. They may come on strong at this point and start screaming while brandishing a weapon, but far more common is some low-key dialogue used to ascertain the resistance level of a potential rape victim and/or shock them, or, in the case of a mugging, camouflage their moving into attack range by distracting the victim with innocuous ramblings. You may realize at this point in this book that you have been "interviewed" at some point in time. Interestingly enough even pickpockets can sometimes use verbal tactics. One ruse is that a pickpocket will call out to a busload of passengers to be aware because his pocket has just been picked. Everyone naturally now checks to make sure they still have their purse/wallet and the pickpocket's accomplices, sitting amongst the crowd, now know exactly where to strike.

Attack/Assault

If you "pass" the interview stage, the next is always the attack. Again, this will vary in nature depending on the type of criminal you're dealing with. Also, keep in mind that the attack and dialogue might come almost at the same second, especially in a mugging scenario where someone is using dialogue to distract you before they attack.

Obviously there are exceptions to the above rules. For example, pickpockets aren't concerned with isolation and prefer to work in crowds, but for the most part, the bulk of human predators will use the above four steps in their *modus operandi*.

What is interesting to note is that traditional self-defense training mostly only deals with the last step in the whole process i.e. the attack has commenced and you must fight your way out. By using the techniques of avoidance and awareness we focus on the first three steps so we never end up in number four if possible.

If I know, for example, that kidnappers are seeking well-heeled American businessmen for kidnap and ransom I'll advise my client to dress like a native, leave the expensive jewelry at home, read a local newspaper and smoke local brand cigarettes etc., and thus blend in with the crowd. If I'm dealing with someone concerned with being chosen by a rapist I'd make sure they took precautions to keep windows and doors locked (most rapists on college campuses get in through open windows). If it's someone concerned with being bullied you might opt to begin a workout program and beef up if underweight or work on your self-esteem so you don't look like a potential victim to every predator.

If I'm about to isolate myself from the crowd, I'll be hyper-vigilant at that point because I know that's when the criminals are going to make their move. Most people on the other hand meander back to their car intent on remembering where they parked, what they just bought, and balancing their check book. They might also be task fixated on their cell phone calling family members to let them know the shopping is done, etc.

Finally, if I'm being interviewed, I'd have some simple dialogues rehearsed ahead of time (salesmen call these scripts) so that I can effectively deal with the interview portion of the attack sequence. Only as a last resort would I then reach into my toolbox for physical methods of fighting my way out of trouble.

Something else worth mentioning about victim selection is the Grayson/Stein Study

Psychologists have known for years that human predators select their prey based on signals given off by their potential victims. In a matter of seconds, the predator acquires a sense of who is and isn't a suitable target. For every victim that is attacked, many more are passed over. What are the criteria that predators use to select their victims?

The Greyson Stein Study

In 1984 two researchers, Betty Grayson and Morris I. Stein, conducted a study to determine the selection criteria applied by predators when selecting their victims. They videotaped several pedestrians on a busy New York City sidewalk without their knowledge.

They later showed the tape to convicts who were incarcerated for violent offenses (rape, murder, robbery, etc.) They instructed them to identify people on the tape who would make easy or desirable victims. The results were interesting.

Within seven seconds, the participants made their selections. What baffled researchers was the consistency of the people that were selected as victims. The criteria were not readily apparent. Some small, slightly built women were passed over. Some large men were selected. The selection was not dependent on race, age, size or gender.

Even the convicts didn't know exactly why they selected as they did. Some people just looked like easy targets. It appears that much of the predator/prey selection process is unconscious from the perspective of both predator and the potential victim.

Video Analysis of the study

Still at a loss of specific selection criteria, the researches had a more thorough analysis of the movement and body language of the people on the videotape. Here is an overview of the results:

Stride: People selected as victims had an exaggerated stride: either abnormally short or long. They dragged, shuffled, or lifted their feet unnaturally as they walked. Non-victims, on the other hand, tended to have a smooth, natural gait. They stepped in a heel-to-toe fashion.

Rate: Victims tend to walk at a different rate than non-victims. Usually, they walk slower than the flow of pedestrian traffic. Their movement lacks a sense of deliberateness or purpose. However, an unnaturally rapid pace can project nervousness or fear.

Fluidity: Researchers noted awkwardness in a victim's body movement. Jerkiness, raising and lowering one's center of gravity or wavering from side to side as they moved became apparent in the victims analyzed. This was contrasted with smoother, more coordinated movement of the non-victims.

Wholeness: Victims lacked "wholeness" in their body movement. They swung their arms as if they were detached and independent from the rest of their body. Non-victims moved their body from their "center" as a coordinated whole implying strength, balance and confidence.

Posture and Gaze: A slumped posture is indicative of weakness or submissiveness. A downward gaze implies preoccupation and being unaware of one's surroundings. Also, someone reluctant to establish eye contact can be perceived as submissive. These traits imply an ideal target for a predator.

In his book, "The Danger From Strangers," author James D. Brewer quotes one of the researchers who conducted the above mentioned study, *"Grayson is convinced that when people understand how to move confidently they can, 'be taught how to walk that way and substantially reduce their risk of assault'"*

How does this apply to Prevention Theory? If you read between the lines of this research, the "Preparation Equals Prevention Theory" makes more sense. The traits described above indicate varying degrees of balance, coordination and awareness. They imply a person's perceived vigilance and potential to fight.

Self-defense training develops the qualities of movement that discourage victim selection and project a "don't mess with me" demeanor. This explains why a person who had formerly been bullied or victimized takes up the study of self-defense and the incidents that originally plagued him or her stop.

Unlike Professor Grayson, I doubt that the solution to reducing one's victim potential is as simple as taking "walking lessons" though the modeling process of NLP etc., could definitely help. True confidence however comes from within and not simply mimicking someone else's gait.

Of course we can break the Selection, Isolation, Verbal and Attack down into subsets.

Selection can be:
- Who do they select? Blondes between 25 and 30 years old for example?
- How do they select them? See Greyson Stein study.
- Where do they select them? Campus or mall?

Isolation could be further broken down to:
- Does victim isolate him/herself by leaving the safety of the crowd?
- Does the rapist kidnap victim and drive her to a secondary crime scene?
- Isolation due to task fixation (a person in a crowd who is task fixated has isolated themselves from others who may be more aware of their surroundings.)

Verbal can be broken down to:
- Innocent patter designed to distract (hey buddy, got a light?)

- Or full on screaming designed to intimidate and bolster the confidence of the bad guy.

Attacks can be broken down to a myriad of types such as:
- Rape
- Robbery
- Mugging
- Assault
- Murder

And all the above can occur with or without weapons and by one perpetrator or several.

But there are only two methods of attack and they are the smoldering or "brewing" type and the ambush or explosion.

Let's deal with the easy one first and that is the smoldering situation. That's where you're in a bar for example and someone who you accidentally bumped earlier is getting progressively drunk and more aggressive towards you. He's probably started posturing and begins to hurl insults, etc. It may not even be directed at you, it could simply be a group of rowdy young guys getting progressively more and more drunk and aggressive. In any event the solution is simple...leave. Don't let your ego get in the way and stay for the fight. The scenario I mentioned in the first chapter about looking after the rock band is a good example of a brewing situation. I could tell the crowd was getting progressively more agitated and the best thing we could do was get the hell out of Dodge. If anyone reading the book is worried about their ego being bruised because they have to "back down" and leave a potentially violent situation remember this; Special Forces troops' main mission is intelligence gathering and not fighting. While they are better equipped than most to deal with esoteric violence, they choose to lie low and gather information rather than scrap with the opposition. If they are forced into a situation by the enemy their adage has always been to "hit and run" or "bash and dash." Not even they want to stay around and get involved in fights when they can possibly avoid them.

The second type is the ambush attack and that is by far the most dangerous. This is the one you can't typically see coming and only awareness and avoidance will protect you against this. Remember a human predator will do everything in his power to take away any advantage you may have, such as witnesses, lights, avenues of escape, and so on. It's what they do for a living so you must remember this and prepare accordingly. It doesn't matter how many black belts you have, how good of a fighter you are, or if you happen to be the champion shot at the local pistol club, if I sneak up on you and cave the back of your head in with a brick, all your skills, weapons, and ability are for naught. Only your awareness can protect you from an ambush. There's a reason in the military we call the area the enemy is going to walk into during an ambush the "kill zone." Fighting your way out of it is almost always not going to happen and the best defense has always been not to get in one in the first place.

6

AGGRESSOR EXERCISE

Unusual, but on one bodyguard course a friend attended they were given the task of planning the assassination of a local public figure. Now, at first bat that may seem odd, but it's designed to teach you to see the problem as the enemy sees it, and by seeing it through his eyes, you're in a better position to thwart him. The attendees not only had to theorize as to how they would do the job but they had to present a plan showing where and how they'd procure the materials necessary for their particular gambit. At the end of the course the plans were presented to the public figure in question as a way of letting him, and his/her security, see how and where they were vulnerable.

Think Like The Bad Guy

I want you to do the same thing. Occasionally, during lunch, or on your way home, put yourself in the shoes of a desperate drug user who absolutely must get hold of some money with which to score drugs. Look around. Who would you choose as a victim? How would you do it? Would you hit them at the ATM? While they're in their car? What about the woman with her arms full of shopping bags?

Once you've figured out who you'd pick as your victim plan how you'd do the actual attack. Would you rob them at the ATM during the transaction or would you follow them to their car perhaps? There's no right or wrong answer here, but by putting yourself in the place of the enemy, you begin to see how he views the world.

Analysis

The next step, the critical step, is then to analyze why you chose that person. Did they look weak and feeble? Were they pre-occupied with something? Did they leave their pocket book or valuables in an accessible place? Were they task fixated at their vehicle while putting their child in the safety seat or balancing their check book?

Now ask yourself, how many times do you do that? In other words, just like my mate on the bodyguard course, you'll begin to see holes in their defense that may well be holes in your own. Obviously then, correct those mistakes as soon as humanly possible.

7

THE THREAT ANALYSIS

C alled a Threat Analysis, it's one of the most important tools in the bodyguard's toolbox. This is a study done of the actual risks faced by a particular client. A politician for example is a prime candidate for assassination whereas a businessman might be sought after by kidnappers looking to reach into the deep pockets of his employer. By performing this study we don't throw our limited resources in the wrong direction. You can do the same thing. Are you a businessperson going to Central or South America next year on business, or are you a housewife in an area where a rapist is known to operate? Perhaps you're a young couple living in a neighborhood plagued by home invasions or work in a part of town where people have been mugged recently. If the rapist was your problem for example it wouldn't behoove you to start worrying about how you're carrying your purse in case you run into a bag snatcher.

It probably doesn't need saying, but just because one threat is prevalent doesn't mean we can ignore all the others. It's really a question of the highest probability. Also, keep in mind that bolstering one's defenses against a particular threat will often produce dividends that will aid in lessening the risk of other threats as well.

To help you with the concept of threat analysis let's break it down a little further. Threats can be divided into only one of two categories; specific and non-specific.

Specific Threat

A specific threat is one directed against you, and more than likely you'll be aware of it. It may be an ex-husband who's threatened to kill you, a former employee that you've fired or a guy in a bar who's just said *"I'm going to kick your ass"* to name but a few. Either way, you have advance knowledge of what's in store for you and probably who the attacker is likely to be.

Non-Specific Threat

A non-specific threat would be things like carjackings, terrorist attacks in which you are in the vicinity, and/or a tourist targeted by local criminals. It's not directed at you per se, no more than a certain fly is targeted by the Venus Fly Trap. The victims in the twin towers and on the planes during the 9/11 attacks were all victims of a non-specific threat.

Clearly a specific threat is more dangerous in the sense that the bad guy wants you and nobody else will do. It's not going to be a case of him looking for someone at an ATM and picking just anybody. Therefore, just as the threat is specific, so must the defensive measures be. Will you take out a restraining order, will you file a police report outlining the communication of a threat, will you hire a team of bodyguards or begin a self-defense course, etc.? Whatever the specific threat is will help you determine the course of action.

Non-specific threats can be just as dangerous. Don't forget the aforementioned victims of the terrorist lunatics on 9/11. They're just as dead as JFK. A lot of non-specific threats can best be dealt with by practicing your awareness and avoidance skills, lowering your profile, and exercising some simple common sense defensive measures. If you do that, and that is the thrust of this book by the way, then chances are good that you'll fly under the radar of any criminal element looking for prey.

Whatever type of threat it is, i.e. specific or non-specific, we can break them down into two main categories which are criminal and terrorist. Those, in turn, can be broken down even further into various types which help us understand who and what we're up against.

Criminals can be broken down into the following types:

Psychological: This is the type such as the gun man who went on a rampage at Virginia Tech and the lunatic who shot up the theater in Aurora CO. These are, understandably and unfortunately, the hardest to predict. Serial killers also fall into this category.

Personal: This is the criminal who has personally targeted you as in the aforementioned specific threat.

Random: The bulk of attacks fall into this category. This is included in the non-specific threat genre and victims are chosen at random by the criminal looking for victims that fit his particular criteria.

Terrorist types can be broken down as follows:

Ideological: These are terrorists who harbor beliefs different to your own. The terrorists who brought down the planes on 9/11 fall into this category.

Economic: These terrorists are in it for the money. Sometimes they start out as ideological but after discovering how much money can be made by kidnapping they quickly shift focus on why they do what they do. Many will still claim ideological reasons rather than admit the real reason they do it. A great many of the kidnappings in Iraq fell into this category. Also note that the IRA would rob banks and steal cars, etc., to raise money for their ideological cause thus falling into both categories. Something else to note is that terrorist groups not sponsored by the state will often resort to extortion, kidnapping, smuggling, drug running, etc., to raise money for their equipment.

Revolutionary: These are terrorists of the various political factions such as The Shining Path and ETA in Spain whose goal is to overthrow the current government. The real danger from these groups is being caught in the wrong place at the wrong time.

Once you've identified the threat, you must assess the bad guy's ability to carry it out. It is relatively safe, for example, to dismiss the small guy in the bar who is so inebriated he can hardly stand up and who has just threatened you with a beating. However, when **Action Directe**, a terrorist group in France, threatened the leaders of Peugeot or Renault, it was George Besse, the former head of Renault, who was killed when he denounced their threat as baseless. Here again is someone falling victim who erroneously believed *"It will never happen to me."*

If you've determined the bad guy has the ability, your next step is to figure out what crime he normally commits, how he does it, and then undertake the relevant counter-measures. That, briefly, is a rough outline of a threat analysis. Following are some questions that you might ask yourself if you were conducting a threat assessment. For reasons of operational security I have not included all the questions on a typical threat analysis which can run into several pages in length and would only typically apply to high risk clients traveling to the world's hot spots. So, ask yourself the following questions:

Are you concerned about becoming a victim? Yes __ No __

Is the threat specific or non-specific? Specific __ Non-Specific __

If Specific

Who is the person making the threat? _____

Are they capable of carrying it out? Yes __ No __

Do they have the means to carry it out? Yes __ No __

Have they carried out that type of threat before? Yes __ No __

On a scale of 1 – 10 what is the likelihood of them carrying it out? _____

Has law enforcement been made aware of the threat? Yes __ No __

Has law enforcement done anything about it? Yes __ No __

Can you remove yourself from the area? Yes __ No __

What measures could you take?

_____

_____

_____

_____

If the threat is non-specific:

Where did you first hear about the threat?

_____

Who has been carrying it out? Individual _____ Group _____

Is local law enforcement doing anything about it? Yes __ No __

Can you lower your profile or adopt any behaviors that will lessen your chance of becoming a victim? Yes __ No __

What measures could you take?

_____

_____

_____

8

THE FORCE CONTINUUM

Comparing levels of aggression with corresponding levels of response is the next topic we must cover from the preamble. It's called the force continuum and it's a scale designed to help you ascertain and justify which level you can resort to while under attack. For example, deadly force is the highest level on the response side and psychological intimidation is the lowest level of aggression on the flip side. Using deadly force against someone who was dressed in a threatening manner would obviously be an inappropriate use of force just as responding with presence would be inappropriate if someone was trying to gun you down.

Levels of Aggression	Levels of Response
Psychological Intimidation – Dressing like a biker, tattoos, scarification, war paint, uniforms.	**Officer (or any responsible person) Presence** Blue light, siren, uniform, witnesses etc.
Verbal Intimidation – Threats, yelling and screaming.	**Verbal Command** – Stop, leave, get on the ground, drop the weapon etc.
Passive Resistance – Usually seen at abortion clinics and protests. Also common during trespass.	**Passive Control and Restraint** – Gentle hands on to remove the antagonist.
Active Unarmed Resistance – Physical resistance such as struggling, punching & kicking	**Active Unarmed Control** – Control & Restraint techniques, strikes, takedowns etc.
Active Armed Resistance – Separated into 3 distinct categories; impact weapons (batons, ball bats, bricks etc,) bladed weapons (knives, razors, broken bottles) and projectile weapons (firearms, slingshots, bows and arrows)	**Active Armed Resistance** – As all three categories on the opposing side have the potential to kill deadly force is a viable option at this juncture.

While the law states you may only use the appropriate response to counter your adversary (the rule of thumb for law enforcement is that they may use one level above whatever they're faced with) there is a danger in doing so.

One night while bouncing, I had to deal with a drunk trying to enter the club where I was working. He was mouthing off and in general just being a nuisance with a potential to become more aggressive. I spun him around at this point and pushed him out of the doorway and a few feet away from our club entrance. Now, according to the law, that was an appropriate level of response. He had been asked to leave private property and wouldn't do so (trespass) so I responded by gently grabbing him and walking him away.

Unfortunately, he went down the road to a trash can, found a bottle which he broke, and then he came back and threatened me with it. Fortunately I won the encounter but don't underestimate how incredibly dangerous that was. One slip and he could have cut an artery and I'd have bled to death before the meat wagon rolled up.

Had I, on the other hand, broken his arms when I first scuffled with him – overkill as far as the force continuum is concerned – he wouldn't have been able to come back with the bottle and I wouldn't have been put at risk.

We could debate this topic for hours and indeed, many do on various internet forums devoted to self-protection. I'm certainly not going to recommend anything other than follow the force continuum and be able to articulate why you responded with the level of violence you did during an attack. However, it would be remiss of me to say that we live in an ideal world and you'll never get in trouble if you do it that way. As evidenced by the above story, there is real danger following either option; in one example the danger comes from the now forewarned and forearmed attacker and in the second it comes from overstepping the law and ending up defending your actions in a courtroom. The decision as to what level of response you're going to use must be your own and figured out long in advance of the actual conflict you might find yourself in.

9

AOJP

In the bodyguard's world it's obviously impossible to be familiar with all the laws pertaining to self-defense in every country you might find yourself working in. In the US alone there are fifty states and within each of those there are various jurisdictions including city, county, state, and federal. Go overseas and it can become even more complicated. Are you dealing with the Westminster system of justice or the Napoleonic code?

What agents do in situations like that is go by some very general guidelines using the use of force continuum outlined in the previous chapter and what is often called "The Reasonable Man" argument. What that means is a jury, a District Attorney, and/or prosecutor is going to ask themselves is what you did in an altercation what a reasonable man would have done in similar circumstances. If the answer is yes then you'll probably get a free pass. If, on the other hand, the answer is no then you might be looking at a conviction, prison sentence and/or fine, etc.

For example, imagine you're out and you witness a guy trying to drag a child, screaming, into a car while the child's mother frantically tries to prevent the abduction. You run over to help and punch the pedophile in the face to get him to let go of the child at which point he drives off. Most people would say what you did was reasonable.

In a different scenario you witness a bag thief, at which point you pull out your concealed pistol and shoot him four times in the face and kill

45

him. Most people would argue here that would not be the actions of a "reasonable" man and you'll probably find yourself charged with a crime.

One guideline that will help you decide – and it dovetails with the above – is that of A.O.J.P. This four-letter acronym will help you answer the question as to whether use of force is justified at all.

Ability

Does the person you're going to fight with have the ability to harm you? Some emaciated nine-year-old hurling threats at you from across the street does not really have the ability to carry out his threats so you can safely leave him alone. Someone with a gun, however, would certainly have the ability so you're moving into a realm whereby you could be justified in defending yourself.

Opportunity

So, let's assume our skinny kid is a muscular adult. If he's across the other side of the street he can run his mouth all he wants. He doesn't, unless he has a firearm, have the opportunity to hit you, or carry out his threat from where he is, so he also is not a justifiable target. There are millions of people in the world who have the ability to do you harm, but unless they're standing directly in front of you and intending to do so, you would not be justified in bashing them all.

Jeopardy

If the same large individual is threatening to break your jaw and he's five feet away and closing you've now met at least three conditions of AOJP. He has the ability, he has the opportunity and now you're in jeopardy. In other words he can hurt you right here and right now. Be very clear on this one. If, for example, someone beats you into a pulp and then walks away, you're not allowed to pull a weapon at this point and go after them. The moment they turn you are not, in the eyes of the law, justified in fighting with them anymore as you are no longer in immediate jeopardy. If you're in a fight with someone who started it, is in the wrong,and who hit you first, who, as the fight goes on, surrenders or quits, you are not allowed, as tempting as it may be, to continue to administer a beating. The instant he gives up or quits you are no longer in immediate jeopardy.

I remember being an instructor on Dennis Martin and Lofty Weisman's (of 22SAS fame) CQB Services Bodyguard Training course in the UK back in the late eighties, and Den set up a scenario whereby you were given a pistol that fired wax bullets and told to confront the burglar in the next room. When the pistol toting security walked in he was confronted with a guy "stealing" his bosses TV set. Of course the security screamed put the TV down and freeze to which the bad guy was told to turn and leave with the appliance. What was interesting was that almost everyone shot the burglar in the back with the wax bullets. Some of them were visibly shocked when they were told, had the scenario been real, they would now be going to jail for a long time. It's human nature to want to punish the wrong doer, but trust me, it's not your job – and you can't shoot someone for stealing your stuff as much as you may like to.

Preclusion

In essence this means did you exhaust every other possibility before engaging in combat or engaging in force only as a last resort. In the eyes of the law, if you can safely and prudently avoid the fight then you should do so. Indeed, in some states you have a duty to retreat if you can.[4] Another way to think of this is that you must, especially as professional, exercise your self-restraint to the greatest extent possible. Remember, you are

---

[4] Remember, this book and the advice within is not to be considered legal advice. Make an appointment with a competent attorney and familiarize yourself with the laws in your area. Some states have adopted the "Castle Doctrine" and other have not. It would behoove you to operate with the confines of the laws in your city.

probably breaking the law if you fight because you want to and must strive to do so only when you have to.

If you can honestly meet all those conditions before engaging the enemy then you should be in good stead from a legal standpoint. Remember, it's not enough to win the fight; you also must win the legal battles afterwards, both civil and criminal.

You might also run across a variation of AOJP called IMOP which involves some other terms for the above. The letter "I" in this instance stands for "Intent," the letter "M" stands for "Means" and the letters "O" and "P" continue to be for "opportunity" and "preclusion." Regardless of which version you learn, they both amount to the same thing. You must be able to justify your actions later to a judge and a jury of your peers.

I realize this is a lot to run through in your head when a fight or situation is imminent, especially when they're as fluid and fast as they often are. For that reason I came up with one simple question to ask yourself in an impending situation which gets to the crux of things fairly rapidly and that is…

"Am I fighting because I want to or because I have to?"

If it's the former you might be at risk of running afoul of the law. If it's the latter you're on more solid ground. Don't make the mistake of assuming you're automatically in the wrong if it's a "want to" situation though. Using the example I gave above about rescuing the child from someone attempting to drag him/her into a car; it's not your child so you could, like so many people do, simply ignore the situation and go on your way. You won't be in any trouble with anyone for that – except perhaps your conscience. If you went to the child's aid though, as mentioned previously, it would be highly unlikely you would end up in any sort of legal hot water even though you were doing it because you wanted to rather than because you had to.

While we're on this legal stuff, let me state that none of what I've written is to be mistaken for legal advice. It would be a great idea for you to study and understand the laws of your particular jurisdiction because as I mentioned earlier what might get you a pass in one State could be an automatic jail sentence in another. You might consider booking an hour of a good attorney's time and getting very clear on some of the basics of self-defense as there is a lot of conflicting information out there even amongst the professionals. I've had discussions with law enforcement officers around the country about the carriage of weapons, rules of engagement, self-defense, etc., and even in the same jurisdiction I've received contradictory opinions. Some of them get confused between Federal law, State law, and then county and city ordinance. Typically, as a rule of thumb, try and remember whichever law is the harshest will prevail. In other words the Feds might not have any issue at all with someone carrying a pocket knife with a blade length of one inch but the city you live in might have passed an ordinance of zero tolerance for any knives at all. You cannot then, go into town with a Swiss Army pocket knife, and claim the Feds don't have an issue with it. While the Feds won't be kicking down your door to arrest you for it, the locals certainly might.

Conversely your local jurisdiction might say growing medical marijuana is ok whereas the Feds have not. If you start growing some you won't have any issues with the locals but you just might find a group of cleanly shaven, armed men wearing dark blue jackets with an alphabet soup of acronyms across the back in big yellow letters, standing around your bed at 4:30 in the morning asking you to go with them for a chat.

Remember also, ignorance is no excuse for breaking the law. You can plead all you want *"but I thought (insert thought here)"* but it will do you no good in court.

Finally, while we're touching on legal stuff here (And one more time I want to stress I am not an attorney and you should seek your own counsel) remember that just because you were not charged with a crime, or that you were acquitted in a criminal trial, that all your worries are behind you. Depending on the statutes of where you live it's possible for civil charges to be filed against you later.

Imagine sitting at home two and a half years after a fight in which you broke the jaw of someone attempting to mug you and there's a knock on the door. It's from a process server presenting you with papers to turn up in court to defend yourself. Don't think it can't happen. It can, and does, all the time. O.J. Simpson famously beat the criminal charge of murder but he lost the subsequent civil trial which is why he moved to FL. (It's one State that doesn't come after your 401K if you've had judgments filed against you.)

In a worst-case scenario, you could have spent ten thousand dollars on an attorney for the criminal trial, lost that and have been fined five thousand dollars only to have to pay another attorney to defend you in the civil trial. Lose that one and you could face losing everything you own. You had better believe the criminal and his family will be in court saying you deprived them of the income of their pure and innocent child who fully intended to turn their life around the night you broke his jaw.

In a best-case scenario in which they fail to get a conviction on either the criminal or civil charges you're still going to have to pay a bucket load of money in legal fees.

10

ADRENALIN

No serious study of self-protection can omit the impact of adrenalin on the system. Adrenalin is a layman's term used to describe a cocktail of various chemicals secreted by the adrenal glands (located just above the kidneys) when the human organism is faced with stressful situations.

I'd be willing to bet that everyone reading this book has had an adrenalin rush at some time in their lives. It might have been immediately following a car accident, it might have been during a fight or an argument. One of my best ones was during a night parachute jump in Borgo on the Island of Corsica during my time with the French Foreign Legion. The night jump was our penultimate jump to qualify for our Para wings with the Legion's famous Deuxieme Regiment Etrangere du Parachutistes or 2nd REP.

Inside the Transal, which is a smaller version of the Hercules aircraft, the interior lighting was red so our night vision wouldn't be effected and we left Calvi doing what the French Air Force – *l'Armee de l'Aire* – called a *"vol tactique."* This is a low-level flight over the Mediterranean hopping up to jump altitude at the last moment over the town of Borgo. Legionnaires who'd been former members of Her Majesty's Para's called the *"vol tactique"* a "Vomit Comet" because at extreme low level over the water the aircraft bucks up and down horrendously, and if you're prone to air-sickness, it's guaranteed on one of these flights.

I was the third man out on my side of the aircraft and began my usual "one-one thousand, two-one thousand, three-one thousand" at which point I should have experienced the violent wrenching of my chute as it deployed. In this particular instance I didn't, and kept counting figuring maybe I was rushing due to nerves caused by jumping in the dark. By the time I'd got to nearly six I realized my chute wasn't doing what it was expected to and my adrenalin kicked in full power. Fortunately, just as I was about to try and pull my reserve (which wouldn't open in time anyway due to the height at which the Legion typically jumps) my main popped. It had been a delayed opening in which the chute stayed balled shut until I reached sufficient airspeed to force air in the canopy so it opened.

Whatever situation has caused the adrenalin, you'll recognize some, or all, of the symptoms listed later. To help us understand it a little better (and that understanding is one of the keys to controlling it) let's talk a little about what happens, physiologically, when you get a shot of adrenalin.

When the brain perceives a threat, it signals the adrenal glands to release adrenalin (a cocktail made up of cortisol, aldosterone and some thirty-eight other hormones) into the system. Long ago, in caveman days, without any options other than running, freezing, or fighting, our systems evolved in such a way that adrenalin increased our heart rate drew blood from the extremities, and fed it into the large muscle groups, legs/chest/back, to aid us in that quest for fight or flight. In other words, our very survival depended on our ability to run like hell, fight like a madman, or freeze in place.

Because we didn't have "tools" that required any fine motor skills, we didn't need blood in places like the hands. Unfortunately, due to the slow rate of evolution, we are left with this response today. That can be a definite problem when trying to put keys in locks, operate phone key boards, load weapons and perform any other skills that require fine motor movement. The scenes you see in horror movies, where the heroine is struggling to put the keys in the door while being pursued by the monster,

52

are not entirely the work of Hollywood's writers. Simply put, the part of the brain responsible for large muscle control gets priority over the part of your brain responsible for abstract thought. Your ability to concentrate is therefore disrupted, as is your judgment and your analytical thinking…in short anxiety overcomes function.

Other side effects of adrenalin that are commonly mentioned are the following;

Feeling Nauseous: This is the body's attempt to get rid of excess baggage for the flight part of the program

Dry Mouth: Some self-defense experts will advise spitting on someone to shock them momentarily which is usually indicative of an instructor who's never been in a real fight.

Sweaty Palms: Some people get like this meeting their bank manager. It makes it hard to hold certain weapons such as knives and sticks or grab hold of someone.

Time Distortion: This is a critical issue to understand, especially during the aftermath. Witnesses will say they saw you choking the guy for hours when in reality it may have only been a second or two. The opposite is true, sometimes it will seem quick and it really is long. Seconds can seem like hours and hours can seem like seconds.

Auditory Shutdown: This can be dangerous for obvious reasons. If you don't hear the shouted warning about a second attacker running at you from behind, for example, you could be in a world of hurt.

Tunnel Vision: This is another dangerous side effect. In the old days it was designed to focus completely on the problem at hand and ignore extraneous stimuli. Again, in a multiple opponent situation such intense focus can be fatal.

Rapid Shallow Breathing: Learning to slow the breathing down is the key to learning to dominate adrenalin and not the other way around.

Butterflies: Again, a normal sensation and one that can lead to the aforementioned nausea.

Trembling: A side effect of the super charging of the major muscles in preparation for the fight or flight.

Increased Heart Rate: Same as the above. Smaller blood vessels are shut down and blood flow is diverted to the major arteries and muscle groups.

Due to this physiological onslaught, mistakes can be made that are fatal, especially if you are unprepared for their effects. It has been discovered that one is less likely to succumb to the negative side effects if one is **a)** aware of the phenomena and **b)** exposed to adrenalin and/or the situations that cause it, on a repeated basis. The latter is the basis of self-defense courses that incorporate stress-inoculation drills. The goal of these drills is to recreate the effects of adrenalin on the system and get you used to handling it. I can personally testify to their efficacy. The training I had long ago in Australia was so intense I'd regularly experience mild adrenalin attacks. By the time I ended up on the door handling real scenarios it was old hat. Another fine example I noticed was in the 2nd REP again. When I'd go up to jump you could see the guys getting ready for their first leap into space with ashen faces, shallow breathing, sweating and nervously laughing. Looking further towards the back of the plane though, you'd see the old hands who were as cool as cucumbers, looking about as stressed as the average housewife does shopping for groceries.

Having said all the above, understand that adrenalin is not the boogie man it is often purported to be. In fact it can be hugely beneficial in any sort of conflict and trying to fight without it would be a huge deficit. It makes you incredibly strong, it speeds up and hones reflexes, it helps blood to pump through the system like a supercharger and helps it coagulate if you're cut, and it heightens all of the senses. Why some people see it as a benefit while others see it as a hindrance is nothing other than exposure. Seasoned combat veterans welcome the effect and raw beginners let it overwhelm them.

Here's something that should help hammer home the above point. Mas Ayoob, one of America's leading self-protection instructors, conducted an experiment in which they injected champion *pistoleros* with epinephrine (the substance used by doctors to kick start hearts after they've stopped beating and for all intents and purposes adrenalin). In all but one instance the champions performed BETTER with the addition of the adrenalin in their systems. This is why scenario based training is so important in any real self-protection program. You must become like the champions in the above example and perform even better when the adrenalin kicks in.

One of the keys to helping control the effects of adrenalin on the system is used by snipers, soldiers trying to shoot, and hostage rescue team members just before entry into a room with a barricaded subject, and that is simply controlled breathing.

By breathing in slowly for a four count, holding for four, letting out for four and holding for four before inhaling again, one can rapidly get on top of many of the symptoms. This is a trick designed to dupe the brain. When it first perceives a threat it releases the adrenalin which starts rapid breathing. When the brain picks up on the rapid breathing it releases more adrenalin and the cycle spirals upwards and out of control. By simply controlling the breathing, and doing it slowly, the brain receives the message that everything must be ok and shuts down the release of the epinephrine and the system starts to calm itself.

Obviously, during an ambush attack, this deep breathing will not be of much use except during the aftermath when trying to regain control as soon as possible.

Something else that may help is understanding that when learning to handle stress, it makes no difference what causes it. Some people for example would rather face ten armed men than approach a beautiful woman in a bar (don't ask me how I know that!!). Others will get that way if they see a spider or a snake. Regardless of what sets you off, learning to control it by utilization of the breathing exercises above, will carry over in other stressful situations. In other words, exposure is exposure. We see a similar phenomenon later when we talk about imagery rehearsal exercises. Your sub-conscious mind can't differentiate between what is real and what is imagined. Ergo, if you imagine something vividly enough, as far as the subconscious mind is concerned, it really happened. It is the same with adrenalin. Regardless of it being brought on by a drill in school or the thought of chatting the cover model sitting at the bar in a night club, you're being exposed, and being exposed leads to familiarity and control.

11

THE OODA LOOP

One industry buzzword you're likely to run into if you hang around self-protection trainers enough is the term "OODA Loop." It was a term coined by Colonel John Boyd (1927-1997) and it stands for Observation, Orientation, Decision, and Action or, alternatively, Observe, Orient, Decide, and Act. Boyd's nickname was "Forty Second Boyd" due to his ability to get on anyone's tail in 40 seconds or less during aerial combat practice. By all accounts he never lost a bet and he attributed his skill to the OODA loop.

It's the process which everyone cycles through, over and over, be they individuals or even corporations, and it breaks down as follows…

Observation

The collection of information by means of the senses (typically sight and sound in physical combat). This could be a known stimulus (example brake light of a car in front which is expected) or unknown stimulus such as a loud noise right before an attack.

Orientation

The analysis and integration of the aforementioned information to formulate one's current mental perspective. This will be affected by many factors such as training, previous experience, and new information as it's unfolding.

Decision

The determination of a course of action based on one's current mental perspective and information perceived during the Observation and Orientation phases.

Action

The physical playing-out of the decision made.

At this point in the process we will observe what has happened as a result of our actions and subsequent feedback at which point the whole thing repeats itself hence the term "loop."

Let me provide you with a slightly more concrete example. You're walking down the street when you notice a gang of youths heading towards you on the sidewalk. (OBSERVATION). You've seen recent news reports and social media clips of gangs of youths beating up and robbing individuals (ORIENTATION), so you decide to cross the road (DECISION AND ACTION). You watch to see what they do next, (OBSERVATION again) which could be, continue in the direction they were going, or, cross the road and come after you, at which point you will analyze what you're seeing and make another decision based on that new information, and so on it goes.

The basic premise is to either disrupt your opponent's loop or make your loop move faster. Years ago I was telling Dennis Martin, one of the UKs premier self-protection trainers, about a tactic I used during brawls with vast numbers of opponents. In this particular occurrence, a large group of guys, some of whom had been ejected earlier, had come back to seek vengeance by bringing a slew of mates with them. They were gathering in the parking lot across the street, pulling up by the carload and grabbing weapons from the trunks of their cars.

The club manager began discussing his elaborate plan to place the desk across the foyer, stand two of us behind it (similar to the concept used by the 300 Spartans during their epic battle against the Persians) with two of us in reserve to jump in should the first two falter and/or be injured.

I decided that was nonsense and figured it would be better to hit them before they became organized. With one of my fellow bouncers behind me who was also one of my students, I ran across the road into the parking lot full speed. As I got close to them they looked up to see me as I went airborne flying into a group of three with a jumping front kick from about ten feet away. It hit the first one in the guts folding him in half, and before the second one could do anything, I had side kicked him. The third was frozen in shock when I caught him with a punch and knocked him out. My student Dennis was by this time wailing into another small group when the manager Alan, and Dennis' brother John, arrived on scene and began wading in to their targets. Within seconds we had them on the run and they had outnumbered us about six to one.

Dennis Martin, on hearing this said "yes, you disrupted their OODA loop" and began to explain the concept much as I'm laying it out here. They have this constant cycle going on of observing what is happening, orienting themselves, making a decision based upon that analysis and then acting upon it. Immediately, after acting, there is a slight mental pause to re-observe the target to see what happened as a result of your actions and the cycle repeats.

In this example, they were expecting the reaction they'd observed a bunch of times before. Outnumbered, we, like normal people, would try and run or take shelter or go down fighting under the surge of superior numbers. When what they observed instead was me running towards them laughing, it literally threw them for a loop (one wonders if that's where the expression came from). While they were now trying to process the new information brought on by their observation and decide what to do, it was too late. We were amongst them causing damage. They couldn't process what was happening fast enough, so, in effect, we had disrupted their loop by performing faster and executing an unexpected action.

Master Sgt. Paul Howe in his excellent book "Leadership and Training for the Fight" gives an amazing breakdown of the whole process but a simple excerpt will help you understand how and why a trained individual is going to process stuff faster, and have a faster loop than the other guy.

"Instead of looking at everything in the environment, walls, trees, cars, roofs etc., I focused on where a person could shoot at you from. If you tried to look at everything, you are already getting behind in the loop because you are overloading your brain with useless information and images."

Master Sgt. Howe was referring to a gunfight in the above example. Someone as experienced as he is, is going to be scanning only where he needs to be, whereas someone without a clue is going to be looking at absolutely everything. It's obvious who's going to move faster and make better decisions.

By the end of this book you're going to know where you need to focus your attention to make your loop faster. You're also going to know how to orient correctly, make correct decisions rapidly, and the correct actions to take in various situations (and you'll also be able to wax lyrical the next time someone brings up the OODA loop).

12

FIGHT, FLIGHT, FREEZING, FRONTING & FOLDING

If you listen to any discussion about fighting, combat, or survival long enough you will hear the term "fight or flight" bandied about. It's become so popular that a lot of web sites and dictionaries talk exclusively about the "fight or flight response" choosing to ignore the third and very real response of freezing. As if that wasn't bad enough, they also omit two other ubiquitous responses which are "fronting" and "folding".

Let's go over all five and learn about the pros and cons of each. We may as well knock out the ubiquitous "fight or flight response" first as that's the one that appears to be the most popular.

Fight or Flight

We touched on this a bit under the "Adrenalin" section, but let's go over the science of it all first. The brain is responsible for triggering the fear response, which is an entirely unconscious reaction. This is why, if anyone ever tries to tell you they're not afraid, they're probably either lying or crazy. When we hear something that goes bump in the night the brain sends out the sensory data – in this case the noise – to an area called the thalamus. At this point the thalamus doesn't know if the data it's receiving is dangerous or not as it could have been the cat chasing a mouse or maybe it's the onset of a home invasion. Because it's far more dangerous to assume it's the cat and have it turn out to be a threat than vice versa, the thalamus sends the sensory input along to the amygdala which then acts to protect you. It sends information further along the chain to the hypothalamus which is what triggers the fight, flight or freeze response. I would submit these first three are hard wired into us whereas the latter two are learned at an early age.

The hypothalamus does this by triggering two separate parts of your body. One is the sympathetic nervous system which uses nerve pathways to initiate reactions in the body and the other is the adrenal-cortical system which uses the blood stream.

The former, the sympathetic nervous system, causes the body to speed up, tense, and become hyper alert. At the same time the adrenal-cortical system is releasing adrenalin into the system as we mentioned in the section on adrenalin. A slew of different hormones and chemicals flood your body and get you ready for surviving combat and other life threatening situations.

These reactions, as I mentioned in the section on adrenalin, are for the most part, a good thing. After all, fear and these responses are what have kept us, as a species, alive for all these years. If we didn't fear things, we'd walk off buildings, into traffic, swim in piranha and shark infested water, and drive 150mph without seat belts, etc. It only becomes a problem when it overwhelms you and causes you to freeze up.

Freezing

Standing stock still is a very viable survival tactic in the wild because most predatory animals hunt on sight and detect movement very easily. By remaining perfectly still they may look right at you and not see you. We're trained to do it in the military. If a flare goes off, running for cover is the worst thing you can do, as the rapid movement is so readily identifiable. Instead we freeze. It is the same thing on patrol. The scout out ahead hears something suspicious and immediately holds his hand up indicating that everyone in the unit should suddenly freeze in place. We'll stand like that until it's determined that it's safe to continue moving again.

When it's not so good is if someone is hurtling towards you, intending to high five you in the face with a chair, and you stand there frozen in place until you get hit. Very often this is simply because of a lack of experience and/or training. Your brain sees the threat and is rapidly running through its memory banks to try and come up with a matching scenario so it knows what to do. While it's doing this, and failing, you're standing there waiting for instructions that aren't coming.

Training, and loads of it, is the best remedy for this problem along with positive self-talk and something called imagery rehearsal (or visualization) which we'll get to later in this chapter.

While perhaps not hardwired, the next two responses are very real reactions to imminent conflict.

Fronting

This is basically a bluff. You'll see the person puffing his chest up, sticking his chin out, and screaming. This is similar to a puffer fish blowing up, a dog's hackles, and a myriad of other animals that try to make themselves look intimidating and fiercer than they really are. They do so in the hopes that the predator will back down and leave them alone.

Folding

As in the game of poker, "folding" is giving in. In the real world, unlike the card game, this would mean complying with the bad guy's demands. It's not one of the big three i.e. Flight, Fight, or Freeze, but it's still a very real response by some people in the face of conflict. Like its counterpart, Fronting, it's done in the hope the bad guy will leave them alone because they're putting up no resistance and thus not inflaming the situation nor antagonizing the aggressor(s). This was the age-old advice regarding how to respond to a rapist for many years and many police departments even pushed this drivel. *"Fighting back will only make him mad, don't resist, give them what they want and they'll be on their way."* Funny, I've never found a male police officer, in twenty-six countries, that would be willing to follow that advice should the shoe be on the other foot.

The problem with folding is that it's no guarantee (like fronting) that it's going to work. In the case of rape it's been found that women who fight back, whether successful in their defense or not, recover much faster psychologically and stand a better chance of surviving altogether. In the case of a mugging you were pretty much guaranteed years ago that, if you handed your stuff over, you'd be left alone. Not anymore. We're seeing more and more cases where, after complying, the victim is beaten or killed anyway.

So, as promised, I'll provide some information about positive self-talk as a method of overriding paralyzing fear.

Positive self-talk is exactly what it sounds like, and it's been validated by the scientific community that you do end up acting the way you think you will. In other words, your subconscious will shape your behavior in line with your expectations.

Having a self-talk "script" is a very useful tool. There are many out there and they can be tailored to your specific goals. One of the best of these that I've seen, and the one that I use all the time, comes from Dennis Martin of CQB Services in the UK and it goes like this

I WILL DO
WHATEVER IT TAKES
TO WIN THE FIGHT
I MAY BE HIT
I MAY BE CUT
I MAY GO DOWN
I MAY FEEL PAIN
I MAY FEEL FEAR
BUT I WILL TURN PAIN INTO POWER
AND I WILL TURN FEAR INTO AGGRESSION
I WILL KEEP FIGHTING...
AS LONG AS I HAVE BREATH IN MY BODY
AND BLOOD IN MY VEINS...
AND I WILL WIN!!!
BECAUSE I *WILL* DO...
***WHATEVER* IT TAKES...**
TO WIN THE FIGHT
I WILL DO WHATEVER IT TAKES TO WIN THE FIGHT!!!

Finally, we'll finish this section with something called "Imagery Rehearsal" or "Chair Flying" as it's known in the Air Force. What it boils down to is that your subconscious can't differentiate between what is real and what is imagined. Your conscious mind can, of course, but your subconscious most certainly cannot.

The easiest way to get that point across is to mention nightmares. Most people have had one at some point in their lives and remember waking up with their heart beating rapidly, panting and in a cold sweat and yet why? Clearly there was no real threat, and yet, you awaken with the physical manifestations as if there was, and all this is because, as far as your subconscious mind was concerned, it was real.

We can take that and use it to our advantage. By taking moments to run through possible scenarios in our mind and see ourselves winning them and thwarting the adversary we are reinforcing our subconscious or programming it if you will, to perform better under the stress of a real attack.

Remember, in a real situation, because of our physiology, analytical thought will all but disappear and you'll be operating on auto-pilot. If the subconscious has been programmed correctly then it will perform accordingly.

In flying circles it's called Chair Flying and begins with a pilot putting on his uniform, sitting in a chair, placing a stick between his legs to represent the joystick and then going through the motions. The top flight aerobatic teams use it before flying, top pistol shots spend the bulk of their time on dry-firing drills, and athletes all use this method to prepare mentally for the physical challenges they're about to face.

The beauty of it is that you can do it anywhere, anytime and in any sort of situation. Look at it as if it's your own virtual reality simulator. One key to making it most effective is to involve as many of your senses as you can. In other words, don't just close your eyes and see yourself in a situation as that's only going to invoke one sense. Instead, close your eyes, see the bad guy(s), listen to what they're saying, smell them, taste the coppery taste of fear in your mouth, feel your fists clench, and the trickle of sweat on your lower back etc. The more senses you can invoke, the more effective this method of preparation will be.

13

THE FENCE

S elf-defense, true self-defense must cover more than fighting your way out of an attack. One of the critical elements missing in most schools is the fight pre-cursor and what to do. In other words, most self-defense courses and martial arts trainers are assuming that the fight has already begun and you are in it. Obviously this is not the case. Unless you've been ambushed there is a whole "dance" before the fight proper, and whether it's someone who obviously intends to do you harm, or someone trying to dupe you as they move in close enough to launch an attack, they have to get into your personal space before they can begin. This is where "the Fence" comes in.

Before we get into the Fence itself it would be incumbent upon us to give tribute to the man who coined the term, Geoff Thompson, who is a renowned self-protection instructor and author in the UK. The principle behind the fence has been around for eons and any bouncer or law enforcement officer worth their salt has been using a version of it for years. What Geoff did was to codify it, and break it down into its components, so it could be better taught to average people who didn't have the benefit of years working on the sharp end.

What it amounts to is using barriers – both physical and psychological - between you and your aggressor(s) in order to protect your personal space and give you a non-aggressive, non-threatening manner with which to defend yourself, hence the term "Fence." If all you did was put up your dukes every time someone got close to you, or assumed your favorite fighting pose in case they launched an attack, you'd look a tad paranoid. If you didn't do that and kept your hands down instead you'd be susceptible to assault. So, by putting up our hands in a non-threatening way, we let the bad guy know we are aware and at the same time we don't cause undue alarm in the minds of an innocent person approaching with a legitimate enquiry.

This letting the bad guy know that we know is the first level of the psychological use of the Fence. We haven't gone physical at all, but by correct use of body language and eye contact we can send a clear message we're not to be messed with. In other words, bad guys looking to ambush someone are looking for someone unaware of their surrounding or visibly afraid and lacking confidence. By standing erect and making eye contact with the person you're letting them know you're ready for their BS. The next step in the psychological use of the Fence is that of voice. Correct use of the voice (verbal command on the force continuum) can be a way of using the Fence. As someone approaches you in an aggressive manner a powerful "Stop" can effectively cause them to freeze in place and keep them there, and keep you safe. I used a version of this in the Legion while working as a military police officer. I had a belligerent drunk in the bar one night who was about to go ballistic. Just as he gave the game away by use of some of the pre-fight indicators (we'll discuss later in this chapter) I screamed at him "Garde Vous" (the French equivalent of "Atten-shun"). He was so conditioned by years in the military he snapped to attention (a perfect example of interrupting someone's OODA loop, right?) and I was able to get control of him during that second or two of conditioned response.

Another one I used was outside a restaurant in London. My client was inside enjoying dinner while the chauffeur and I were outside in the Merc waiting for him to be done. A gang of four troublemakers sauntered by and made as if to vandalize the car. I stepped out of the vehicle and they began to posture as if they were going to come back and start a fight. I wasn't worried about dropping them but I was very concerned about bringing undue attention to my employer, his vehicle, and the very upscale part of town we were in so, as they began to approach, I dropped back, swept my coat and put my right back on my hip as if to draw a concealed pistol.[5] They froze in their tracks. They began to look at the big black Benz, the size of me and the way I was dressed, the attending chauffeur and you could see in their eyes they were putting it all together and figuring I must be some armed diplomatic protection. They immediately gave up bluffing, flipped me off and legged it down the street. That's another perfect example of the psychological application of Mr. Thompson's Fence in action.

If they were to ignore your verbal commands or the body language and keep advancing, it is at this point you'd go into a physical "Fence" and pick up your hands and keep them between you and your antagonist. There are many ways to accomplish the hands up pose. Some people fold their arms (if you do this don't have the arms intertwined), some put their hands up, palms facing the aggressor, some place only one hand up like a police officer telling a driver to stop, some point at the person while others do what is called a "Jack Benny" (named after a popular talk show host who used to stand this way when talking to guests) with one arm folded across the chest and the other on the chin like Rodin's statue.

---

[5] FYI – You cannot be armed as a private body guard in the UK and this was a complete bluff on my part to avoid getting into a brawl. Keep in mind, I had the physical skills to back myself up if the bluff failed.

Jack Benny's classic stance

This last one is my personal favorite as it puts one hand up to ward off or block attacks to the head area and one down low to intercept kicks and/or attacks to the belly area. Anytime I work security in a nightclub and must get within "bad breath" range of a possibly dangerous person I adopt this stance.

Most instructors teach only one version of the Fence. Listen to someone like Canada's Rich Dimitri (highly recommended) and his is a relatively low level version for dissuading drunks from picking fights in bars. Listen to "Southnarc[6]" (also highly recommended), however, and because of his work as an undercover narcotics agent in a very violent Southern city, his will be more in line with dealing with the serious criminal element attempting to either kill you or rob you or both. There is absolutely nothing wrong with either approach and it's interesting to notice the two different takes on the same subject because of these stellar instructors and their respective experiences in different environments.

For me, having worked both nightclubs and in the military, and as a bodyguard I utilize both versions, and as a result, tend to teach both.

---

[6] "Southnarc" is a pseudonym for an undercover narcotics agent in the South of the US. He is an excellent teacher of extremely close range combat with guns, knives, and bare hands.

Low Level Fence

As mentioned, this is your classic bar room set up by the local bully. It will involve an approach with a verbal assault first, such as

"Have you got a problem?" "Do you have a problem?" "Have you got a problem with me?"

"You were looking at my girlfriend" "That's my girlfriend"

"Are you looking at me?" "What are you looking at?"

If you've hung around in bars long enough you've no doubt witnessed a version of this or maybe even been a victim of it. The problem is that no matter what you say (almost) will result in you getting clobbered. Tell him you were looking at his girlfriend and you'll get punched because she belongs to him. Tell him you weren't looking at her and he'll accuse you of calling him a liar, or asking *"why not, do you think she's ugly?"* The point is he really doesn't care what your answer is going to be...he's leading you along a carefully crafted script so you walk into the trap and he is then justified in hitting you.

This is all part of a stylized ritual aimed at establishing dominance over the interloper into the pack and not aimed at actually, seriously, hurting someone (of course, there are still plenty of people in prison who had no intention of seriously hurting their victim who subsequently died after hitting their head the wrong way). Rory Miller, an author of several very good self-defense manuals brilliantly describes this ritual as a "Monkey Dance" which is about as close to perfect a description as you can get.

So, let's analyze it a little bit and see what the correct approach would be

Step number 1. As he approaches, put your hands up in whatever position you've opted for. A good one, for several reasons, is both hands up with the palms facing towards your attacker. 1) it shows him, and witnesses, that you're not holding a weapon; 2) by not clenching your fists you're not demonstrating any aggressive tendencies; 3) perhaps most importantly is that you don't look like the aggressor to any witnesses who may be present (and you can bet there'll be witnesses because most of these clowns are playing to an audience); and 4) you're still in a great position to hit him, and hit him hard, with palm heel strikes.

Step number 2. You should try and circle as you talk with the person. Stepping backwards can cause you to trip over obstacles you can't see (which can activate his prey drive) which can be humiliating or fatal depending on the circumstances. I'm aware of a guy falling backwards in a parking lot dispute and banging his head and dying. Circling round puts you in control and keeps the situation confined to a small area. It also isn't confrontational like standing in front of someone can be. If circling is impossible, i.e. jammed between two parked cars, do not back up.

Step Number 3. Never contradict the person. If they say, for example, *"You were looking at my girl"* and you say *"No"* the next words out of their mouth will be *"Are you calling me a liar?"* You cannot win at this point. Say you're not a liar and you've admitted you were looking at his girl. Say yes, and you've justified, in his mind, a fight by calling him a liar. Instead, agree with the person but then deflect it. Here are some examples of what I'm talking about:

Example One:

Him: *"You were looking at my girlfriend"*
You: *"Yes, her name is Alexandra, right? I think we went to school together."*
Him: *"No, her name's not Alexandra"*
You: *"She's not Alexandra that went to Nazareth High School?"*
Him: *"No dickhead"*
You: *"Aw mate, I'm sorry then...I could have sworn she was a friend of my sister's. Here, let me buy you a drink, ok?"*

Example Two:

Him: *"You looking at me?"*
You: *"If your name's Brian and you're a cop I am? "I'm supposed to meet Brian the police officer here to buy his car."*
Him: *"No my name's not Brian and I'm not selling any f**king car."*
You: *"Oh, sorry buddy. I'm supposed to be meeting some off-duty cop here about buying his car and his description's a bit like yours. You haven't seen anyone else like you in here tonight by chance?"*
Notice I've slipped in the fact there is a police officer supposed to be meeting me which hopefully will put the clown's plan on hold.

Example Three:

Him: *"You got a problem?"*
You: *"Yes, tons of them mate. In fact, I've got more problems than a math book. I just got fired and I found out my wife's having an affair. On top of that some jackass stole my dog, and my car got repossessed. I figured I'd come here and get a drink or kill myself. How's it going on your end?"*

Make sure you never say *"Calm down"* to anyone in this situation. Again, like the "liar" line the result is scripted and predictable. *"Calm down? I am calm. You want to see me when I'm not calm?"* Another top tip is using a common name. For example, in the scenario where the guy asks are you looking at him reply with *"Yes, I met you at John's party a while ago right?"* This serves two purposes. 1) by using a common name such as John, there's a very good chance the guy actually knows someone by that name; and 2) that concerns him, because if you do have a mutual friend, he's going to make an ass of himself and cause a problem with the friendship if he rearranges your face.

Role playing is a vital aspect of training and becoming confident in dealing with this type of confrontation. So, you must practice because unexpected problems will occur. Having dealt with them in training you'll be confident in dealing with them in the real world. For example, what happens, if when you answer the question about *"were you looking at my girlfriend?"* with *"yes, her name's Caroline right?"* and it actually is Caroline you immediately have to follow up with *"Caroline Kone-Brucato from Boston right?"* otherwise both you and Caroline are about to have a lot of explaining to do. (Notice the last name is non-existent gibberish which avoids the highly improbable occurrence of guessing her real first and last name)

A question often arises during training sessions in this low-level Fence and that is what do you do if he slaps your hand out of the way? For me, personally, that constitutes assault and I'm going to defend myself. I've heard people try and say they wouldn't do anything other than raise them again, but what if on the next slap he's knocking them out of the way to hit you in the face? You are legally justified in defending yourself, and just to reiterate, once he's put his hands on you he has already assaulted you.

Serious Criminal Assault

The Fence can (and must) be used during a serious criminal assault, i.e. the type of attack we see repeatedly on reality TV shows that air video of criminal attacks. In these, professional criminals with no other objective other than to use you as a supply source, will try and work their way in close enough by using deceptive dialogue to gain a position from where they can launch an attack. They're not dumb. They know about concealed weapons, mace and OC, cell phones, self-defense, and avenues of escape. What they do is utilize a plan that will eliminate most of the aforementioned protective measures. If for example, they can get in close enough by putting you off guard by asking for directions, the first time you're going to realize you're under attack is after he's just slugged you, or worse, his mate has been using the distraction to sneak up and grab you from behind. It's very important to distinguish between this and the MD or monkey dance. This is no low-key dominance ritual being played out between two competing males of the species. This is a full-on attack and they have no more qualms about killing you than you have feelings for the sandwich you ate for lunch.

Before I go over the following, please don't delude yourself that if you do carry some type of self-defense weapon, that you don't need what we're talking about because you'll get your weapon out in time. Almost every cop in the country has heard of the twenty-one-feet drill which is the distance a man can cover and get to you before you can access your pistol. I demonstrate another one at my seminars around the country where I get a volunteer and tell them where on their body I'm going to hit them, when I'm going to do it and with which hand. To date I've never had anyone successfully block me and I'll do it five times in a row.

Step Number One: Once again the first step in this type of approach is to get your hands up between you and him. Again, in this instance I'll revert to both hands up and palms towards the guy for the same reasons we talked about in the low-key assault. It's non-threatening, ready to hit and looks non-aggressive to witnesses.

Step Number Two: Ask the approaching person to stop where they are and ask their questions. At the same time, spin off to either your left or right on a ninety-degree angle. Like the cornering we practice in the low key this is again non-confrontational, but more importantly, it will expose his accomplice, if he has one, sneaking up behind you. This is done using a combination of verbal commands and physical gestures.

Step Number Three: If they don't comply, we must immediately escalate and put more venom in our command and say *"STOP."* If they continue at this point, the next step is to say *"Back Up",* and if that doesn't work *"Back the F**K up."* Many criminals and human predators will only register what you're saying with the addition of profanity. Another piece of dialogue that works well in the United States is *"Give me five feet."* That's because most U.S. corrections officers learn this command during training to use on an inmate trying to work his way in close enough to attack. If the con doesn't immediately back up he's given a shot of OC spray. Like my example earlier with the Legionnaire, there's a good chance your criminal assailant has been through the prison system at some time and will be institutionalized. Hearing the command will cause a split-second hesitation as he tries to figure out how you know he's been in prison and how you know the commands you're using. For all he knows at this point you're in law enforcement or corrections.

The moving off the line and use of a command such as *"give me five feet"* are both further examples of the OODA loop. He's expecting you to fall victim to his (or their) plan like the last victims he targeted. You OBSERVE his action, however, and ORIENT yourself by processing the fact that this could be an attack. You move off the line, and what you see here will help you DECIDE what your ACTION should be. He is expecting you to be distracted and let him get close. When he observes you putting your hands up and moving off the line of attack he's momentarily confused and now must re-observe what you're doing exactly. Then he has to re-orient himself to your new position (at this point you're two moves ahead of him), make a decision now whether to continue with his plan (which is rapidly unraveling due to your actions), and then act based upon his decision.

14

SEPARATING
THE BAD FROM THE GOOD

Go out and about enough and you're going to have to deal with people who will get in your personal space, and shaping up to them in your karate stance on the off chance they're bad guys, isn't practical. Good criminals however know how to convince (con) people that they are also legitimate, until such times as it's too late to do anything to stop their attack, so we must have some guidelines in place to separate the two.

Fortunately for us, no matter how good the criminal is, he will often give away his intended attack by body language. This is the sort of thing you learn to read very early on when you grow up on the wrong side of the tracks, but if you've lead a sheltered life, you won't have a clue. There are a slew of giveaway idiosyncrasies, but the most common four are quite distinct and worth studying. Do this by watching video clips of attacks on store clerks that air on such TV shows as "Wildest Police Videos." In fact, an excellent drill is to watch such clips and see if you can correctly guess the exact second they're going to launch their attack.

The four biggies are as follows; Grooming, Glancing, Weight shift and Hands Round the Waist Area.

Grooming

Grooming is the term applied to any touching of the face, brushing the nose, rubbing the ears, playing with the hair or hands up near the face. It is a classic pre-fight indicator and one you should be very aware of. Almost all criminals do this and so do most people when they're being deceptive so be especially leery of it.

Classic grooming indicating deception

Glancing

For law enforcement the glance is a giveaway that the suspect is about to run. In that instance he is looking for escape avenues. For targeted civilians the glance will precede the attack and is being used by the bad guy to ensure there are no witnesses, cameras, or law enforcement around. It will typically be furtive and fast and may be repeated more than once as he continually scans the area. Sometimes, the bad guys will look at a target right before they launch their attack, which is especially prevalent in law enforcement when attempts are made to grab for an officer's gun.

Furtive glancing looking for witnesses, cameras, cops, and escape routes

Hands

Just like the good guys, bad guys keep their weapons accessible around their waist line. It may be in a back pocket, under the waist band, front pocket, etc., but often it will be near the center of gravity. Hands moving in that vicinity therefore are also good pre-fight clues and indicative of the fact he may have a weapon concealed in that area. Be especially wary of anyone who's hand or hands you can't see. Bodyguards are trained to scan constantly between hands and eyes because eyes will conceal the intent and the hands will conceal the weapon. If someone is getting within range with at least one hand out of sight tell them to show it to you or get ready to escape or deal with a weapon attack.

What's in his right hand?

Weight Shift Balance

The weight shift is the all-time classic indicator of the punch/kick being just seconds away. The most common example is the right foot stepping backwards and the body blading, but shifting from foot to foot is another good indicator. This dropping back of the foot is called "blading" because the body ends up angled at approximately forty-five degrees. The most common is the right shoulder dropping back which is the set up for the big right hand punch that's about to be launched.

Body now "bladed" and right hand loaded to launch

The above four are by no means exhaustive, but are the best four to rely on. Other instructors talk about the face becoming pale (blood draining from the extremities to fuel the major muscle groups as mentioned in the section on adrenalin), shallow rapid breathing, thousand yard stares and so on. The problem with all of those is they can be easily misinterpreted. If a person for example is arguing with you after a near miss in traffic, adrenalin may cause the pale face and shallow rapid breathing despite the fact the person has no intention of assaulting you. The main four however are very rarely confused for anything else but what they are, pre-fight indicators.

Obviously, one on its own isn't as certain as two or more. For example, someone may be looking around to make sure it's safe to cross the road (after a fender bender with you for example) and someone else might be reaching in their pocket to grab their driver's license. It's when we see several of them clustered together that we need to be extremely concerned.

Again, just as with the low-level conflict, you absolutely must go out and practice this as a scenario drill. Anybody who thinks they're going to read this book and somehow absorb the techniques by osmosis is seriously deluding themselves. Can you imagine for one minute any military or law enforcement training that doesn't involve scenario training? If the pros,

81

who deal with extreme violence on a day to day basis, practice scenario training then you should as well. Put another way, would you put faith in a police force that only read about practicing to be a law enforcement officer but never actually practiced high speed driving on a skid pan, how to handcuff, or how to shoot? The answer is obvious so get some likeminded friends and play around with both the low-level threats and the serious crime versions as well.

This sort of training pays off big time. One night I was cleaning up my business before leaving for the night and I heard my friend outside talking to someone. I walked out to find him engaged in a dialogue with a guy claiming he needed help pushing his van to a gas station. The bad guy had wrongfully assumed that my mate was on his own and chosen him as his victim.

My arrival on the scene visibly upset him but he continued with his pitch about his truck running out of gas, the cops telling him if he didn't move it they'd have it towed and some other palaver. On several occasions, while we were heading to the street to give this guy a push, he tried to get behind us but I made sure Jamie slowed down even more than he did and wouldn't let the guy outmaneuver us.

As we started walking to the alleged van and listening to him giving us his sob story the guy asked if either of us had a light and proceeded to whip out his cigarettes. I told him neither of us smoked. Five minutes later, at which point we arrived where his car was supposed to be (now, miraculously missing) he pulled out a lighter and lit one of his smokes (so much for asking us for a light).

We wished him well at that point and left him alone. Amusingly enough, I had a Secret Service mate visiting me a few days later. I was relaying the story to him when I looked across the street and saw the same guy talking to some potential victim at the bus stop. I told my Secret Service mate and his partner *"that's the guy"* and I went careening across the street and grabbed him at the bus stop. I told the stunned passenger who was in the process of leaving with this guy *"let me guess, he just told you his truck is out of gas around the corner, and he needs help pushing it to a gas station before the cops arrive right?"* The passenger/potential victim looked aghast and wanted to know how I knew and I told him what had transpired the other night.

The crook kept claiming his truck was miraculously, coincidentally, out of gas again so I told him we wanted to see it. Before we went another five feet I told him that if we walked around the corner and the truck wasn't there I was going to slap him, at which point he broke cover and told us there was no truck. Unfortunately, there wasn't much my Secret Service mate could do because at that point he hadn't committed a crime, and there wasn't much I could do because there were two sworn law enforcement officials present, so I sent him on his way with a warning of what would happen if I saw him in the area again.

Both the victim at the bus stop and my mate Jamie admitted they'd fallen for his spiel hook, line, and sinker, and if left to their own devices, probably would have been victims of a mugging or worse. Astute readers will also notice that this ploy to lure the victim away from everyone else was the "isolation" part of SIVA and the story was his "verbal." He'd already chosen his victims and all that was missing in both instances was the "attack."

15

STEPS TO TAKE

O k, now that we've got some of the theory out of the way, let's get into the practical side of things. We're going to begin with the soft skills. Those are the techniques that involve everything we do other than fighting somebody else. Looking at a group of guys, for example, who are walking down the street towards you, making you feel uneasy, and causing you to cross the road to the other side, is practicing soft skills.

Assessment Time

The first step in our plan is to develop the habit of gathering intelligence. Remember General Norman Schwarzkopf aka "Stormin Norman" of Operation Desert Storm fame? He spent weeks before committing to action by having Special Forces behind enemy lines gathering intelligence. At the same time this information was coming in, so was imagery from overhead U.S. satellites. This enabled the General to formulate a plan that would maximize his troops, take advantages of enemy weaknesses, and win in the shortest time possible with minimum casualties. The old adage from the military, i.e. "that time spent gathering intelligence is seldom wasted," proved to be true then just as it's true now.

So, how do we do this in the civilian world? Obviously we don't have satellites at our disposal and/or compliments of SF soldiers to deploy. It's simple really. We do it by taking five to ten seconds when exiting a building (the mall for example) or your home to pause, survey your surroundings, and take in information. The best way to do this is to break the area you're looking at into a foreground, a middle ground, and background. Begin by looking at the foreground and do it from right to left and not left to right. Why? We read from left to right and so, as a result, we tend to skim over minor details when looking in that direction. By forcing ourselves to look from the right to the left we tend to take in more information. The other step to keep in mind is that you search the foreground first, and then the middle, and then the background last. That's because anyone in the foreground is going to be the most dangerous due to their proximity.

When we do the sweeps we're looking for things that don't seem right. For example, a few months ago, I left a book store in an incredibly upscale neighborhood and noticed two guys dressed in wife beaters and baggy jeans leaving the car park in a car that clearly cost less than a happy meal. Next to the book store were a gentleman's tailor with suits beginning at $2,500, an art gallery, a nail salon and day spa, and an upscale day planner store. All the other cars in the parking lot were an array of the crème de la crème of luxury automobiles. It didn't jibe with me that those guys would be there and in the market for anything in that price range. Sadly, I missed getting the license tag due to it being dusk, but upon arriving at my car, I found I'd become victim of a spate of robberies where a local gang was targeting SUVs for lap tops and guns by punching out the door lock. The models they were picking were domestic and therefore the alarm didn't go off when the lock was punched as the car assumed it must be the owner coming through the door. They were in and out in fifteen seconds and of course the real danger was that you'd catch them in the act which would put you at risk of being shot by the lookout man and driver.

We're also picking out where we parked our car and the most expeditious route to it. We're looking for people who might be loitering near or en route to your vehicle. A favorite of sexual predators at malls for example is to wait beside a victim's car in a van. As the victim approaches, the door slides open, the victim is grabbed and dragged into the car, in less than three seconds, and carted away. By pausing for the five seconds before you blindly head to your car you would have a chance to spot the suspicious vehicle and go back for assistance from mall security. What if it's not directed at you? What if you're on vacation, and instead of wandering out of a store or hotel into the middle of a local riot or coup, you spot the melee and return inside? The possibilities are endless and all it takes is a few seconds to pause, look around, and assess what you see happening.

On a personal note, my neighbor in Wilmington NC learned this technique from me and used it upon returning home from a trip to the beach. She noticed a screen hanging off the window and feet marks up the front wall of the house. She called 911 and the police turned up hoping to catch a burglar inside. Fortunately, or unfortunately, as the case may be, the bad guy hadn't made it inside and everything was ok. However, given the large amount of burglaries that turn into murders when the thief is caught by the home-owner, it's

Man Stabbed to Death

Charlotte, NC – A man who stabbed a stranger to death in his Charlotte home will spend life in prison.

Antoine Young pled guilty Thursday afternoon to murdering Chris Radok in Jan 2011. Prosecutors agreed to life in prison in exchange for not pursuing the death penalty.

Prosecutors said Young beat Radok with a bat and stabbed him multiple times with different knives.

"This was very savage, one of the worst crime scene pictures I've had to review over and go over," said prosecutor Gabrielle Macon.

very possible a tragedy was prevented that day, just by following the simple intel gathering trick.

Just to hammer this point home, my friend "Radar" became the first murder victim of 2011 in Charlotte NC by walking in on a burglar who grabbed a knife and stabbed him to death. Very sad and all too common.

Places to use this technique are; leaving a store, exiting your vehicle, leaving home, arriving home, leaving and arriving at work, to name but a few. It can also be used entering a room or a bar. In this case you should be weighing up whoever is inside. In most occurrences it will be perfectly harmless and people will just look at you, and you at them, out of idle curiosity. Occasionally however you've gone into a bar when you're from out of town and it's the wrong bar. If you don't want to upset the locals just beat a hasty retreat and everything should be fine. If you must stay for whatever reason, then the way to assess them is to look at them fairly quickly and then break eye contact away to one side or the other. Looking up or down can sometimes be misinterpreted as being either submissive or dismissive.

Know The Way Out

An old Special Force's adage is never go in somewhere if you don't have a plan to get out. This applies in self-protection by knowing where your exits are. This is particularly important in hotels, aircraft and any building you're not familiar with for obvious reasons. What if you're in a mall and a crazed lunatic opens fire on the crowd? What if you're in a hotel or ballroom and it catches fire? Knowing where those exits are is going to put you so far ahead of everyone else it's not funny.

A fun but serious game played by my team members in the UK on bodyguard assignments was to cover one of the team member's eyes, and if he couldn't immediately identify the exits by pointing in their direction, he bought the other guys' dinner.

You can use the same type of training at home as your kids do at school and you probably do at work and that is to practice a fire drill every six months. It's absolutely stunning how many homes burn down every year in the US and how many people perish within unnecessarily. Grab the kids and run through where the exits are and also identify a fire rendezvous point. That's a place where you all gather after the fire in case you didn't get out as a group. That enables you to quickly do a head count and know if everyone made it out safely. If you live on the second floor you can purchase a simple ladder from your local home improvement center that will enable you and the family to safely climb down from the upper floors in case the downstairs is ablaze. Remember, the bulk of house fires start in the kitchen so it's entirely possible the downstairs will be engulfed by the time you realize you're in danger.

Another place to know how to escape from, and one often overlooked by the experts, is the trunk of your car. Getting in is easy, right? How do you get out and how do you do it if it's dark? Do you hide a flash light in there just in case? Do you know how to activate the safety release that most modern cars come with? Do you know how to get out of yours if it's an older model? Every year, a slew of people are transported unwillingly in the trunks of their own vehicles by carjackers, murderers, and rapists.

We'll cover some more of this in the travel module of the book concerning airlines, hotels, etc.

3 Second Rule

Get into the habit of locking your doors within three seconds of getting into your house, car, or hotel room. If a predator is following you to take advantage he has a limited amount of time to get into where you are by following you through the door. By locking the doors immediately, you deny him that access. Far too many people get into their car, for example, and balance their checkbooks or open their new CD and figure out how to put it in the player.

One woman at a local real estate office I spoke to could have avoided a nasty assault and potential pack rape if she'd followed this simple rule. She was talking on her cell phone, writing down info in her day planner which was on the roof of the car, while she stood in the open car door with one foot balanced on the door sill. Two attackers attempted, in broad daylight, to drag her into their car, punching and pounding her for a scary fifteen seconds before her screaming alerted enough people nearby. Had she got in the car, locked the doors and then made the call they probably wouldn't have even seen her.

The same is true at home. If you're loading groceries into the house and it requires multiple trips, even though it may be an inconvenience, lock and unlock your doors each time. Complacency and the attitude of *"oh, it will never happen to me"* will come back to haunt you if you get lazy on your security regime. Remember, complacency is the enemy of good security.

Lower Your Profile

This falls under the advice of "don't look like a victim". This is especially true when traveling to areas away from home. We've all seen pictures of the ubiquitous loud, obnoxious, American tourist replete with Hawaiian shirt and draped in cameras. Sadly, a lot of people actually dress like that, and when you consider that in a lot of third world countries the average person earns in a year what the American earns in a week, little wonder our tourist is looked upon as a piece of corn ripe for the picking. The attitude of the bad guy in the third world locale is that you make plenty of money so you can always buy another camera or watch.

So, while this is important anywhere, it becomes doubly important around tourist resorts and landmarks frequented by tourists. Think about it from the criminal's view point. He wants a victim who is task fixated, which is almost all of them standing around agog at one of the natural wonders of the world. Once he's chosen you and swipes your stuff, he knows the chances of you spending $3,000 to return and testify, in the unlikely event of his capture by local law enforcement, over the theft of a $1,000 camera is slim to none. By lowering your profile you lessen your chances of being chosen as a potential victim.

How do we do this? There are several ways to consider. One is to buy local clothing so you don't stand out as much. Some friends of mine on executive protection details go so far as to carry local newspapers and smoke local brand cigarettes. Any opportunist criminal is going to see the local clothing, newspaper and cigarettes and assume you're a native. Even if he realizes you're not, he'll assume by the carriage of the newspaper that you're a frequent enough visitor, and savvy enough about the location, that you don't fit the profile of the unaware victim he's looking for.

In real life, the following applies as well. Leave the fancy car behind, don't wear your Rolex or expensive jewelry, eschew the Hartmann briefcase, don't stay in five star hotels and/or flash cash, etc. I know it's fun to work hard and spend your money on the status symbols, but you really do have to pick when and where you wear them. Walking around a third world country with a Rolex and you may as well wear a sign that says "mug me." One of my former EP clients had two completely different wardrobes (at my behest). One was for his work in London and New York's financial districts and it consisted of suits made in Saville Row, shoes by Church, and a watch that cost the same as a small house. His other, for trips to Florida and India, consisted of clothes from the Walmart equivalent, a Timex, and shoes that cost less than a hundred dollars.

If you're in the military or law enforcement and traveling aboard, you may want to re-think the screaming eagle haircut as that's the equivalent of wearing a "take me hostage because I'm an American soldier or LEO" sign around your neck. Another thing to do is don't wear anything that has a political or religious saying on it. Many years ago, in Africa, a group of US and UK teenagers were massacred by rebel soldiers who mistook their cheap military surplus clothing for mercenary uniforms. I almost made the mistake once of running with a red bandana in Los Angeles when bodyguarding the rock band "Warrant." It was a day off and I was working out at Gold's Gym near Venice Beach. My team mate pointed out that, only a few blocks up the road, was the turf of two of LA's most notorious gangs, the "Bloods" and the "Crips" who indicate their affiliation by wearing red or blue bandanas. Without his timely intervention, I may have been canceling any future birthdays and appearing on the seven o'clock news as the latest victim of gang warfare.

Make sure you don't become task fixated, and look alert as you move about. Don't walk too fast, and by the same token, don't dawdle. Be aware of what type of shopping bags you carry and what they say about you, and don't drape yourself in souvenirs...criminals love tourists for those aforementioned reasons.

The Buddy System

Special Forces usually travel in four man teams. Executive protection specialists travel in teams of anything from two to twenty-four members, juvenile gangs and bikers all travel in packs. The common denominator here is that there is safety in numbers.

As a recon diver in the French Foreign Legion the first rule that I was taught about SCUBA diving is that you must NEVER do it alone. You practice what is called "The Buddy System" in which you always dive with at least one other person. That way, if an accident should happen, someone is able to render aid either by helping the victim directly, or going to get help.

I want you to adopt the same methodology whenever possible and that is adopt the buddy system and at least go out in pairs. Take a workout partner to the gym, car pool with someone, go shopping with a friend, etc.

Criminals who prey on people have all said that controlling one person is relatively easy. Controlling more than that becomes an exercise in frustration and is much harder. Trust me when I say criminals are opportunists. If there are two potential female victims exiting a mall and one is on her own while the other has two friends with her, the criminal will take the one on her own.

Buddies don't have to be real either. Imagine you're a criminal and you're trying to force your way into a woman's house and she screams out *"John, Tony...get the shotgun and come quick."* John, Tony, and the shotgun are all imaginary but the criminal has no way of knowing that. The same ruse can be used by a lone woman concerned about getting into an elevator with a guy standing inside who makes her uneasy. All she has to say is *"you go on ahead, I'm waiting for my husband and his friends."*

91

Whether the friends are real or imaginary there is no question that there is safety in numbers.

Study Time

Make sure you study local crime trends whether at home or traveling. Most people spend more time working out what the weather will be like before traveling somewhere so they can pack accordingly than they'll spend looking up what they're going to face locally, crime wise. In the resource section of this book you'll find links to various web sites where you can log into and research any location in the world for an update. There are also companies in the private sector such as the very famous Kroll International, who, for a fee, provide Fortune 500 company execs with detailed reports on what is going on in any area in the world. Local news stations are a good source, as is the internet. In a lot of places the local police will have a resource officer who will be able to help. As a bodyguard, I always contacted local law enforcement and asked them about parts of town to avoid and so on.

By knowing what is going on you'll be in a much better position to lessen your chances of being targeted. For example, my home town is currently experiencing a mass crime spree in car break-ins with gang members hitting SUVs looking for both lap tops and guns. We're also enjoying a spate of home invasions. Preparing to deal with those two scenarios is going to be a lot different than for someone living in an area prone to carjacking and a serial rapist.

In the former, I might make sure to secure valuables out of sight in the trunk or not bring them at all to deal with the car break ins, and fitting panic alarms, a panic rooms, and upgrading my locks to deal with the home invasion scenario. In the second example however, I'm going to find out what model is the favorite for the carjacker and make sure I don't drive one and be hyper-vigilant whenever I'm stopped in traffic. If I was a female, with regards to the rapist, I would take self-defense classes, read and practice the techniques in a book like this, and carry OC spray. (If permitted in my local jurisdiction.)

Would your plan change if you were going somewhere exotic on business and found out they were kidnapping Americans, and in your second-choice destination, it was renowned for pick pockets. In the first case I might lower my profile and go native, arrange the meeting via conference call, or go with a team of close personal protection specialists. In the second example, I'm going to leave the bulk of my money somewhere safe, carry traveler's checks, and keep a dummy wallet stuffed with newspaper and expired credit cards that I can lob away from my mugger while hoofing it in the opposite direction.

You get the idea, I'm sure. Take the time and learn what's going on in your neighborhood, and the city in which you live, to deal with local crime problems and utilize the resource section of this book to dig up info on local crime trends in the area you have to go for either vacation, business, or both. The advanced knowledge will pay off in spades one day when it prepares you for what's about to happen.

Crime Scene Number 2

Never ever leave crime scene number one for crime scene number two. You've almost certainly heard this advice before but it is of paramount importance. Paul Pfingst, a District Attorney in San Diego CA said, *"Murder is one thing, but torture, mayhem and savagery – it takes more time for these crimes. Every torture case I have prosecuted involved a victim isolated and completely controlled."*

It's a chilling statement, but true. Someone who wants your money is going to hit you now, take it, and immediately flee the scene in a bid to place as much distance between the crime scene and himself. Any sexual predator or serial killer on the other hand, is going to have to go hunting to find his victim, subdue them, and take them back to his lair which will be set up according to his particular twisted fantasies. There have been cases of victims kept alive for years, abused on a daily basis, and discarded once they get beyond their prime or "usefulness".

Rape victims are not the only ones at risk here. Think of a kidnapping victim in a foreign country. You're going to be attacked at one location and then moved to another. Your greatest chance for survival will be during the first assault because the second location will be especially designed to keep you out of sight – and sound – of any potential rescuers.

You have options and chances at crime scene one. Time is on your side at that moment, not the aggressor's. Do whatever you have to do to escape. Go limp, fight back, and scream. Yes, it may mean being shot and/or killed, but the critical question to ask is *"if someone is willing to kill you in broad daylight in a parking lot, think of what he'll be more likely to do in an isolated spot that he controls?"*

Code Words

Make sure you have a code word that you practice with your significant other and/or family members or people you hang out with regularly. Again, this is a page straight out of Bodyguarding 101. You need some discrete way of alerting other members of the team to a potential threat without alerting the threat himself. The code word can be a signal for example that means *"honey, grab the kids and head to the car as fast as you possibly can"* or, simply, *"We've got trouble."*

When I worked security at the Town & Country Club in London, the DJ was given the code words so he could, via the PA system, alert every single security member without causing a panic amongst the audience. If we had a bomb threat for example the call might go out for *"Mr. Brown is needed in the office"* which would let us know we had to begin searching the premises. We had another in the event of a fire and so on. Imagine instead if he'd announced there was possibly a bomb in the club? That sort of panic killed a slew of people in a club in Chicago, shortly after 9/11, when someone let off tear gas inside. A stampede ensued because the patrons thought it was a chemical attack by terrorists.

Make up your own, make it something you wouldn't use inadvertently, and practice it occasionally. The one I figured out with my ex was *"Honey, why don't you go buy something with the credit card."* Now the word "honey" was a term of endearment I would never normally use so that let her know immediately that something was up...and of course I'd never tell her to go buy something, especially on my credit card (we had separate accounts).

Businessmen who go through anti-kidnapping training are taught similar codes. During a "proof of life" call for example they might ask *"did all five kids get their report cards?"* which lets the listeners know there are five kidnappers. Once again, it is not enough to read these and think *"wow, great idea."* You absolutely must sit down with your kids and significant others and practice them until you have them down pat. You also should do a refresher every once in a while. I don't know any professional security specialist worth his salt who doesn't train and practice scenarios on a regular basis to keep the knowledge fresh.

The "What If?" Drill

This is another one straight out of the bodyguard's playbook. Someone once said of bodyguards *"they're professional paranoiacs"* and it's probably got some truth in it. Our job is to prevent an attack from happening in the first place so we spend loads of time avoiding routines and so on. Another major part of the job is being hyperalert in the event of an attack on the principal. To do this, we play the "what if" game. What if gunmen burst through the door right now? What if that truck in front of us slammed their brakes on and blocked us in? What if the guy over there suddenly pulls a weapon from under his coat and begins firing? By imagining these worst-case scenarios and running through possible options, you've shortened the OODA loop we talked about earlier, which means you'll be out-thinking the opposition, and moving faster than anyone else who'll have to perceive the threat, assess what they're plan is, and then implement it. You will be light years ahead because you foresaw the attack in your mind's eye before it happened and formulated a plan of action already.

Now that doesn't mean you spend your whole day doing this – unless you're a close personal protection specialist – but do it for some common scenarios occasionally so you have already run through some options in your mind. Do it next time you're sitting at a light in your vehicle. What would you do if a guy walked up with a gun and wanted your car? Do it on the way to your car in the parking deck…if the guy coming towards you pulled a knife and told you to go with him, what would you do? You don't have to do either of those every day to be ahead of 99% of the population. Doing it once or twice, every now and then, will suffice.

It was interesting to note that on the Motorcycle Safety Federation course that I used to do every couple of years that one of the drills was identical to this. We were taught when riding to always be thinking *"what if that car suddenly turned in front of me?"* *"What if the car in front suddenly jammed on their brakes?"* *"What if that oncoming car came across the median and into oncoming traffic?"* and so on. Once again, they prepare you in an easily practiced way to be moves ahead of the average person during a catastrophe.

Think Like The Enemy

One of my good friends in law enforcement took part in a bodyguard course for witness protection which involved an exercise whereby they had to plan how to assassinate a public figure. I attended another course that incorporated a similar idea except ours was to plan the kidnapping of an executive. In both cases, real people were targeted (unbeknownst to them), and afterwards presented with the plans of how we planned to kill and/or kidnap them. This was done in the former case to alert the VIP so he could better protect himself, and in the latter, it was a case of that and possibly drumming up some business by the company in question.

Regardless of the motive, the exercise is brilliant because once you look at the problem from the enemy's viewpoint, you can see where the weaknesses in your defense are and plan accordingly. Later, in the chapter on home defense, I'm going to have you look at your house as if you were a burglar trying to break in and see if you can spot any weaknesses that need fixing. Here though, in this exercise, the idea is to go out one day and play the part of a junkie in need of money to buy a fix. Who would you pick as your victim? More importantly, why would you pick them? Is it because they're small in stature? Is it because they're task fixated and therefore easy to sneak up on? Is it because they stupidly flashed a wad of cash at the store they were in or maybe they've left their purse unattended for a second to sort out the toddler in the stroller. You get the idea. The goal then is to ask yourself *"why did I pick that particular person, and am I ever guilty of doing what they did?"* If the answer is yes then shore up your defense. When I run the "How to Be Your Own Bodyguard Course" it's a two-day training event with both lectures and hands on training. One of those hands-on sessions is this one, usually done over lunch at the mall. During one of the classes in Tampa Florida, two of the female students came back from lunch, and this exercise, absolutely stunned and shocked at how easy it had been. One lady told me she'd picked four people just leaving the hotel and entering the Mall entryway. Remember that criminals are opportunists, so the harder you make their job, the more likely it is that they'll pick an easier, softer target. Remember, their goal is money, not necessarily YOUR money. Anyone's will do and ensuring it's not yours is YOUR number one priority.

16

MISCELLANEOUS SECURITY

Right, in miscellaneous security, we cover all the minor facets of a good security plan that aren't addressed in the major sections. In other words, these apply to both home and on the road.

ATM Security

Day Time Only: Do not, if possible, ever use an ATM at night time. Time and again, people using ATMs are attacked and robbed under the cover of darkness. Be hyperaware of the lighting around one if you absolutely must use it at night. Enterprising thieves have been known to knock out the security lighting of the ATMs they intend to hit.

Scan First: Use the intel gathering ploy you were taught in the first chapter. Who's in the area? Do they look like they belong there or are they loitering? What vehicles are nearby? Is anyone in them? Is the engine running (look for smoke from the exhaust pipe)? Are there hiding places nearby that somebody could use? Is the security lighting intact?

Think Like a Criminal: Is the ATM easy to run and hide from? You should put yourself in the predator's shoes and think like him/them. If you were going to rob someone using this ATM, where would YOU hide? Now, check that area and what do you see? Is it a viable target or is it relatively safe?

Use the Buddy System: Use the buddy system wherever possible. It's much harder to rob and control two people compared to just one. A friend of mine was robbed at a large Mall in broad daylight, in the parking lot. He heard footsteps running up from behind him, but before he could turn, he was whacked on the head with a 2x4. He awoke on the ground to find a woman in a car reaching out over his prone body while she used the machine. To add insult to injury, he said she looked at him like he was some homeless drunk who'd picked that spot to sleep.

Avoid Routine: Remember, one of the bodyguard's key tools is to avoid routine behavior. Do not make regular deposits or withdrawals. The same rule applies, by the way, if you make deposits for your small business. Turning up at the same time on the same day every week, loaded with money, is courting disaster.

Get it and Go: Once you have your money, stash it and go. Too many people hang around counting their money which makes them task fixated and enables the bad guy to approach undetected.

Counter Surveillance: Just because you used the ATM and weren't robbed doesn't mean you can afford to drop your guard. Hagakure, the Samurai's book of how to conduct oneself as a warrior, mentions *"After the Battle Tighten Your Chin Straps."* What that's referring to is that the most likely time for a counter attack is immediately following a battle when a lot of inexperienced soldiers will drop their guards and relax.

Just because you weren't mugged at the ATM doesn't mean you can relax just yet. A common ploy is to follow the person from the machine and mug them out of sight of the cameras on the machine and/or the parking lot. The same rule applies if you go into the bank. You should exercise caution and maintain a heightened sense of awareness for at least 20 minutes after leaving the ATM/bank.

Lock it All: If it's a drive through machine make sure all your doors and windows are locked before you get there. I'm aware of two instances where someone was taking money from the machine and the bad guy jumped in the car on the passenger's side though the UNLOCKED door. Assuming it's a walk-up machine lock the car doors when you leave even if you're only going to be inside or at the machine for a minute.

Beware of Surfers: At some locations, especially in popular areas at lunch times for example, there may be a line of people waiting to use the machine. Be aware of someone attempting to surf (look over your shoulder) who might be trying to get your PIN (personal identification number), or see if you withdrew a sufficient amount of cash to make you a viable mugging prospect.

Lost Bag/Wallet: If your bag is lost or stolen, beware of scams designed to get your PIN. A common one is for someone, allegedly from your bank, calling you and asking you to verify your PIN as they've had a report of an unauthorized attempt of someone using your card. They claim they need to verify the PIN to ensure you're the actual owner. If you're naïve enough to give it to them, you've just given them all they need to start cleaning out your account.

Dumb Stuff: Watch out for, and be aware of, stupid emails and messages that do the rounds via email or on social media from time to time. There's one that claims if you're being driven around at gun point from ATM to ATM just enter your PIN backwards and it will alert the authorities as to what's going on. Think about it for a minute and see if you can figure out why it's a nonsense idea.

Let's assume it actually worked, (more in a minute as to why it can't possibly), and you type in the number backwards unbeknownst to the bad guy(s) and it spits out your cash while alerting the authorities. By the time they get the message you're already on the way to another machine. Just what is law enforcement supposed to do? You could be five machines away by the time they get alerted.

Here's the big problem that I'm sure you've all spotted. What if your PIN is the same forward as it is backwards? 1221, 1331, 2442, 2222, et al. If you had a PIN like that, you would be sending false alarms all day long.

Use your common sense and critical thinking skills when you see posts along these lines.

Telephone Security

Unlisted Number: If you have a landline seriously consider an unlisted number. Yes, your phone company will charge you more for this (because they claim it's more expensive not to print your name in the phone book I suppose), but it's worth it. When the phone rings, it's almost always only going to be someone you've given the number to instead of nuisance callers or pranksters.

Initials Only: If you do decide to list your name, make sure that you use an initial only in lieu of your full first name. This is imperative for women who live alone. If a sexual predator is looking to get his jollies, all he has to do is sift through his local phone book and find a listing for Sally Brown for example. S. Brown on the other hand could be Simon Brown or Steven…he has no way of knowing.

Male Voice: If you are a lone female consider having a male friend put the message on your voice mail/answer machine. That way if someone does call they will assume a man lives in the house as well.

Hang Up: If you receive an obscene phone call, hang up…FAST! There's all sorts of advice out there about keeping whistles near the phone and blowing them to rupture his eardrums etc. Sorry, it's another urban legend. The receiver on the other end will only put out a certain level of volume so all your whistle is going to do is hurt your ears, not his. Also, what if you did hurt his ears and you ticked him off to the point where he decides he's going to come around and punish you for it. Don't engage the person in any way, shape, or form. Just hang up. That is the fastest way to get rid of them. In the event you get a serial caller who will not give up you can contact the phone company and they will take you through the various methods of dealing with it. You might also have to change your phone number if it becomes problematic. I am personally aware of one friend who was still getting calls despite having an unlisted number and changing it. Local law enforcement officers weren't interested and told the girl in question that the caller had a right to privacy so they couldn't try to find out where he was calling from. Fortunately, I had a friend in federal law enforcement who took the case on and tracked the phone to a girl whose boyfriend was borrowing it to make the calls. He knew the victims' number because they were both in the same off-roading club at one point, and being the treasurer, her number had been listed in the member's directory.

Keep A Log: In the event it becomes serious i.e. in the case of a serial caller, keep a log of every time they call. This is relatively easy nowadays due to itemized billing from the phone company however not every company offers it and there are ways of masking the number the call came from, so a log will help if there is a subsequent legal case.

ICE: If you have a cell phone, program the word ICE into the directory. This is a clever trick that is making the rounds. ICE stands for *"In Case of Emergency"* and so under the ICE entry you want to put the number (or numbers) of people to be contacted in the event of an emergency. For example, if you've been hit by a car and are comatose the responding emergency services personnel will grab your phone and look for ICE in the directory. If they find it, they can call your emergency contact and let them know what is going on. Originally, some people thought this might be an urban legend but it is not. Snopes (a site for verifying urban legends) confirms it's legit. Of course, there are some problems with it such as what if the phone is also damaged and how do we match the phone to the victim etc. However, there are too many possibilities of it working for us not to use it.

Also, keep in mind there is another email saying that if you program ICE in the phone it will make your phone susceptible to some virus doing the rounds, etc. Needless to say this is not true. Feel free to program ICE in your phone with your next of kin or emergency contact numbers under it.

Don't Be A Good Samaritan: When I was bodyguarding in the UK a very common scam was being perpetrated by Indians and Pakistanis on the English. A woman from either of those two countries would appear on your doorstep covered in blood (fake) claiming to have been in a car accident/hit by a bus etc., and could she please use the phone to call a relative. Once inside she'd phone her relatives alright, only they were relatives in the home country and not local. After chatting away for as long as they could pull it off they'd leave. The first time the suspecting home owner knew anything was amiss was once they received their next phone bill. It would be exorbitantly high due to international call rates to India or Pakistan.

The other ruse of course is to gain access to the home to either case the place, attack the home owner, open a window for surreptitious entry later, or steal something. If someone comes to your door asking to borrow the phone etc., tell them to give you the number and the message and let them know you'll make the call for them. If they're genuine this won't bother them a bit. If it's a scam you'll find out pretty damned fast.

Wrong Numbers: If someone calls you and then claims it was a wrong number just say no problem and hang up. Too many people fall victim to giving away personal information when asked *"well, if this isn't Bob's number, whose is it?"* or *"So this isn't 6754 Mayberry St?"* Remember just say *"you have a wrong number"* and hang up the phone.

Info Overload: This point dovetails with the preceding one. Be very aware of what information you give out over the phone. There are tons of methods of getting information out of people this way which go under the banner of "social engineering." When I worked as a private investigator in the UK, one of my gigs was to track down people owing money to a car rental company from overseas trips. I used a program that gave me the neighbor's phone number and I'd call saying I'd met (insert name of neighbor we were chasing here) while they were on holidays last year and they'd left personal belongings at my place. Did they have any way of getting in touch with them? Usually they'd then give me the life story of the person involved since they'd got back from their travels. Now, in this instance it was legitimate, but the bad guys know these ruses as well and are very adept at getting info out of unsuspecting people even to the point of having recordings of crying babies in the back ground to make you drop your guard.

Also, remember to be careful of what info you give out if you've called someone. Too many companies still ask for social security numbers, for example. Identity theft is at an all-time high and an SSN is the first bit of info the bad guys needs to steal yours. Refuse to give it out and ask for an alternative method to ID yourself.

Beware of Kids: The preceding rule is a no brainer for you but what about your children? A lot of young kids answer the phones and they have no idea what is safe to say and what isn't. A predator can gain all sorts of information from an unsuspecting naïve child. Either don't let your kids answer the phone if you're not there or train them in what they can and can't say.

Cordless Phones: Obviously a lot of people have replaced these and even home phones are becoming outdated, but if you're one of the few that still have them, the following advice is relevant. I'm personally aware of a guy who used to take his cordless phone and drive around trying to get a dial tone from his car. The phones have a range of about 400-500 feet and a lot of them were the same brand and/or frequency. It never took him long to find a dial tone while driving at which point he'd sit outside and make his long-distance calls. High end cordless phones come with changing frequencies etc., to prevent this type of attack, so make sure you spring for a good quality one or turn the receiver on your cordless unit to "off" until a call actually comes in, or until you intend to make an outgoing call.

Taxi Cab Security

Use a Reputable Company: In the United States, in most cities, most cabs are owned by reputable companies. In London, however, and many other cities in the UK, there are unlicensed taxis and using them, in some places, you're literally putting your life in the hands of the driver. In Djibouti for example, where I was stationed with the French Foreign Legion, all the drivers chewed the local narcotic called Khat which meant they were quite literally stoned while driving. If you find yourself in a third world hell hole for business, try and use hotel transport or have a local business connection pick you up.

Keep Quiet: There's nothing wrong with being sociable with the driver if he's so inclined but don't reveal any personal information. In kidnapping rife cities around the world, that information dump can come back to haunt you. Another thing to remember, along the same lines, is avoid any discussion about religion or politics. Again, doing so can put your life in danger.

Don't share the taxi with someone you don't know: In a lot of big cities here in the States, when taxis are short, it's not uncommon to share a taxi with someone. Be careful...especially if you're a lone woman. Another time to be extremely careful with the sharing of cabs is in third world countries. In Mexico for example, many tourists have reported being robbed by taxi drivers. The driver picks you up at the airport, sometimes with an accomplice (allegedly a fellow traveler going in the same direction) and heads to a deserted location where your money, luggage and sometimes even clothes are taken from you. Often, the robbery is accompanied by a beating.

Make sure the driver's photo matches him: Before you climb in the cab make sure the photo of the driver matches him. A common swindle is for the driver to rent his car out to his unlicensed cousin or neighbor to pick us some extra dollars while he's taking a break. Unfortunately, the unlicensed friend is unlicensed for a reason. There have also been cases where the driver has been beaten up and is in the trunk and the bad guy is driving the cab keeping all the money.

Make a note of his name and license number: I'd always make sure the driver knew I was copying down his license number and name. I'd tell them I did it in case I came back that way again at a future date so I could ask for the same driver. Another mate who used to bodyguard with me would tell them it was a hobby of his, like train spotting. Doesn't matter which ploy you use but it lets them know you have a record of them so it's unlikely they'll try and rip you off.

Make sure you pick the cab and he doesn't pick you: This one is especially important in countries where kidnapping is rife. Don't opt for the car that seems a little too convenient and instead seek out another one.

Make sure the meter is at zero when you get in the cab: An old scam amongst drivers was to "forget" to reset the meter when the next fare climbed in thus adding the previous trip to your bill. Make sure it's been reset when you climb inside. Another option is to establish a flat fee before you head to your destination. If you fly into JFK in New York, this is almost how all the cabs from the airport work. You tell the coordinator where you're traveling to and he writes a flat fee on the piece of paper and then relays that fee to the driver. That way there's no being driven forty miles out of your way on the scenic route to pad the driver's fare.

Try not to put luggage in the trunk. If you do, make sure you see to the loading, personally!

In 3rd world countries it's better to work out the fare in advance: This dovetails with the above and is always the best option in most third world countries. Again, it ensures the driver will drive you the most direct route to wherever it is you're heading and leaves little room for feeling ripped off or arguing over what might seem too high a price later. The price for these trips is usually readily available with a simple search of the internet and/or travel sites.

Sit directly behind the driver: The safest place for you is undoubtedly directly behind the driver. It's very difficult for him to pull a weapon out and attempt to control you with it when you're sitting thus.

This is especially important if you're traveling with your wife or girlfriend. The natural inclination is to have the woman in the back and the man up front but it's easier to deal with a driver who turns out to be a bandit from behind than it is sitting beside him up front.

Don't accept food stuff from the driver: One ploy in certain countries around the world was to accept part of the driver's meal. The driver is capitalizing on the need of the tourist to not offend him by refusing the 'generous' offer and of course the food is drugged.

Taxis are not always all bad. In most countries for example they are an incredible local resource and they know the best restaurants, the parts of town to avoid, and so on. In many cases they're better resources than the concierge at the hotel, and if you're in a third world country at a cheap hotel, there's not going to be one of them available anyway.

In case you missed this story under situational awareness baselines, when I was in Djibouti with the Legion, a bomb was planted by Al Qaeda in a nightclub frequented by French military personnel. Nine of my colleagues were blown to bits and I accompanied our Captain down to the site of the bombing. The next day I was talking to one of the Legionnaires who'd escaped the blast by coincidence because he left the club a few minutes prior to the detonation.

What he said next was chilling. He said it was the first time, ever, that he'd come out of a club and hadn't been assailed by taxi drivers screaming at him to use them. Anyone who's traveled to places like that has invariably witnessed the above. You would walk out of a club looking like you were ready to call it a night and drivers would leap from their doors screaming *"Warrior warrior, avec moi warrior"* or quite literally drive their cars at you flashing their lights etc., all the time screaming and beckoning from the window.

On this night, he walked outside and there wasn't a taxi in site. That's a little like not seeing a hot dog at a ball game here in the States. Unfortunately, he didn't think much of it at the time and walked away to find a taxi elsewhere. That's when the bomb went off. It was obvious to us later that all the taxi drivers had been alerted to the fact that the bomb was going to go off and to keep away. Not even one of them bothered to alert the authorities or the patrons of the club, which to my way of thinking meant we should have issued a directive to not use them ever again.

UBER: Since writing the original version of this book Uber has become a thing. Just like taxis, there have been attacks going both ways i.e. drivers have been attacked and killed, and passengers have been attacked by Uber drivers.

There is now a feature that Uber has added to their app where you can send a message to a friend who can now track your whereabouts on their phone while you're being driven to your destination. My recommendation is that you use it.

Finally, if you are overseas and find a good driver, pay him well and keep him on call. They can be worth their weight in gold.

Public Transport

A lot of people in third world countries make use of public transit. Unfortunately the bad guys know this too and frequent these modes of getting around because the pickings are rich. Here are some tips to remain safe.

Sit Strategically: It's not always possible, especially if the particular mode of transport is crowded, but do your best to sit where you don't have anyone behind you. This might be in the very back of a bus for example or in seats that line the sides of a train carriage and face inwards. There are attacks on public transport all the time, even in civilized places. Remember Bernhard Goetz who was the passenger who was being mugged in NY on the subway in 1984? How about the mental patient who -went on a "stabbing rampage" in New York, or the gang attacks on London's underground? At the time of writing this updated version, there was an attack on the train in Seattle by a gang of juveniles. At least by keeping your back to a wall you eliminate the possibility of being attacked from behind.

Keep an eye on your valuables: Public transport is a place of rich pickings for a pickpocket or thief. It's often so crowded that getting close enough to someone to lift their stuff without arousing their suspicions is dead easy. Also, people tend to exit quickly just as the doors are about to close, so if they suddenly grab your bag as they make the leap for the doors, you can't do anything about it. The safest place for your bag is between your legs. If you put your bags to one side you're making it easy. If you have two bags and place one on each side you're leaving yourself wide open for the team of thieves who'll one-two you. They do this by grabbing one bag and running. When you turn to give chase, you lose the other one as well as the two thieves bolt in opposite directions.

Study your fellow passengers: This is the same technique we use on an aircraft. Don't just blindly walk into a vehicle of any type full of people without glancing around first and making note of your fellow travelers to see if there's anyone who gives you pause. Maybe you can move to another carriage or wait for another bus. Maybe you just want to move to the other end of the carriage, or change seats, etc. Either way, by looking around first, and evaluating who your sharing your personal space with, you'll be better prepared in the event something kicks off.

Don't fall asleep: Personally I can't fall asleep on public transport, even if I haven't slept for 36 hours (don't ask me how I know) but I've seen plenty of people who do. I've seen the same people wake up after they've already passed the station or stop at which they meant to alight. Also, someone asleep or drunk on public transport is obviously going to be a prime candidate for a pickpocket or thief. Remember, crooks like easy and it doesn't get any easier than taking something away from someone while they're catching forty winks.

Nightclub & Restaurant Security

Alcohol Dangers: Alcohol is responsible for more murders, deaths, and fights than almost any other cause. Recently I was on a self-protection forum with some English constables who cited a study in the UK where some 98% of people in cuffs on any given night were under the influence of alcohol. Now, that doesn't mean don't drink, but it does mean two things; 1) drink in moderation, and 2) be very aware of the potential dangers when you're somewhere that serves alcohol in large quantities. I'm noticing a trend, (and maybe it's just that I'm getting older) of more and more people staying home on New Year's Eve simply because of the risks involved in going out into an intoxicated mob at a bar, and then having to cope with the risks of drunk drivers on the way home.

Don't leave your drink: One of my idiosyncrasies when I bounced was to always get a fresh drink if I left mine for a minute. A lot of my co-workers ribbed me about being paranoid until they met Goldie and heard his story. Goldie was a Torres Strait Islander who worked the door and trained in the karate school with us. One night he went to break up a fight, and when he returned to pick up his orange juice, a girl nearby piped up and said, *"I don't think that's yours."* He told her it was and she responded with a story about some other guy had it earlier. Goldie's sixth sense went off and he bagged the drink. Later, they had it tested independently and it contained rat poison in sufficient quantities that it would have killed him. Another old door colleague called "Cyclone" went on a rampage for a few days. It was discovered later that someone thought it would be funny to slip an LSD tab into his drink. This was all late seventies and early eighties way before the scare about "rufies" and GHB – so called date rape drugs – being dropped in to drinks of unsuspecting girls in clubs. My own ex-wife, and her girlfriend, thought it would be ok to accept a glass of champagne in an upscale club from two guys who'd overheard it was my wife's friend's birthday. On their way home an hour or so later they both got violently ill and had to stop the car to throw up. They had both eaten different things at dinner and attributed the fact they both got sick at the same time to something put in the drink. Who knows what would have happened if they'd been in the club when they were overcome. More recently, Mike, the husband of one of my students, got violently ill and began throwing up after drinking a drink originally intended for his wife. Everyone is fairly sure that the guy who bought the drink thought it would be funny to slip a roofie[7] into it. The point is, if you leave your drink, even for a second, buy another one and be very wary as to who's plying you with alcohol.

Don't accept drinks from strangers: This rule dovetails with the one above. Do not, under any circumstances, accept drinks from strangers. I'd go out on a limb and say a vast percentage of the date rapes that occur wouldn't if everyone followed this simple rule.

Beware the enchantress: In certain parts of South America right now there is a scam going on where women are painting a certain drug between their breasts and inviting unsuspecting tourists to stick their heads in between them and smell their new perfume or lick them. The tourist blacks out from the effects of the drugs and is helped out of the bar "after having one too many" by his new friends who promptly steal everything he has and leaves him up an alley next to the club. Again, I'm not advocating that you should avoid all contact with locals, especially enchanting ones that want to invite you to stick your head in their cleavage, but be careful. Maybe ask around if that bar has a rep for mugged tourists, do your homework and read up on local crime trends, go with a mate and make sure one of you stays out of the cleavage and off the booze as designated driver and chaperone.

Discretion, the better part of valor: If someone starts getting belligerent, leave. Check your ego, make your excuses, and get out of

---

[7] Roofie and rufie are common street names of Rohypnol which is a drug with similar qualities to Valium. Side effects include sedation, muscle relaxation, reduction in anxiety, and in many cases, amnesia, which is why it's used as a date-rape drug.

there. It doesn't matter if the vitriol is even directed at you. I've seen bar fights between two people turn into bar brawls between everyone in the place in mere seconds. If you sense that it might go pear shaped, leave as quickly and as quietly as you can.

Face the entrance: An old trick of police officers and security personnel the world over, whether on duty or not, is to sit where they can see who comes in to any restaurant or bar they happen to be in. Again, history abounds with tales of mad gunmen and robbers walking into restaurants and opening fire on people inside. At least by facing the doorway you get to clock and assess people as they enter. One day I was in a friend's tattoo parlor in the States comparing pistols with a mate who'd just bought a new Colt 1911–A when in walk two large black guys wearing long overcoats in the middle of the hot and humid North Carolina summer. We never got to find out whether they were indeed going to produce weapons and attempt to rob us because we turned when they walked in and they could clearly see ours in hand and ready to go. Their eyes got very large and they began spouting some nonsense about *"oh, this is a tattoo shop, sorry dog, we had no idea."* Spotting them on the way into the shop, and turning so they could see the weapons in hand, was the key to avoiding a potential shootout and/or robbery in the store.

Know where the exits are: A game my mates and I used to play in the UK while at dinner after work was to come back from the restroom or bar and cover one of the guy's eyes with your hands and say *"exits mate?"* He would immediately, with eyes still covered, be expected to point out all the exits into and out of the club. If he couldn't, drinks or dinner was on him. The obvious practical application in our line of work was being able to, in a fire, shootout, or bomb blast, etc., grab the boss, hit the floor, and know in which direction to be crawling without sticking our heads up to look. If I was taking a client into a club I would physically go and verify all the exits and make sure they were functioning and weren't blocked or locked (something which used to happen with too much frequency, sadly).

17

PLOYS

Gambits and ploys are various methods to get you to let your guard down so you can have your bag snatched, your pocket picked, or your home invaded. There are too many to list them all but this primer should give you enough of an idea to at least make you aware that the lengths some people are prepared to go in order to take advantage of you.

Ketchup Squirting

In this ploy, a team of people work together to rob you. One stands behind you and squirts you with ketchup using one of the small sachets and then points out the problem *"Sir, you have ketchup on your coat."* At this point, the other team members move in to "help" you clean up the mess by removing your coat and holding your packages etc. While you're distracted they then take your wallet, bag, purse, or anything else of value.

Babies & Kids

Sad as it may seem, children are often used by unscrupulous parents to trick and deceive. One ploy is to leave a toddler on the floor. When the Good Samaritan picks the kid up to find the parent, their stuff is stolen. Another ruse is to have a kid knock on your door and ask to use your phone. While they're inside they steal from you, or open a window/back door for an adult accomplice to enter later.

Crowds

Elevators and crowded areas are a favorite for these ploys in which pickpockets, working in teams, will distract their victim while the other cuts their bag and/or goes through their stuff. Another one is someone yelling out on a subway car *"Hey, my stuff's been stolen, there's a pickpocket on the train."* Everyone, of course, checks that their stuff is still intact and thus reveals the whereabouts of their wallets/valuables to members of the pickpocket team who are scattered amongst the passengers on the train and watching.

Gaining Entry

Fake uniforms, pens that don't work, crying infants, stage blood and so on are just some of the ways criminals will try and gain entry into your house. If someone comes to the door with stuff and you're not expecting a delivery find out where it's from and call the company involved if necessary. If the delivery man's pen doesn't work don't let him follow you in to the house while you get one that does. If you hear a child crying outside don't open the door. If someone comes to the door, covered in what appears to be blood, make them wait outside while you call emergency services. Ted Bundy, one of America's most notorious serial killers, lured most of his victims with ruses and props.

The list of such scams and ruses goes on and on and on. Sadly, new ones are coming down the pike all the time. For that reason, I'm not going to list them all here because a) I don't know every single one of them, and b) by the time I did, there'd be new ones out there. This is where your own awareness and cynicism must come in to play. Be very aware of anyone coming to your house unannounced. Be very aware of anyone invading your personal space. I know it sounds sad, especially when traveling to foreign lands, to put up such a defensive barrier, but unfortunately criminals and predators prey on human kindness. You really must keep your guard up always.

Teamwork

One scam involves three guys working in concert with one another. One will move in front of you and then all of a sudden lean over to tie his shoelaces. While you stop, and are subsequently distracted, the other two will move up, shove a weapon in your side and march you down an alley. If you see this happening get ready to move fast and start fighting back immediately. This attack will even happen in broad daylight.

18

TRUST YOUR GUT

Everyone in Hollywood knows who Gavin De Becker is, and if you've ever read his book, "The Gift of Fear", you'll know it could be written on one page and re-titled "trust your instincts." Mr. De Becker's message is spot on. Far too many people ignore their sixth sense, their "spidey sense", their gut, and/or their instincts to their own detriment.

I've trained and worked out with a lot of law enforcement officers over the years and one of the things they tell me is victims are always saying *"I knew there was something about that guy"* or, *"he just creeped me out."* Of course, this was right after ignoring that inner voice and falling victim to the guy, during their subsequent session with the officer filling out the criminal complaint.

Way back when we didn't have alarms, sensors, police officers, armies, or even doors and windows. Our very survival depended on our ability to sense danger and avoid it or prepare for it before it happened. Unfortunately, years of living in civilization mutes that sixth sense to the point where people can't hear it, choose to ignore it, or, ignore it because they're afraid it will get them labeled paranoid or politically incorrect.

During my time in the military I've spoken with plenty of vets who've talked about how sharp that sense becomes again after just a few weeks in a combat zone. Suddenly, years of ignoring the warnings to the point where the instincts have atrophied, goes out the window and senses become hyperalert. We were taught in the Legion, during the commando course, that if you're sneaking up on a man you must never look at him directly or think about killing him. To do either can enable him to pick up your approach. Instead you stare off to one side and keep him in peripheral vision and think about anything else other than the kill.

If you want to get some idea of how muted this gut instinct has become just sneak up on a few of your friends and see how easy it is. Now, go try and sneak up on any small woodland critter such as a deer or a rabbit. See how close you can get before it senses you and flees.

Now, while some part of this damping down of our instincts comes from living in a society that is supposed to be civilized, and one that employs people to do your own protection, more is down to political correctness. We're being taught to ignore our natural feelings in deference to some abstract morality. A case in point is when the actor Danny Glover went to New York City and found he couldn't get a taxi cab to stop for him after dark because, he claimed, he was black. A huge political and media maelstrom ensued with the Mayor, the commissioner of cabs, etc., all leaping on the political bandwagon saying something would be done and racism is alive and well in America etc.

Excuse me!!! Racism? Mr. Glover conveniently neglected to mention how many drivers of those taxis were black or Asian themselves. Think about it for a minute. Have you been to New York City? Now, how many times have you climbed into a cab driven by a white guy? I went a few months ago and out of seven cab rides I never had one white driver. It's not that the drivers weren't stopping because they were racists, for God's sake. They weren't stopping because the majority of the times that they read of a robbery and/or murder, it was being committed by either a black suspect or a group of black suspects. Their own sixth sense was kicking in when they'd see a group of black youths trying to flag them down late at night and they were being criticized for it and were being labeled "racists".

There's a move afoot to stop labeling the race of the suspect in crimes because apparently, that is being seen as racist. No, if a green man with aerials on his head has just robbed a bank it makes sense to publish those details so the police don't waste time stopping black, brown, yellow, and white men. It's not racism, it's common sense, and it's using our senses the way they were designed to be used.

The castigation of profiling is another example of politically correct madness. Let's say there's a group of people in town who all have swastikas tattooed on their foreheads, and within that group is a smaller group who take guns into banks and rob them. The PC crowd would have you waste resources by checking children and people without swastikas so as not to offend anyone. They'd even go as far as to allow some of the swastika crowd go without a search at all so as not to offend them. Wrong again. Your senses, the sixth one and all the others, have told you the swastika crowd is dangerous, be wary around them. If the innocent members of the swastika crowd don't want to be searched all the time, perhaps their time would be better spent policing their own kind.

Let's put this in perspective. Someone who was bitten badly by a dog when they were young is acting perfectly normal when they're cautious around all dogs. Someone who nearly drowned in a pool when they were very young is acting perfectly normal when they're cautious around bodies of water. But, if that same person is careful around young males wearing hoodies because a disproportionate number of them mug people and beat them up, suddenly they're racist profilers.

To be blunt, it's better to be safe than sorry. If your gut is telling you something, listen to it and then heed its warning. One day you'll be hugely thankful that you did.

19

VEHICULAR SECURITY

One massively important facet of self-protection is vehicle security. The reason for that is eighty percent of all attacks on VIPs in the bodyguard world occur while he's in a vehicle. Homes are relatively easy to defend via the use of panic rooms, fences, guards, alarm systems, firearms, hardened windows and doors, and so on. Work places for high level clients are generally the same and usually come with guard posts, fences and razor wire to name but a few. Vehicles on the other hand are limited, even with armoring, in the amount of protection they can provide. One only has to look at the recent conflict in Iraq to see how true this is. More than half of the U.S. servicemen's deaths have come about while they've been on patrol in their vehicles from improvised explosive devices a.k.a. IEDs.

Outside of the realm of the bodyguard and the military there is the civilian equivalent such as road rage and car jackings, and given the amount of time the average American spends in their vehicle, it makes sense for us to practice certain behaviors that will lessen our chances of being targeted.

Vehicle Choice

While not politically correct the SUV stands far above every other vehicle type as the best from a security viewpoint. With apologies to their opponents, occupants of SUVs generally survive accidents whereas the occupants of the smaller vehicles do not. An SUV provides a vantage point above most other vehicles. This means that you can spot situations developing before anybody else can. Also, if you do spot a situation developing, or a gang of individuals is heading your way, you can use the SUVs all terrain capabilities to go off road and/or push other vehicles out of the way. Real SUV's such as the Range Rover and the Hummer are virtual small tanks in this regard and not a lot will stop them. From a broader viewpoint, such as a natural disaster like a hurricane, the SUV can be used to get you and your family to safety. While I was in the process of joining my local Red Cross chapter, I discovered they have an arrangement with the local Hummer dealership, that during the event of a natural disaster, Hummer owners will be called upon to ferry their personnel around.

The above points are so important that I'm going to bullet them again here, for added emphasis.

- **You have a greater chance of surviving an accident in an SUV than a regular car[8]**
- **By being significantly higher than other traffic you have a better vantage point and can spot potential trouble before anyone else.**
- **If there is trouble the SUV can go off road.**

---

[8] When a SUV strikes a passenger car, there are 16 driver fatalities in the passenger car for every driver fatality in the SUV. This if from a presentation by the National Highway Safety Administration before the US Senate.

- The SUV has the ability to push other vehicles out of the way, if necessary.
- The SUV can go further during a natural disaster, with debris on the road and flooding etc. than a regular car.

On Star™ & Its Equivalent

On Star™ is a service that provides – for a price – layers of service and protection for your car. The basic package will alert emergency services if your air bags deploy and you don't respond to the call from the operations center. It will also open your locks if you've inadvertently locked the keys in the car, and provide GPS tracking in the event your car is stolen or carjacked. I'm personally aware of a young woman in a nearby town who rolled her car coming home and ended up in someone's front yard without their realizing it. Her family was frantically looking for her and it was all over the local news. Eventually, a passerby saw her car in the front yard and assumed it was for sale. He went in to ask the owner of the house, an old lady, how much she wanted for it. It was then that they realized what had happened. The car had rolled into her front yard and ended up on its wheels. During the subsequent autopsy, it was determined she had been alive for several hours. With the On Star™ system in place, and its ability to alert emergency services in the event the airbags deploy, she would have most likely been alive today.

In another example, one of the "current affairs" programs on television was doing a show on the unwillingness of cell phone companies to triangulate and locate phones. They played a chilling 911 call from a young Hispanic woman who'd gone off the road and into the Everglades during a storm in Florida. She was in touch with emergency services via her phone but they couldn't locate her. On the tape you could hear her final moments, drowning, as the car sank into the swamp. Again, with that system in place, they could have located her in seconds and dispatched emergency services immediately.

However, it's not only useful for situations such as the ones above. At our local Cadillac dealership they found out exactly how great the GPS tracking system can be. One Saturday morning one of the salesmen couldn't locate a particular black Escalade he was looking for. After questioning all the other salesmen present they finally determined it must have been stolen. They filed a report with the local police. Once that was done, On-Star™ was contacted. The car was found just north of Richmond Virginia and State Troopers stopped them, recovered the vehicle, and took some car thieves out of circulation for a while[9].

Finally, by pushing the emergency button you will automatically be connected with the authorities in the event of an emergency such as a road rage incident, a traffic accident, or a motorist needing assistance, etc. Their web site and radio ads abound with real life examples of people being saved every day by having this service on board. From a self-protection view point you really couldn't ask for more.

By upgrading you can have the navigation service and hands free phone both of which are viable services from a self-protection standpoint. The navigation is a god send for anyone (especially a lone female) driving in unfamiliar territory and the hands-free phone is definitely a plus from a driving safely point of view. Many states are enacting laws that will make using a hand-held phone while driving an offence so the ability to use hands free is going to be a definite benefit if for no other reason than that.

When I began writing this book, On Star™ was only available in cars made by GM, but now On Star™, or similar services, are available in

---

[9] The Troopers in this case waited to do the stop over the Chesapeake Bay Bridge. They had a car on the other side and an unmarked tailing them until the bad guys got on the bridge. Their reasoning was none of the four were likely to jump over the side of the bridge in a bid to flee.

pretty much any vehicle. You buy an after-market device and pay your subscription and get the same security services as mentioned above.[10]

Gas Tanks

Your new empty mark on your car's gas gauge is now the half way mark. This is *Standard Operating Procedure* - SOP - with regards to security driving when protecting a principle and needs to be adopted by you as well. Suddenly finding yourself on empty when being chased by a bunch of gang bangers or followed home by a stalker is nerve wracking and unnecessary. Just imagine your vehicle has a really small gas tank and now needs to be topped up more often. Is that a little inconvenient? Sure, but you won't think so the time you need to evade someone or you get lost while driving late at night. Remember, fill it up, and top it up often.

It also happens to be better for your vehicle. If you let the gas tank get down near empty, the crud that floats around the bottom of the tank works its way more easily into the fuel system, and can cause major problems that are expensive to fix. So, there you are, yet another good reason to keep topped up.

Safe Havens

On any route you travel on a regular basis you must know your twenty-four hour safe havens. What are they? Simple, they're anywhere that is open and manned on a twenty-four-hour basis, so in the event of trouble, you can head for one of them instead of all the way home. When I looked after the soap star Emma Samms after her wedding in London, my partner and I drove the day before along the same route we were going to be taking with her, as well as along our alternate routes. On the dry run we plotted all the hospitals, police stations, and fire stations in the event of an emergency on the way to her reception at Pinewood studios. By doing so,

---

[10] In the interest of disclosure, I am not in any way connected with GM, On Star™ or any of their associates or affiliates. I'm getting no money for plugging their product.

should we have had a problem, we wouldn't be driving along the motorway looking for signs as to where the nearest hospital was.

Former President Ronald Reagan was saved by his Secret Service personnel who knew exactly where the nearest hospital was when he was shot by Hinkley. In the car, his USSS agent was doing a standard pat down for any injuries and the President assured him he was fine except for a cracked rib. During the pat down the agent, Jerry Parr, discovered blood and screamed at the driver to take them to the George Washington University Hospital as that was the closest. Once again, another example of knowing where things are that will save you during a crisis.

Your twenty-four-hour havens are such places as gas stations, grocery stores, hospitals, fire stations, police stations, industrial plants with 24 hour security, airports, and military bases. Plot yours. Most people drive very similar routes all week long such as the ride to work, the ride to pick the kids up, and the drive to the store. Spend a weekend and go out and locate all the nearby safe havens.

If it's a deadly serious situation such as a gang of people pursuing a lone female, or being shot at by someone after a road rage incident, don't bother stopping and getting out of the car. Drive straight through the front door and watch how many people turn up and how quickly they do so. Your life, and that of your family members, is far more valuable than the front doors of a gas station or grocery store. Whatever you do, don't do what most people do and head for home. That is a mistake. Head for the safe haven instead.

Report Incidents

Many criminals take advantage of people's urge to help and the good Samaritan in all of us. By stopping to render assistance you put yourself in a very vulnerable position and the news is full of stories of good Samaritans being set up and attacked. The best thing you can do is keep a cell phone and charger in your car and report any stranded motorists, flat tires, etc., to the relevant authorities. Do not stop and help anyone yourself no matter how innocuous the scene looks.

Sanitize Your Car

Too many people give away too much information when it comes to their vehicle. The next time you're parking your car check out some vehicles in the parking lot and try and guess what type of person the owner is before you walk up and look inside. You'll see bibles, pornographic magazines, shotgun shells, baby clothes, hair brushes, and sports equipment, etc. What does your car say about you? Are you a lone female? Are you wealthy? Are you in law enforcement? What about your politics and/or your religion?

During the classes on "How to Be Your Own Bodyguard" we've even found people who've left their mail on the front seat with their home address clearly

Samaritan Robbed.

Martinsville Ind. – A man was beaten and robbed when he stopped to help a man he believed to be a stranded motorist, the Morgan County Sheriff's Dept said.

Chief Deputy Robert Downey said the 61-year-old victim, whose identity was not made public, was driving late Tue night. "As he approached a red, 4 door car, a man waved him down and said he had a flat tire," Downey told 6 News. "He stopped to help and when he went around he didn't see a flat." "Then he was struck in the face with some type of object, possibly a rock." Another man kicked the victim and the 2 stole his wallet before driving away.

readable from the window. If a sexual predator wanted the home address of a potential female victim, he just got it without all the hassle of following you anywhere. What if a burglar wanted a sure hit? If your car is at the shopping center it means you're not at home. Again, by reading the address from the mail, you've given him a huge head start. The correct method is to go over your car and remove anything that might tell a criminal anything about you.

Religious and political stickers can cause people to vandalize your car if they share a different viewpoint. Try and be the "grey man"[11] and give nothing away about who you are or what you do. Some people allege putting a gun sticker on the back window can keep people away. Maybe, but what if the criminal wants a gun? You've just told him there's a chance there's one in your car, and if you've just gone into one of the many locales where a weapon is not allowed, he knows it's in your car. The same people advise leaving a set of hand cuffs hanging from your rear-view mirror and/or law enforcement magazines lying on the seat of the car. The idea is to create the impression the car is owned by a policeman, giving pause to anyone thinking of stealing your car or messing with the driver. It's sound in theory, but then again it's a double-edged sword. For every person you deter from messing with you there's probably a couple more who'll break your window, or key your car just because it's owned by a cop. This is especially true in today's political climate and what would appear to be a war against the police in certain parts of the country.

Know Your Car

In the Foreign Legion we used to have competitions between the company sections as to which group could change the VLRA (all-terrain vehicles used by the French in Africa) tire's fastest. It wasn't done for fun or the kudos of winning. In a war zone, or the middle of a battle, the faster you can change that tire and get mobile again the greater your chance of

---

[11] A "grey man" is someone who goes unnoticed. He doesn't draw attention to himself by word, action, deed, dress, or mannerism.

survival. The same is true for you. Every second you spend on the side of the road trying to figure out how to change a tire is a second that increases your risk of being hit by a passing car or attacked by someone pretending to come to your aid.

Take time to familiarize yourself with how to change your tire and make sure the components for the jack and so on are where they should be. Years ago gas stations serviced your car when you came in to fill up by checking your oil and tire pressure. Nowadays they don't do that which means the onus is on you to check those things regularly. Incorrect tire pressure is not only a cause of poor gas mileage but it can also cause blow outs and flat tires. Blow outs can kill you if you lose control and flats can be the cause of your problems if you're targeted by a criminal while stuck on the side of the road.

Knowing your car isn't just knowing where the jack is either. It's being aware of how everything works. Someone driving down the road, trying to change something on the GPS or radio who isn't 100% familiar with the process, is distracted and a distracted driver is in a perilous position. What about how to escape from the trunk of your car? Many new versions come with latches inside...does yours? Ever tried it? What about the locks? Running for your car with someone chasing you, are you confident you're going to hit the right button to lock all the doors? If you hit one button do all the doors lock? Some models require you to hit them twice. What if you're attacked in your car and ordered on to the passenger side? Can you get out? One car I owned had the locks set up for children and only the driver's door could open the others. It's a disaster to realize you're in that predicament once you're at knife or gun point in your own car being driven somewhere against your will. Go practice and learn the idiosyncrasies of your particular model. This also goes for anyone else's in the family that you drive on a regular basis.

Carry The Right Gear

Make sure you have the following in your car at all times;

A fully inflated spare tire: This should be obvious, but you'd be amazed how many people change a flat, throw the deflated tire in the back with every intention of getting it repaired, then never get around to it. The next time they get a flat they've now got nothing to change it with.

A jack: The same thing goes for the jack. I helped a student one night who had two pieces of his jack but was missing the third. Are all the components of yours there? Do you know how they work?

Jumper Cables: This is another must have. A lot of cars end up with a dead battery and all they need for a quick jump is a set of cables. It goes without saying you should learn how to do this, but owning a set gives you the option of asking who you want for help, rather than depending on someone who actually has a set.

Flashlight: A good flashlight is key. Most lights – interior and under the hood – give off a paltry glow. Maglites™ are a cheap and effective improvised weapon as well. You can use them to see what you're doing, signal people, warn them of your presence, light your way, and defend yourself with them if necessary.

Water: Every day there's another story of a motorist who's gone off the edge of the road down a ravine and survived by living off scraps of food in the car. Water is necessary for the same reason. It can be used if the radiator boils dry and it can be used to hydrate yourself when stranded.

Duct Tape: Duct tape is the miracle product that can be used for a thousand and one different purposes. Keep a roll handy as you'll never know what sort of running repair it can help you with. I'm even aware of one person who used it to spelled out HELP in their back window when they were stranded. How about reattaching a broken rearview mirror, holding on a fender, an improvised rope, repairing a fan belt or split hose.

Flares: Obviously they can be used in the event of an accident to alert other motorists, but how about hiding one under the passenger seat. Imagine being pushed over there by a criminal and being able to access one of those.

1st Aid Kit: This is another no brainer but make sure you know how to use everything in the kit. A lot of people buy fancy first aid kits and don't have a clue what's in them or how to use them. Speed is usually of the essence if the kit must come out so take the time and do a course. They're cheap and one day you'll be hugely thankful that you took the time to learn how to administer proper first aid.

8 Day Nightmare

An 18-year-old Maryland college student is being treated for dehydration, cuts and a hip injury at the hospital after being trapped for eight days when his car ran off the road, down a steep embankment and landed upside down in a shallow creek bed.

Survival Blanket: These are small and usually silver and can be found at camping stores. They work by trapping body heat in which can be the difference between life and death if your car is broken down in the middle of winter. It can also be used as an emergency shelter, provide shade, and a host of other uses. As I write this particular section of the book the news is all about the Dominguez family. They were missing in upstate California in the freezing cold, after going on a search for a Christmas tree. That's exactly the sort of emergency that the blanket is designed for. A couple of those in the car could have been slipped into pockets and once again can mean the difference between life and death.

Tool Kit: A basic tool kit is a necessity. Think of it as a first aid kit for your car, and just like the first aid kit, learn how to use the various elements within. Most community colleges run simple courses for the layman on basic car maintenance and repair. With the right tools you can get yourself back on the road in no time.

Types Of Car Crimes

The following list details some of the types of crimes associated with motor vehicles. We will cover most of these in more detail in other sections of the book.

Drive by shootings: Sadly there isn't a whole lot you can do about these, but be aware of them and hit the ground should you ever find yourself in the unfortunate position of being in the proximity of one. It seems every day the news covers a story about some innocent victim being caught in the cross fire of one of these attacks on some perceived enemy. This is very much a candidate for the "what if" drill and visualize hitting the deck should you ever hear the pop of the guns going off. The safest place in the event of stray rounds is always going to be on the ground if you can't get behind solid cover.

Road Rage: This is another hot button item that is constantly in the news. According to the latest statistics just over 70% of Americans have been involved in a road rage incident and it even reached the stage a few years ago where people in California were taking shots at other motorists from their cars. Indeed, as I'm doing this re-write, the man who shot and killed a young girl in a road rage incident while merging with traffic has just turned himself in to law enforcement.

Carjacking: Carjacking would probably have never been invented except for the efficacy of the vehicle manufacturers and their anti-theft devices. They reached a point where they became so effective the enterprising criminal realized the only way to get the car was to wait until you were in it and had de-activated all the devices yourself.

Bump & Rob: This was a major problem a few years back in Florida (remember what we said about tourists), where criminals would identify rental cars by the stickers on the back and then pretend to get in an accident with you by bumping you from behind. When you alit from the vehicle to swap insurance information etc., you were robbed.

Police Impersonators: This is another big local crime in the Carolinas. They call them "Blue Light Bandits" because they stick a blue flasher in the car and pull over lone motorists at night. Nine times out of ten it's a sexual predator targeting lone female motorists.

Overhead Missiles: A slew of motorists are killed or seriously injured every year by this ploy which involves someone dropping objects onto cars from an overpass or bridge. In South America the criminal element go one step further and have friends lie in wait several hundred yards down the road. After you're hit by the falling missile it's a natural tendency to pull over and check the damage. The other members of the gang lie in wait down the road at the most likely place for you to stop and rob you once you have.

Drunk Driving: This is another no brainer and it kills thousands of people every year all over the world. It goes without saying not to do it yourself but, you also have to be aware of other inebriated drivers out to get you. The risk is greatest between the hours of midnight and 3 a.m. with Sunday, typically, being the most dangerous day of the week (bars closing on Saturday night) and New Year's Eve being the most dangerous day of the year. Police estimates in the States are that one in thirteen motorists is driving under the influence between 10 p.m. and 3 a.m. every morning.

Parking Safety

Think Ahead: Think about what the area will be like if you return after dark. Too often people find a spot that looks fine in broad daylight, forgetting that, when they return later that evening, their ideal spot might be in pitch darkness making it very easy for a bad guy to conceal himself while he lies in wait.

Lock It: Get in the habit of locking your car every single time you leave it even if it's only for a second. Ask yourself this…how long would you need to steal a car that had the doors unlocked and the keys still in the ignition? 80% of stolen cars are unlocked when stolen whether the keys are in them or not. Will a locked door stop a determined thief? No. Will it deter them or slow them up long enough they'll look for a more opportunistic target? Yes!

Attendants: In big cities always choose car parks with attendants if possible. Statistics prove that far less vandalism and theft goes on at attended parking centers for obvious reasons.

Buddy Up: Ask security to walk you to your car, if possible, if you're at all concerned. How about working overtime at work? Is there a colleague in the office who can walk you to your car?

Look: Scope under the car, around the car and in the car as you approach. It's not that common, but bad guys have been recorded as hiding in all three of those locations while waiting to ambush a victim.

Loitering: If someone is loitering near your car, leave and get security. Too many victims are recorded as saying afterwards *"I thought there was something weird about him."* Don't take a chance and trust your instincts instead!

Drive Away Fast: Your goal is to drive away as soon as you possibly can. Do not sit around balancing check books, fixing make up, or looking at your phone. The sooner you get moving, the better.

Driving Safely

Tire View: This is critical and very easy. Always make sure you can see the bottom of the rear tires of the car in front over the hood of your own car. In other words, while sitting at lights in your driver's seat, you should be able to see the back tires of the car in front, where they meet the road. It doesn't matter what vehicle you're in, this ensures you have room to pull your steering wheel to left or right and get out of there without hitting the car in front. So many motorists and terrorist targets have set themselves up for failure over the years by getting within inches of the car in front. The bad guys then pin you in by driving up on your rear fender making it impossible to move out of the way.

Gas tank half full

We've already mentioned this one, but it's worth mentioning again. Your new empty mark on your gas gauge is the halfway mark.

Know your 24 hour safe havens

Another previously mentioned tip that's worth mentioning again. Learn the twenty-four-hour safe spots on routes you travel frequently.

AAA

Are you a member? You need to be. And if you don't have an AAA in your country, join its equivalent. It's incredibly cheap given the peace of mind it buys you knowing that, if you break down and can't affect a repair yourself, the pros are on their way. They also help with route planning and a slew of other associated services that help keep you safe.

Seat Belt

It should go without saying to wear your seatbelt when driving. It's been proven again and again that they save lives in the event of accidents. How long does it take to put one on? What's the return on that investment of time?

Hide valuables

We've already mentioned hiding valuables when you park the car and leave it but it's also important to do so while driving. When I lived in the UK as a bodyguard, one ploy used by local thieves, was to have one crook down the road near the crossing or traffic light whose job was to scope what was on the seats of the car. If he spotted something of value he'd use his cell phone to contact his buddy up at the cross walk. This guy would then walk up to the car, put a hammer through the window, and snatch whatever it was off the seat.

Two Seconds

Arguably the Metropolitan Police in London UK have some of the best police drivers in the world of law enforcement and some of the best training. Most police officers in the U.S. are lucky to get a day or two on a skid pan whereas their cousins in the Met get seven weeks of training with regularly scheduled refresher courses. One of the things they're insistent on is maintaining a two second gap between their car and the car in front. What does that mean? Simple. As the car in front passes an object in the road, a street lamp for example, you begin to count *"one thousand and one, one thousand and two"* You should be able to count out the entire two seconds before your car passes the same object. That simple formula works no matter how fast you're driving and will give you sufficient time to react should the guy in front do something drastic.

I know it's not easy to do always. In the city where I live, people see a gap that size and immediately try and squeeze four cars into it. Doesn't matter, back off and repeat again. The chances of you ever rear ending someone just went down so low as to be almost non-existent.[12]

Brakes & Tires

There are two things you never want to skimp on with regard to your vehicle and that's both brakes and tires. These are the two things that are going to ensure you stop in time and you stick to the road when you need to. A lot of people spend money on expensive accessories for their vehicles and ignore these two life savers. Pay as much as you can and get the best you can.

Cruisin' In The Rain

I used to think this was an urban legend, but it's absolutely true. Using your cruise control in the rain can lead to dire consequences. I'm not sure of the exact details, but it's something to do with hitting a puddle and the tire speeding up due to lack of traction. That in turn dupes the sensors which try and apply the brakes and voila, instant accident. Whatever the mechanics of the problem are don't matter…just remember, if it's raining, do NOT use your cruise control.

Trouble Overhead

As previously mentioned overpasses can be dangerous. There's a disturbing trend nowadays for thugs to drop objects from overpasses and bridges on to cars below. One of the worst cases happened recently in Germany when the sons of some U.S. servicemen decided to drop stones onto passing cars. They killed two women and injured five other people.

---

[12] In this city of NASCAR fans, who all think every drive is a race and sitting two inches from the bumper in front is how you're supposed to drive, thirty-five vehicles ended up in a pile up a few years back when one up front stopped to watch a topless girl on a jet ski on the lake.

Even something small dropped onto a car traveling seventy miles per hour is going to hit like a bullet.

Look: Get in the habit of scoping out every overpass and bridge as you approach them. If people appear to be walking across you're probably ok. If they're stationary be very aware.

Lane Change: If you do see people loitering on overpasses be prepared to change lanes if possible. If not, get ready to vary your speed. The people throwing the objects are timing it based on your speed remaining constant. By suddenly accelerating or decelerating you can throw their aim off.

Keep Rolling: If you are hit by something from overhead don't stop immediately if you can help it. Obviously, this is going to depend on the extent of the damage to your vehicle and/or injuries to persons in the car, but as mentioned previously, in certain South American countries, the people dropping the rocks on passing vehicles are often part of a team. The rest of the team will be stationed further down the road in the proximity of where you'll stop after being hit. When you get out to assess the damage the other gang members appear and rob you blind.

Road Rage

You'd have to be living in the Stone Age to be unaware of the problem road rage has become in the last few decades. It has reached a level nowadays where people in California shoot at one another over some perceived transgression on the road. In one study entitled the Mizell report, commissioned by the AAA, it was found that in a roughly five-year period over 10,000 accidents were attributed to aggressive driving and over 230 of those involved fatalities. The AAA has also determined that the problem is only getting worse, compounding annually at approximately seven percent. Eighty five percent of offenders are male and the bulk of them are poorly educated.

Understand this, if nothing else. Aggressive drivers are a part of venturing out on the road today just as the weather is. During inclement weather you adjust your driving habits to ensure your safety by doing things such as turning on your wipers, slowing down and increasing the distance between you and the vehicle in front. Dealing with road rage and aggressive driving is much the same. Learn how to adjust your driving to deal with the problem.

Signs: Make yourself a small sign that says "SORRY" and carry it on the front seat. If you inadvertently cut someone off or cause a problem simply hold the sign up to let them know you made a mistake. Many of the incidents are due to misunderstanding and assuming the other guy cut you off on purpose. The problem with using hand gestures to attempt the same is that many can be misinterpreted as gang signs or offensive gestures.

Don't Look: Do not exchange gestures or even look at the person if you can avoid it. By looking straight ahead and refusing to make eye contact you can often diffuse the situation.

Tag Time: If they persist, make a note of their license tag and make and model of car. If you have a cell phone handy report the incident to local authorities. Out on the highways in the United States you can usually hit *69 for a direct line to Highway Patrol. Chances are other people have reported their aggressive driving as well which bodes well for you and badly for them.

Detour: Be prepared to leave the highway if necessary or turn off a side street and take a detour. Again, by removing yourself from their vicinity, you can often defuse the situation. Remember what I said about Special Forces Teams and how they avoid every fight they can.

Back Off: Do not, under any circumstances, attempt to outrun other motorists. Back off, slow down, or turn off the highway/street and let them get away from you. High speed evasive driving is only used in life and death situations, by law enforcement and/or personal protection teams, in cars that are specifically modified for the job, and driven by highly trained security drivers/specialists.

Last point is don't be an offender yourself (you wouldn't, right?). Don't tailgate someone you think is going too slow, don't cut people off, don't race people, don't pace them and slow them down in a bid to punish them, use your turn signals and pay attention when you're driving. You wouldn't do this stuff out of the car on foot in a mall, what gives you the right to do it in your vehicle?

One final point about road rage is that a recent study discovered that people with stickers all over their cars were more likely to be offenders than people in cars without stickers. It might be due to them seeing the car as an extension of themselves and their beliefs but whatever the reason they've been deemed more likely to be the culprits. It also didn't matter what stickers were on the car so even the hippy with the peace and love to all and the religious ones were just as likely to offend as any others.

Car Jacking

Carjacking, like road rage, is another fairly recent phenomenon. It arose out of the fact that car manufacturers began to make alarms and locking systems on vehicles that were so effective that crooks couldn't steal the cars any more. Their solution was to simply wait till you unlocked everything and put the keys in the ignition before attempting to take your vehicle, typically at gun point.

The first level of defense is preventative again. What sort of car do you drive and what parts of town do you drive in. Many car-jackers target specific makes and models, and if you know what those makes and models are, maybe you would consider driving something more low profile. I'm not suggesting for one minute you should give up your right to drive what you want or where you want, but if the particular car you drive isn't important to you, if it's just a mode of transport, why not buy something they don't want? I did this in the UK. The least stolen motorcycles were anything by BMW whereas the most ripped off were Harley Davidson's. In fact, Princess Di's brother had his first Harley stolen within a week of owning it and his replacement was stolen two weeks after that. Kids would work for the gangs and ride around on bicycles looking for suitable targets. When one was spotted, the kid would call on a cell phone and soon thereafter a refrigerator truck would arrive with four behemoths inside armed with 2x4s. They'd shove a 2x4 through the spokes on each wheel and the four of them would hoist the bike into the back of the lorry. Even if it was alarmed the insulation of the refrigerator truck would baffle the noise and soon after the bike was shipped to a market overseas or chopped up to be sold for parts.

Task Fixation: To my knowledge nobody has been car jacked driving down the highway. It's always when cars are stopped such as at busy intersections and or traffic lights. Therefore, when should you be hyper-vigilant? Obviously when you're at either of the above locations. What do we see people doing instead? Putting on makeup, reading books and reports, chatting on the cell phone, fiddling with the radio, eating, grooming, and so on. This is why the criminal *"appears out of nowhere"* according to the brain-dead, task fixated motorist, relaying what happened later on to law enforcement.

Lock Up: Keep doors and windows locked. In some cases that I'm aware of (from local law enforcement) the driver of the car has looked up at the noise of the passenger door opening only to see the armed bad guy sliding into the seat.

Leave: If you get into the habit of stopping in traffic so that you can see the rear tires of the car in front, where they touch the road, it will mean you're far enough away that you can hook the wheel either left or right and get out without hitting that vehicle. Too many people make the mistake of driving up inches from the bumper of the car in front thus trapping themselves. Included in this bit of advice is the following; be aware of what lane you choose. It's better, where possible, to be in the extreme left or right hand lane so that you can get out to one side. If you're in the center lane it won't matter that you can avoid the car in front if you're stuck between cars to either side.

Don't Argue: Never argue with the carjacker. Hopefully your car is insured and/or has On Star™ or Lo-Jack™ (or their equivalent). All you do by fighting them is dramatically increase your risk of being shot, stabbed, or killed. No vehicle is worth dying over, especially if it's insured. If you can't drive away, and they want your car, let them have it.

Be a good witness: The best thing you can do at that point is to be a good witness. Do you know your car's tag number? You should! Can you describe the guy(s) to law enforcement and/or the type of weapon they were brandishing when they took your car? What clothes where they wearing? What color was their hair, how much did they weigh, how tall were they? Did they have any distinguishing marks or tattoos? Can you tell emergency services which direction they went in? All of that will be a lot more helpful to the law enforcement personnel trying to catch these guys than any heroics on your behalf.

Report It: You'd think most people would report the crime immediately, but apparently some don't. Every second is going to count, and if you do have a tracking service, they're going to require a police crime report number before they can activate their tracking system anyway. The sooner you let law enforcement know, the sooner they're going to be able to get your vehicle back.

Exceptions: There's one exception to all of the above and that is if you have children in the car. There have been cases where the carjacker has struck so fast he's driven off with the child still inside strapped into their safety seat. Obviously, this is an incredibly difficult situation to find yourself in. All I can tell you is try and get your message across that you'll comply but you want your child first. Some criminals are going to want to avoid the kidnapping charges that driving off with your child is going to bring. Others may not even hear you due to the panicked state they find themselves in at the time.

Possible Solution: I'm always stunned by certain experts who preach a blanket approach to various crimes as if they only ever happen one way and are perpetrated by one criminal. An example is the advice that if mugged to throw your wallet/money one way and run the other. Well, that may work in one case whereas the next time it might get you killed by a ticked off mugger angry at your trying to dupe him.

In June of 1995 in Charlotte, North Carolina there was a case all over the news. Five "gang bangers" tried to steal a woman's car from the forecourt of the Hilton Hotel in the University area. She threw the keys

141

down and ran off shrieking into the lobby of the hotel. One of the kids shot her in the back as she was running away despite the fact she had handed the car over. I bet I wouldn't have to look very hard to find another example of where someone did that and survived.

Keeping that in mind, one such strategy if you have children in the car is to throw the car keys away from your vehicle. While the bad guy goes to recover the keys you recover the kids and bolt as far and as fast as you can. I'm not going to say it will work as evidenced by the example above. Each situation will have its own merits and drawbacks. Be aware that the strategy exists, and be aware of the risks.

Bump & Rob

The bump and rob was a ploy that got a lot of media attention worldwide back in the late eighties/early nineties due to a spate of the crime in Florida, targeting tourists. The bad guys would come up behind a target vehicle – more often than not a rental car – and drive in to the rear bumper at low speed. When the hapless victim pulled over to sort out insurance details, etc., they'd be robbed. In perhaps the most infamous of such cases a German tourist was run over and killed in front of her mother and two children by the bad guys as they made their getaway.

Wait: Fight the immediate urge to get out of your car and see what damage has been done and instead take a second to look around and assess the area you're in and the car and driver that (accidentally) hit you. If you think it's necessary, signal them to follow you to a populated area by driving very slowly to such a location with your hazard lights on. In some jurisdictions this is not legal, so be aware of your local laws. If they try and drive away, take down their tag number and the make and model of their car, if possible.

Call it In: Use your cell phone, if you have one, to immediately call the police and alert them to the accident. Let the other driver see you on the phone as soon as you possibly can.

Be Hypervigilant: If you do get out of your vehicle to assess the damage be hyperalert. This is when it will go pear shaped if it's going to.

Use some common sense here as well. If you're a large male and the driver of the other car is a mother in a mini-van with kids you're probably going to be ok. If on the other hand you're a slight female and the car has four swarthy looking individuals in it, you might want to stay put until law enforcement or reinforcements arrive. Don't feel bad about telling the driver of the other car that you're going to wait inside your vehicle through a crack in your window. If he's halfway human he'll understand your dilemma.

Police Impersonators

Often called blue light bandits these guys impersonate police officers by sticking a blue flashing light on the dash of their car (like an unmarked police car) and pulling you over at night. Sometimes they rob people and other times they sexually assault lone female drivers.

Rules Apply: Typically there are rules that apply to officers on traffic duty and one is that they should be wearing a uniform. If they're not this should be the first thing that should set your sixth sense off. A real police cruiser will also more than likely have way more than just one flasher on the dash. Most unmarked cars nowadays have strobe headlights that flash alternately and blue lights doing the same behind the radiator grill.

ID Please: If you are at all suspicious, and you should be if you don't think you did anything wrong, it's dark, late, and isolated and/or you're a lone female driver, wind down your window a crack and ask the officer for his ID. If he's legitimate he'll show it to you without hesitation.

Call It In: Police officers involved in traffic stops will always call it in to their dispatch before getting out of their car and approaching yours. If possible – and not all country roads have great cell phone signals – call 911 and tell them where you are and ask them if a police officer has just pulled over a car out there.

Leave Slowly: If you're still concerned turn on your interior lights and hazard lights and drive slowly to somewhere populated and well lit. The key here is having the interior light and flashers on and driving slowly. Speeding away at fifty is called a pursuit and that excuse will not work in

143

any subsequent trial. Most officers are now aware of lone female drivers being taught the above, and while they might not like the added drive, they will understand and follow you. This is another good time to try and call 911 and let them know what you're doing and why.

Being Followed

There is not a lot more terrifying than being followed by another vehicle, especially if you've already had a run in with them, tried to drive away, and noticed them tailing you. This is exacerbated even more so if you're a lone female motorist and it's a car load of guys behind you.

Determination: Determine first that you're being followed. I've been convinced sometimes that someone has been following me due to the fact that they were behind me for miles only to find out they eventually turned off somewhere along the way. You can make that determination in several different ways.

One is to drive around the block (make sure you know you're not turning down a dead-end street or cul de sac) or round a shopping center or through a parking lot and seeing whether or not they're still behind you. There should be no earthly reason to be followed by someone if you drive round a block and go back out and on your way.

The next method is to vary your speed. Slow way down and speed back up…does the car you suspect is following you do the same?

Counter Measures: These are your counter measures to help you throw off pursuit by somebody should the need ever arise. We used to do these *de rigeur* while on close personal protection assignments to make it hard for any team of bad guys trying to follow us to build up a pattern of movement.

Safe Haven Time: Early in the book we discussed safe havens for motorists. If you're on one of your regular routes and know there's one in the vicinity, head for it.

Emergency Lane: If you're on the freeway/motorway and you think you might be being followed, pull over in the emergency stopping lane for about a minute and a half. Anyone trying to follow you now has a huge dilemma; does he stop behind you and give the game away or does he drive on past and now lose you due to the fact he can't possibly know whether you're stopped there for a while, leaving immediately, continuing on your way, or turning off at the very next exit.

When I worked as a private investigator this was always a nightmare scenario when trying to tail someone. A lot of other situations such as the suspect running a red light can be dealt with relatively easily, but this one always presented major headaches.

Over the Hill: This is a valuable one to know if you're not on a roadway with an emergency stopping lane. As you go over a hill or round a sharp turn pull over and stop. Anyone tailing you will give the game away by jamming on their brakes and/or slowing as they come around the corner or over the crest and see the car they're tailing has stopped.

Should I stay or should I go?

In the Foreign Legion during the Commando Training we talked about what to do in the event of going down in an air crash and surviving. The question always arose as to whether to stay with the wreckage or attempt to hike out of the area. Here are some simple guidelines to follow if your car is broken down and you happen to be stranded and faced with the similar dilemma of leaving your car to walk for help or staying with it hoping someone will come along and find you.

If your vehicle is broken down stay with it if:
- The weather is bad and going out in it would be risky. (This one is fairly obvious. Every year people die in winter storms when their vehicle becomes stranded and they attempt to hike for help. You really need to be well equipped for such a venture and have experience at cold weather survival if you do attempt it. It's much easier for rescue teams to spot a stranded vehicle than a stranded person.)
- You've called someone (friend, AAA, etc.) and help is on the way.

- The nearest place to walk is too far (see more on walking later in the section on bug in bags).
- Law enforcement regularly travels the road you're on. Obviously, this is going to mean fairly major highways, etc., and not rural back roads.
- You're in a secure, populated and well-lit area.

Walk for help if:
- A safe location is within walking distance. (This will depend on your health and the contents of your bug in bag, to some degree, and whether doing so would leave a small child, disabled person, etc, alone in the car.)
- You have no way of letting anyone know you have broken down (this could happen despite having a cell phone because you could be in the country or mountains, and out of range of any cell towers).
- Your vehicle can't provide protection from the weather (cars can become death traps in extremely cold or hot weather once the gas runs out and the heating/cooling system no longer functions).
- You have the proper gear for the walk.
- The weather is not too extreme

Stay hidden in the vicinity if:
- You have called for help but are in a bad area. (Cars that don't belong in an area will quickly gain the (unwanted) attention of locals who may decide to steal it, vandalize it, or take the tires. If any of the former is happening and you can see it occurring resist the temptation to run out and confront them. That's just going to compound any problem you have.)
- A group of people or an activity nearby makes you nervous. (See previous point)
- Your car might be the type to attract attention i.e. a luxury sports car in a bad part of town.

Consider A Driving Course

Most automobile clubs such as the AAA will be able to direct you to defensive driving courses which address a lot of the above issues and some related to handling under extreme conditions. Another side benefit of some of these courses is that it will lower your insurance premium (check with your insurance agent if they have a program like that and any such courses they endorse).

BMW offers a brilliant two-day course in South Carolina near their plant in Greer. They teach you emergency braking procedures, obstacle avoidance, skid pan control, cornering, threshold breaking, and so on. They also have a unique "wall of water" course where they shoot jets of water in the air to represent obstacles that must be avoided. Unlike other courses, the water wall doesn't hold up the show while you get out to dig the plastic cones out from under the car.

Other courses are more specifically geared for security driving and are worth considering as well, especially if your business takes you overseas. They cover in much more detail things such as running road blocks, performing J-turns, bootlegger turns, and so on, and in most instances, you'll get to perform the maneuvers in real time in old model cars destined for the scrap heap.

Yet another option used by a lot of bodyguards and security drivers is a rally driving course. This is, in some cases, the absolute best option when it comes to high speed handling in traffic and built up areas. Lofty Wiseman, of the famous 22 SAS, told me this tip while training with him in the UK. The problem with a lot of the aforementioned security courses is that they're conducted on old disused air strips and the roads are flat, there are no parked cars, pedestrians or curb stones etc., to impede your progress. Unfortunately, any attack you come under will probably be under real world conditions such as those mentioned above. Rally driving deals with negotiating incredibly narrow country roads, sometimes covered in gravel or snow, on the side of perilous drops into the void, at incredibly high speeds. Those skills transfer perfectly to narrow city streets lined with vehicles and trees, etc.

Last, but not least, if you live in an area where it snows, there is an excellent course conducted in Colorado every year that teaches you how to drive in the snow and on ice. You'll spend two days driving rear wheel drive, front wheel drive, four wheel and all-wheel drive vehicles round snowy tracks to learn the vagaries of the different systems and their handling under those conditions. You should also seek out advice on what sort of survival emergency gear is good to carry in the car during winter and make sure you have it. You can pack an amazing amount of survival gear in a small bag in the trunk that could literally mean the difference between life and death. For a complete list see the resources page on H2BG.com

Confronted by a mob of protestors

Since writing the first edition of "How To Be Your Own Bodyguard" a lot has changed. As you've no doubt noticed, I've added a section on Active Shooters, and Riots and Flash Mobs. Since the protests in Ferguson Missouri various groups have decided to make their objections known by forming road blocks across interstates, highways, and thoroughfares. For someone with little experience in violence this can be one of the most terrifying events you will ever face. It's also serious. In the race riots in Miami in 1980, several motorists were dragged from their vehicles and beaten to death. A lot of readers will remember Reginald Denny, the truck driver who was hauled out of his 18-wheeler during the LA riots and almost killed.

Read posts on the internet about what to do and you'll be confronted with the usual band of tripe by internet warriors from the safety of their mum's basement screaming *"run them over"*. While a lot of people no doubt wish they could do that it's not viable advice. The following is.

Don't Be There: I know this sounds trite, but we still have far too many people who are oblivious of their surroundings due to task fixation until it's too late. You should always be looking as far ahead as you possibly can when driving so events don't catch you unprepared. If you're doing that and you notice a wall of protestors or a riot formed ahead, do your absolute best to get out of there before you become ensconced in a mass of cars and unable to move.

Running Them Over: If avoidance has failed, now we have to deal with the elephant in the room, i.e. do I run them over? This is not a law book, and I am not a lawyer, but little changes with regards to the laws of self-defense just because you find yourself in a car when attacked.

The simple answer is, providing they're not a threat i.e. they're lined up on the roadway but not actually attacking anyone, you are NOT allowed to run them down or hit them with your vehicle, which could be cause to charge you with vehicular assault. However, if they begin dragging people from vehicles, flipping them over, breaking windows, or setting them alight, a reasonable person is apt to assume that there is an imminent threat and is now allowed to use self-defense to get away and save themselves, or family and friends who are in the automobile with them.

If you're going to exercise that option, here's what you need to know.

Lock your doors: This might seem obvious, but again you'd be amazed at people who drive around who don't wear seatbelts and/or lock doors. Nor do they lock them when they leave their vehicle.

Put your windows down ¼ to ½ an inch: This might seem counterintuitive, but they're actually stronger in this position than if they're fully up. Obviously, you don't do this if there is tear gas or chemical warfare of any sort going on.

Passenger Concerns: Get any passengers to lie down as best they can and cover themselves up:

This is for two reasons. One; if the windows, sunroof, or windshield are broken, they're not hit and/or cut by flying or broken glass shards, and two; in the event of children being in the car, it will help them in being less afraid and traumatized by what's going on outside.

Seatbelts: Some experts say leave them on while others say take them off. The former say use it to make you harder to drag from your vehicle while the latter are saying if you have to bail because your vehicle catches fire you're not hampered in any way. My personal viewpoint is you leave it on until such times as you see vehicles being flipped and/or hit with Molotov cocktails, etc.

Windows Up: In the event of tear-gas being used on or by the protestors then you'll want to put the windows back up and turn the recycled air button on or turn your air/AC off altogether.

Call 911: You can, but understand that sometimes the cop cars are right in there with you or are already flipped over and burning. A couple of police officers on their own are hardly likely to enter the mob to try to get you out of your vehicle if everything has gone pear shaped.

Using Your Vehicle As A Weapon: If you have reached the point where you're going to drive into the mob to get away, resist the temptation to hit them fast. You will be far more effective tapping the horn, having your hazards on and driving very slowly in a bid to push them out of the way and then gradually accelerate as you make your way free.

The problem with driving fast is that now you break legs and bodies begin to pile up under your car which will stop its forward progress, and at that point, it's very likely you'll be dragged from the vehicle and killed (more on "Mob Mentality" in a bit). Not a lot of people know this, but the terrorist attack in Nice France, on Bastille Day 2016, (where the terrorist plowed into the crowds with a large truck) was stopped because the truck's undercarriage and drive shaft were clogged with body parts and not by any police action. Assuming you did make it you'll have to deal with the legal aftermath as opposed to simply pushing people out of the way using the vehicle's mass.

Mob Mentality: The mob mentality is a very real psychological phenomenon. Individuals inside a mob lose their own identity and take on the mob's identity instead. People, who would normally not be violent, will get caught up and not hesitate in breaking windows, looting, vandalism, and even murder, so you need to take that into consideration when making your defensive plan.

On Being Armed: In some states and some countries you may have the right to be armed, and have your weapon with you inside the vehicle. These weapons may be anything from firearms to tear gas.

To begin with, let's talk about the weapon everybody has and that's the car itself. A bullet is pitiful when compared to the damage that a car can cause at 30mph. Stay in your car, and use it, before you ever think about descending from it and using a firearm. This is where the SUV reigns supreme. They're usually too heavy to flip over, they keep you up and away from the mob, you can see over them for the best route out, you can get off-road in your bid to escape, and push other vehicles out of the way. You might also want to consider "run-flat" tires for whatever vehicle you're running as some mobs have put down sharpened spikes, etc., to try and stop cars from getting past.

With regards to your next most effective weapon (the firearm), you'll need to have it on your person and not on the seat, dashboard, or center console. That way, if you must exit the vehicle and flee, your weapon is with you. Also, if someone breaks the window they won't see your gun lying there and grab it.

The least effective weapon at this point is probably the tear-gas or OC spray. As I've mentioned before, trying to use it from inside the car can cause a type of vacuum effect and the gas will come back in on you and it's probably just going to piss the mob off.

So, in a nutshell, avoid using weapons if you can, but if you can't, do nothing as long as they do nothing. Get out of there using your vehicle as a way to push them clear, if they turn violent. The car is your best weapon (windows are slightly down if there's no chemical warfare going on), and if you do have a gun in the car, make sure it's on you.

20

BUG IN/BUG OUT

U tterly important, and oft times ignored, the Bug In Bag – BIB – is a critical piece of kit. Although you should have some elements of it on you at all times it becomes both easy and important to have one on you in the car.

A Bug in Bag is a small backpack, or equivalent, packed with some simple items that will help you get home (Bug In) in the event of a breakdown, blackout, or similar emergency. The Bug Out Bag is similar in content except it is usually bigger and contains elements to camp out and survive in the wilderness should it ever become necessary to leave home and head for hills.

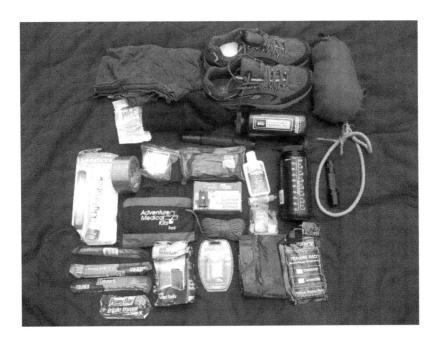

My Bug in Bag Contents

One only has to see the cataclysmic events of 9/11, the subway attacks in London on 7/7, and the great Northeast blackout in the last few years to see the wisdom in carrying something so simple. During all the above examples some people were forced to walk home twenty plus miles. In the case of the power outage/blackout, that arduous trek had to be done in the dark, without food, water, or any method of lighting their way, while wearing high heeled and/or dress shoes. People trapped in the subway in London died due to the lack of simple medical equipment that is an essential component of any good BIB. Outside of huge events like this, and as previously mentioned in the section on vehicular security, every year around winter time we hear of someone dying who left their stranded vehicle to go and get help. With a little forethought and planning, and taking a bit of advice from the Boy Scouts about "Being Prepared", tragedies like this need not occur.

One of my Fight Survival students Randal F. was honeymooning in Scotland late 2007 when he and his newly betrothed hit a rock in the middle of a small country lane and broke their rental car's axle. Randal had fortunately listened to the training about the BIB and had his with him. While it wasn't a long walk back to their accommodation, his new wife, Sandy, was impressed that they had everything they'd needed, should they have been caught further from shelter than they were and forced to stay out in the elements overnight.

While the contents of your individual bag will vary depending on your needs and where you live etc., some basic items should include:...

Father Dies

In Oregon last month, James Kim, a 35-year-old father of two, died of hypothermia during a fruitless search for help after he made a wrong turn onto an unsecured logging road and the family became stranded in their car in the rain and snow.

NY Times, 1/9/07

Walking Shoes	Water	Bandana
Power Bars	Flashlight	Batteries
Lighter	1st Aid Kit	Whistle
Compass	Dust Mask	Survival Blanket
Multi-Tool	Swiss Army Knife	Poncho
Hands Free Light	AM/FM Radio	Handi-Wipes
Duct Tape	Para Cord	Chapstick
Sun Screen	Gloves	Pry Bar

I have, for your convenience, a complete list under the resources page on H2BG.com with links to the best types of all the above gear.

Water, food, and shelter are our most basic needs, so let's deal with them first.

154

Water: The first thing you should keep a supply of in your bag is water. I went to the expense of buying some Nalgene water bottles but a couple of store bought bottles of water are fine. You'll primarily use this for hydration but it can also be used for wound irrigation, and as witnessed during film footage of the day the twin towers came down, washing foreign matter from your eyes and face. I also throw in some water purification tablets in case I run out of water and have to use some from a questionable supply.

Food: Next is something that will last a long time, provide nourishment, and not take up too much room in your kit. Think of things like beef jerky, dark chocolate, Kendal's mint cake, or power bars. Reading about those who had to walk out of the city during the power outage I learned they couldn't purchase food even though some had cash because registers wouldn't work, stores didn't have lights, employees had left and locked up, and credit cards couldn't be processed. If you anticipate a long walk – you live in the countryside for example – you might want to include some freeze-dried foods available at camping stores or some Army ration packs – MREs – available online or at your local Army Navy surplus store. Power bars and jerky etc., are good for short bursts of energy but you may want something more substantial if the hike is going to be a long one.

Shelter: Shelter begins with **clothing** and the first thing you'll want to have in your bag is a **pair of training or lightweight hiking shoes**. Some people's feet were so torn up after walking out of NY City in dress shoes and/or high heels during both the outage and 9/11 that they resorted to walking home bare foot. Personally, I prefer shoes that go up at least to the ankle which are going to offer support in the event of rough terrain. You might also consider water proof or Gore-Tex versions if you live in an area where the weather may be extreme. Normal training shoes in snow, slush or floodwater are going to get very uncomfortable very quickly. Don't forget to **include socks** if you normally wear loafers or high heels.

Next, you'll want a **lightweight waterproof jacket or a poncho**. Some of these fold up and zip into their own pockets so they end up taking up almost no room at all. Again, if you live in Colorado or somewhere equally cold you'll want something a little warmer or **a fleece liner** for the above.

I keep a spare **thermal shirt** in mine as well which is designed to work in a multitude of weather extremes and also wick away sweat from the body and a **pair of shorts** might be useful if you live somewhere hot.

Another important but often overlooked item is some sort of head coverage. In colder climes I'd opt for a **woolen watch cap** whereas in the South I'd be more inclined to go for a **soft hat with a brim** in case the hike home was in the summer during the day. Eschew the ubiquitous baseball cap. While I agree it's better than nothing it's not going to provide enough protection against the sun beating down on the back of your neck.

Gloves are another good addition. Again, you'll want warmer ones for cooler climates but even in hot weather a pair can come in handy for climbing over stone walls, handling rope, and a plethora of other purposes.

Still under the shelter banner, but off the body, we come to items such as ground sheets, tarps, and space or survival blankets. Again, these take up almost no room at all and can be used as temporary shelter from wind or the elements, as a litter to carry the wounded, insulation against wet or cold ground, and in the case of the survival blanket, as a signaling device should you be out in the middle of nowhere.

While it's probably more appropriate for the BOB, some friends carry a bivvy bag (sleeping bag) and/or a one-man tent available from Army surplus stores. If your walk home is only 20 or so miles it's probably not a necessary item, but for someone living in rural Montana it might be. It all depends on what you anticipate your situation to be given the local environment and season.

First Aid: A small first aid kit would be my next priority because in most disasters, emergency services personnel will be stretched thin. Also, if you're trapped, as some of the victims of the subway bombing in London were, it can be hours before help turns up. Knowledge of first aid and some basic gear could literally mean the difference between life and death.

You can buy these first-aid kits pre-made in camping stores or simply build your own out of a small waterproof camera bag or a large zip lock baggie. The zip lock is good because it allows you to see the contents of the kit. The waterproof camera pouch is good also because you can slip it on your belt.

A good kit will include most of the following...

Aspirin, or similar	Imodium (anti diarrhea)	Band Aids
Safety Pins	Latex Gloves	Butterfly Clips
Antiseptic Wipes	1st Aid Book	Sterile Gauze
Antibiotic Cream	Hydrocortisone Cream	Tweezers
Scissors	Calamine Lotion	Thermometer
Elastic Bandage	Mouthpiece for CPR	Antiseptic
Insect Bite Wipes	Laxative	Lip Balm
1st Aid Tape	1 Sling Bandage	Eye Pad
Finger Splint	Wound Dressing	Antacid

The most important part of all of the above is knowing how to use it. I'm a graduate of, and cannot recommend enough, a Wilderness 1st Responder Course. It is far more in depth than a regular first aid course as it deals with the possibility of being stuck in the wilds for several weeks before professional medical assistance will arrive. If you can't spring for the time or money for one of those the Red Cross regularly schedules 1st Aid courses and/or CPR courses. Do not include something in your kit that you don't know how to use.

Another important point is to go through the kit every six months or so and upgrade or replace any items that may have passed their "use by" date. Alcohol swabs or sterile wipes will often dry out in the heat of the summer and most medications have a limited shelf life. For a complete list of who I recommend to train with check out the resources page on H2BG.com. This will save you a lot of money and heartbreak.

If you are going to build your own and keep it in a transparent zip lock bag I recommend compartmentalizing the gear into even smaller bags. Keep all your meds in one for example, band-aids and gauze in another and so on. That way you don't have to rummage through the bag looking for whatever it is you need. Instead, you can just grab the relevant item and go.

Bandana: The humble bandana is my next piece of *de rigueur* kit as it dovetails nicely with the 1st aid kit. How? To begin with it makes a great (temporary) tourniquet. Most first aid courses used to advise against the use of tourniquets, but sometimes you just can't get around the need for them. This resurgence in popularity is due to military operations in the middle east where they discovered they kept soldiers alive, and at the Boston Marathon bombing, twenty-seven victims are alive today due to the application of improvised tourniquets. The key is to mark the time you apply it on the victim's head with lipstick or a marker or equivalent and loosen it for a few minutes every twenty minutes.

After twenty minutes the flesh begins to die because it's been deprived of oxygenated blood for too long. By releasing the tourniquet you permit the capillaries to open and carry fresh blood into the limb before tightening back down again. If you don't do this the chance of them losing the limb is great.

Another possible use is to roll the bandana up like a do-nut. Wounds with objects sticking out require this kind of bandage to protect them. Finally, it makes a great improvised triangular bandage or sling in the event of an injured arm, wrist or collarbone.

Other than for first aid, the bandana can be used as...well, a bandana. Great for keeping sweat out of the eyes while you're working on something. It can replace a broken strap on your bag, tie something or someone up if necessary. It can be used as an improvised weapon (ask a Filipino Kali Instructor how to do this), or dunked into the out of reach hollow of a tree to soak up water trapped inside if you're stuck in the wilderness. Use it as a dusk mask or to cool off. How about carrying or collecting things in it? You can tie extra stuff to your back pack with it or protect your head from the sun. How about an emergency coffee filter? Emergency toilet paper, anyone? An ice compress, a signaling device, an emergency canteen plug and also as emergency kindling in case you need to light a fire.

You get the idea, and now you know why I carry more than one in my BIB.

Lights: The next thing we need is light. It's no fun trying to apply your first aid equipment in the dark, and if we look at our other major scenarios again, 9/11, 7/7 in the UK, and the great northeastern power outage, all required portable lighting. What if your car breaks down in the middle of the night on the way home? What if the power goes out in your place of employment?

If you're doing a micro pack then you should have at least one light, but I actually carry several sources in mine.

First is a hands-free lamp that looks like an upgraded version of one of the old miner's lamps. They come with straps and you slip them over your head and turn them on leaving your hands free to use and a light that moves to illuminate wherever you happen to be looking. They're worth their weight in gold if you happen to need both hands free to work on someone's injury, etc.

Next, is a small anodized aluminum torch such as those made by Maglite™. Another great version of these is a Surefire with an on/off button on the end cap which makes it ideal for tactical shooting. If you did have to resort to a firearm during such an emergency the last light you'd want is one permanently strapped to your head!!

My third light source is one of those high-power key chain LED lights that you see at sporting and camping stores near the cash register for about a dollar. They can be used on your key chain, but I also keep a couple near the lid of my BIB so I have a light source to look for things in my bag in the dark, much like you use the light under the hood and in the trunk of your car.

Fourth light source is a survival candle. These are slow burning, fat candles that provide heat in a confined space. We did some winter survival in the Legion and they will actually increase the ambient temperature in snow cave. The candle is a longer burning light in a situation like those trapped in the subway during 7/7 experienced. It allows you to conserve the battery in your flashlight and there's something psychologically warming about a naked flame as opposed to the mechanical glow of a flashlight. You can also use the candle to sterilize things, heat things up, and start fires, which you can't do with the flashlight.

Fifth light source is a bunch of those chemical light sticks that you snap in half to activate which can burn intensely, or for a long time, or in infrared, etc. You can find different colored ones for different needs and they can be used for illumination, are safe around explosives, and have a multitude of uses from signaling to vehicle marking.

Last, and not technically a light source, I carry a Bic lighter and a couple of boxes of waterproof matches. I used to use a Zippo given to me during my time with the REP in the Foreign Legion but the fuel evaporates and that's something else to carry. The Bic lighters seem to last forever and are practically indestructible.

Duct Tape: Next on my list is the ubiquitous duct tape. If you can grab the dark green military grade stuff as it's stronger than the more common gray is. Duct tape is amazing and there are books and web sites devoted to the myriad uses of the stuff.

You can use it to repair rips in your BIB, tape up a gaping wound, wrap spare batteries around the outside of your flashlights, resole your shoe, tie bits of your car back on, improvised hand cuffs, and the list goes on. As there are already books devoted to its uses I'd recommend getting a hold of one rather than me writing another one here.

Trash Bag: I keep a couple of trash bags in various sizes in the bag. They take up almost no room at all, and like duct tape, have a million uses from improvised ponchos to carrying water, and emergency cold weather survival coats (another layer and stuffed with leaves etc.) to sealing a sucking chest wound when coupled with the duct tape. I'm not talking about the small ones but rather the huge "lawn and leaf" bags or the heavy duty "contractor" bags available at your local home improvement store.

They can also be used to compartmentalize your stuff within your BIB and keep the clothes, for example, dry.

Para-cord: Para cord is available from your home improvement or local Army/Navy store. It's nylon cord and wraps up into a small bundle that can be chopped into specific lengths when needed. Again, the amount of uses for something like cord in an emergency is limited only by your imagination. It can lash a knife to a stick to make an improvised weapon, it can be used to make snares, tie someone up, replace a torn strap on your BIB, and lash things together to make shelter should your short trip become a long one.

Make sure you get the good stuff. It comes with seven strands of smaller string on the inside that each have a fifty-pound breaking strain and the whole thing still woven will hold almost 200 pounds.

That means if you take a 3-foot length of the stuff and unravel it you'll have almost twenty feet of string available.

Multi-tool: Originally there was a Leatherman™ and that was it. Nowadays it seems there is a plethora of multi-tools available. In case you've been living in the dark ages, they're a little like a Swiss Army knife on steroids and come with many different blades and tools attached in a handy leather belt pouch. Are they as good as the authentic tool? Almost never, but try carrying your full-blown home tool kit around with you in your BIB and see how far you get. You can buy them in various configurations with pliers, blades, an assortment of screw driver heads, rulers, nail files, saws, scissors, wire strippers, bottle and can openers, and many companies have now gotten in on the act.

Swiss Army: One could almost be guilty of overdoing it by carrying the above multi-tool and a Swiss Army knife but the multi tool is a tad more robust if you really must take a screw out of something. On the other hand the SAK can be dropped easily in your pocket and takes up almost no room. There is an absolutely mind numbing array of variations on their knives and they come with some that have more tools than your local home improvement store on them. They can also have attachments such as compasses and magnifying glasses and pens and tooth picks et al that the multi-tools don't. I also like the fact you can stick the SAK on your belt and not arouse much undue attention from security personnel whereas a multi-tool can cause them to have conniptions.

Radio: You'll be wanting an AM/FM type and there are several versions of these. One uses batteries and the other has a small cranking handle that, after winding, will give you about 25-30 minutes of listening time (some of the newer crank types actually have a USB port built in which will allow you to charge your mobile phone, etc with it). Information, in any sort of national emergency, is going to be critical. Is it a terrorist attack or is it something more benign? Is someone coming to get you? Should you be evacuating? Has the situation become worse? The lightweight and small size of these definitely makes them worthwhile.

Pry Bar: At first blush that probably seems like a crazy idea but there is a titanium version available that's incredibly strong and very small. Think for a moment about the plight of the people trapped in the wreckage of the underground during the London terrorist bombing. I remember reading one account of a guy whose leg was trapped under a seat and they couldn't get him free. With the pry bar that probably wouldn't have been an issue. What about opening a door that's jammed, be it on a fire escape, a house, a car, or an elevator? In a pinch it can be used as an improvised weapon as well. If my kit was for getting me out of the city safely in the event of a disaster I'd definitely have one of these in it.

Dust Mask: These are cheap and readily available. People who inhaled the dust from the collapsed towers on 9/11 are still coughing 9/11 and many people went down from smoke (and other contaminants) inhalation. A couple of these in your kit and the problem is solved. Remember your bandana is a viable alternative if you don't have these.

Whistle: You absolutely want a whistle in your kit. Remember the movie with Nicholas Cage about the two firemen trapped under the rubble of the towers. Blowing on a whistle to alert someone to your presence is a lot less strenuous, and more effective, than trying to yell and shout. Remember the code for SOS too. Three short blasts, three long blasts, and three short again is universal for someone in distress.

162

Compass: A compass isn't a bad idea. If all you're going to be doing is hoofing it out of the city to the burbs, then it's probably not necessary. However, if your car breaks down in the country side a compass would be a god send, especially if you end up in the woods. It will also work if the satellite system goes down unlike a hand-held GPS unit. If you haven't already it's a great idea to learn some land navigations skills.

GPS unit: An alternative to the compass would be a small hand held GPS unit. They can be used to backtrack along your path, and in the city, will list the names of streets and landmarks.

Fire Starter: Available in camping stores this is a piece of magnesium and a flint in a handy little unit. Again, if you're only concerned about the long walk home from the city, this is probably overkill. However, in the country side, during hostile weather conditions, it's an absolute necessity. Don't forget that it can be used as an improvised signaling device as well.

Handi-wipes: In the old days we'd use toilet paper but these are better and have more uses ranging from the aforementioned TP to a refreshing rest and wipe down to washing hands and cleaning a wound.

Sunscreen: Don't only consider a power outage and walking in the dark. What if this is broad daylight like 9/11 and you're forced to trudge home in the middle of the summer, with the sun beating down on you. Sunburn is dangerous and can absolutely exhaust you prematurely. Carry this in the handy stick form and use it often.

Sunglasses: Along the same vein as sunscreen, are sunglasses. Keep a pair in a hard case in your kit for the same reasons cited in sunscreen. Sun blindness can be a real problem and hits you before you even realized it's happening. Sunglasses therefore, especially in the south, are a necessity.

Batteries: A lot of your kit will require batteries. A handy tip taught to me by the legendary Marcus Wynne was to tape spare ones of the required size to the various lights by use of liberal swathes of duct tape. Or, you can purchase cases which hold various size batteries from someone like Pelican™ and keep spares in there.

Bungees: Bungee cords are another piece of kit that have an almost endless supply of possibilities for use. Replacing torn straps on your bag, holding car doors shut, strapping things down, they can (almost) eliminate the need for learning how to tie knots.[13]

Cash: I'm amazed at the amount of people I see on the web with their BIBs itemized who always leave out cash. Imagine being in the woods stranded and walking out to a road and needing to pay for a ride, bribe someone, buy food or rent a room. Cash is king…just make sure you ensure it's well hidden in the bag liner somewhere.

Knife: I carry a large fixed blade in my kit. In the event of an emergency I'd strap it on so it was close at hand. Any camper can tell you a knife is a survival tool all in itself, and given the human predators that seem to surface during calamities – think looters and rioters – the knife makes an excellent deterrent and weapon.

Pistol: In jurisdictions that permit, I carry a pistol in my bag as well. Like the knife it's going to be on my person the second the walk begins. It's effective for self-defense, against human predators and wild ones, and hopefully a deterrent in the event of an attack that you have advance warning of. A lone female, broken down in her car on the highway and awaiting help she's phoned for, is going to feel a lot more confident if she's armed and knows how to use it, than a similarly unarmed female.

This list of kit is by no means exhaustive. It can also vary depending on the size bag you want to carry to the part of the country you live in. I've worked with some executive protection teams whose medical kit alone would rival that of an old-school ambulance and take up almost the entire back of an SUV and met people carrying kits that fit in their pocket. I also know people who've got more than one. They have one in the locker at work up on the top floors designed to get them out of the building, and a second bigger kit in the trunk of their car. The small one only needs a

---

[13] Caveat: Thousands of people every year end up permanently blinded when using bungee cord. The hook doesn't engage and the end whips loose. The injuries can range from inconsequential and painful to the surgical removal of the damaged eye. Be careful.

smoke hood, a small first aid kit and a flash light to enable you to get to the car.

When I went through my commando training at the center on the Red Sea in Djibouti we learned keep one load of gear in our backpack and to have a smaller "belt kit" that slipped into pouches on your web belt or in your pockets. In the event you had to move fast you could drop your big back pack and resort to the belt kit and still have a fair chance of survival.

As previously mentioned you might, if you're of that mind-set, have a Bug Out Bag at home as well. It's a big daddy version of the BIB and includes all the same stuff with the addition of three days' worth of freeze dried meals or "Meals Ready to Eat" MREs from the Army/Navy store, a tent and a sleeping bag. The concept there is, should it become necessary, such as when Katrina hit Louisiana, that one can grab the big BOB from the garage wall and go, confident in the fact they have everything they need to sustain themselves for three days or more. My ex-wife used to laugh at my preparedness until we had a power outage in our house one night. I went to the garage, grabbed my large back pack, dragged out the gas camping stove and some tins of soup and we ate like champs in the light of the candle. Our neighbors meantime sat around wondering whether it was going to last long enough for them to have to go book a hotel room or stay with relatives in another state or part of the city.

The last issue that must be addressed when it comes to BIBs is that, if I were you, I wouldn't tell anyone at work that you have one. Throw it in your locker, and if anyone asks, just tell them it's gym clothes. It's a sad indictment of man's inhumanity that there are cases of people robbing and or killing others for their kit during times of emergency.[14] If you tell your co-workers, and God forbid, there's another 9/11 you might just find someone has broken into your locker, stolen your goodie bag, and bolted with it.

---

[14] These will probably be the same people that make fun of you for being prepared!

The other question arises as to whether this is paranoia to have one of these. Trust me when I say there is a chasm between paranoia and preparedness. Cops and firemen go to work every day equipped with belt loads of gear to deal with whatever emergency they should be faced with. They're not labeled nuts or paranoid because everyone knows that's the sort of kit you need in an emergency. Well, if you know that, where's yours for your emergency? It may never happen but the old adage applies here: "Better to have and not need, than to need and not have."

21

HOME DEFENSE

Some people think of home security and they think it means securing their home from break ins when they're NOT at home. That's fine, but that is only dealing with one part of the problem, and given that the average home owner has their contents insured against theft, it's the minor part.

The crime that's sadly on the increase is that of home invasion, which is when the bad guys attack your home while you, and your family, are inside. When it originally began to make headlines in the media it was usually a disgruntled drug dealer going around to get even with his competition. Unfortunately, once criminals realized how easy it was, they began attacking anyone's home, providing it looked like a viable target. Another reason for the uptrend is in line with the advent of car-jackings and that is that the alternative is too risky. Convenience stores and banks, long the desired targets of criminals, have hardened themselves to the point where the crooks are being caught due to cheap surveillance cameras and security measures. They also know there's a huge chance that another customer will walk in on them, or a silent alarm has been tripped and the police are only moments away. In the privacy of your home, however, they have all the time in the world and have been known to make meals, stay overnight, take naps, sexually assault members of the family, and go on jaunts to empty out bank accounts with one family member while the others remain behind as hostages. Chilling stuff.

In one of the worst examples in recent history a doctor's wife and two daughters were killed and the house set on fire to destroy the evidence.

Notice again the location and remember my reminder earlier about crime happening anywhere. Also, notice the ubiquitous "you don't think about those things happening" statement from the local Reverend. Not a criticism of him, but rather a fine example of the attitude that far too many people have, and that the crooks are counting on.

Before we move on from this discussion of home invasions it might be a good idea to learn the three methods by which they typically gain entry into the house. They are:

All Out Assault: This is when the attackers hit your abode without any warning at all. Asleep or awake, the first warning you get is the sound of a window breaking, a door caving in under the force of kicks, or someone running into your house.

Surreptitious Entry: This is when the bad guys enter your house (Typically when it's dark) through a breach in your

Cheshire, Connecticut (AP) 2 parolees with long records were charged Tue with breaking into a Dr.'s home, forcing a hostage to withdraw money & setting fire to the house.
The Dr.'s wife and 2 daughters were killed.
Dr. Petit Jr. was the only survivor. The 2 men were charged with assault, sexual assault, kidnapping, burglary, robbery and arson.
"They're just a lovely family," said Rev. Ronald Rising, a neighbor. "It's just awful to think it could happen to a family like that in this community. You don't think about those things happening."

perimeter such as an open or unlocked door or window.

Deception: This is where the criminals will prey on the milk of human kindness and use ploys to gain entry. They may send a female accomplice made up to look as if she's been in an accident to ask to use the phone or they might come to the door asking for directions to a nearby landmark. Either way, once the door is open the rest of the gang invades.

Just as we had corresponding elements in our force continuum we have corresponding methods here. For every way the bad guy has of gaining entry, be it during a home invasion or the more traditional burglary done in your absence, we must have defenses in place. The easiest method I'm aware of is one taught to me by the renowned Marcus Wynne. His originally contained four "Ds", but I took the liberty of adding the fifth. The five "Dees" are as follows;

- **DETER**
- **DETECT**
- **DELAY/ DENY**
- **DEFEND**

The military and bodyguards alike utilize the same system when we protect an objective by using concentric rings of increasingly difficult layers of security. Assuming you make it through the first layer the next layer will be even tougher and so on and so forth until you reach a very hard target with a last line of defense. We must again take a page from the pro's playbook and do the same with our homes.

Deter

Our first objective therefore is to deter them. The outermost ring then becomes the city you live in. Is it a dangerous metropolis or relatively safe? Next comes the side of town in which we live followed by the neighborhood and/or subdivision. Assuming they were the best you could afford, you'd begin to consider such things as a neighborhood crime watch group, alert neighbors, street layout - cul-de-sac or cut through – is it a

169

gated community with private security, lighting, the police, etc. Do you have a sign on the front gate saying beware of the guard dog? Do you have a large dog? How about alarm company decals or signs? I recommend a generic sign saying it's alarmed rather than specific companies as enterprising crooks have been known to go as far as acquiring the plans of the security systems for the various companies in town so they know how to circumvent the system. Don't forget also, you don't need a dog or an alarm to put the signs up and create a deterrence. Most bad guys aren't going to verify whether you actually have either when there are so many other targets out there rich for the plucking.

A further deterrent would be keeping curtains on your windows and not displaying your valuables as some people do in certain upscale neighborhoods. I once wrote a blog about the citizens of Myer's Park, a suburb of Charlotte, who seemed to be stunned that they were enjoying a spate of burglaries. These are the same neighbors that never had curtains on any of their windows, flaunting their valuables in a competition with the neighbors to see who had the best "stuff." Is it any wonder the robbers hit them? It must have been like window shopping, no pun intended. Another point is to keep the hedges around the house trimmed down. Criminals don't want to do their stuff in the open so, if there's no apparent hiding spots from which to operate, they'll pick another weaker target.

Finally, something else to consider is that some home invaders have chosen their victims based on the car they were driving at the time and simply followed it home. I'm not suggesting buying a jalopy if you've worked hard for your money and wish to enjoy a luxury automobile, but if you are going to drive something that screams "the owner is wealthy," at least adopt some of the counter-surveillance measures from time to time that we mention in the section on Auto Security. On the subject of vehicles, a recent poll of burglars revealed that one of the biggest deterrents to someone breaking in during daylight hours was a car parked in the driveway.

Detect

Let's assume that we haven't been able to deter them from attempting to hit your house. Your next layer of defense is to detect them as soon as you can. The sooner you detect them the sooner you can prepare yourself to deal with them either by contacting the police or the alarm company, fleeing the premises, securing yourself in your safe room, arming yourself, or a combination of the above. Detection methods run the gamut of CCTV camera systems hooked up to monitors, motion detectors, sensor pads, and alarms to infra-red beams that activate when you walk through them, dogs and real live security guards if your budget extends that far. Without a doubt one of the cheapest methods, and most effective is the motion detector hooked up to some powerful flood lights.

I was on a surveillance gig once in Canada, lending a hand to the local private investigators, by flying in to Canada in advance of a murder suspect and identifying him to their people as he came out of arrivals. During a later stakeout of his residence we had planned to get into the back yard so we could make sure he didn't climb over the fence and escape that way. The suspect's house, and the neighbors, all had the new-fangled motion detector floodlights on their property and there was no way around it, if you tripped them you just couldn't get close without anyone looking out the window being able to see you.

The other great thing about motion detector lights is that the bad guy has absolutely no way of knowing whether someone who just saw or heard him has turned that light on, or if it's been triggered by your movement, and who can take the chance it was a motion detector only? (Of course there are ways to circumvent them but for reasons of security I'm not going to reveal them here.)

The CCTV cameras I mentioned above are now within almost anyone's budget. I've seen them at the large consumer warehouses for only ninety-nine dollars which includes the TV monitor and four cameras that you can place anywhere wirelessly. Some of my colleagues on high level protection details are using these systems now in hotel rooms. In other words, an agent will sit inside and monitor the screen while the cameras are placed discreetly in plants etc., along the hallway. Doing it that way can play down that there's even security in place. No visible guards mean no valuable VIP in the vicinity to the uninitiated. However, someone watching the screen inside, can have all the same static post points for live guards on his monitor with cameras in their stead.

Something else to consider is gravel garden beds and/or driveways etc. Sneaking across this stuff without making a noise is nigh on impossible and it's cheap and easy to maintain.

If you're going to use an alarm company consult several and get written quotes and read the small print. Years ago I used one of the major players and their rep neglected to tell me I was locked in to the contract for five years. I found that out when about a year into the contract I was offered a better deal. When I contacted *** they told me I could only escape the contract by buying out the monthly fee multiplied by how many months/years I had left to go. I also discovered if you didn't send them a written, (yes, you read that right) notice within a seven-day window of the expiration of their contract you'd automatically be signed up for another five years. Guess who I never used again and guess who I tell everyone about at my seminars to avoid like the plague?

Make sure their installers are licensed and bonded and find out if you own or are renting the equipment. Is the system monitored (better) or does it just make a noise designed to scare away intruders? The very best ones are monitored which will eliminate the increasingly expensive false alarms (fines are being levied in some cities in the States for false alarms going to the police or fire department) as the operators can listen in and determine if someone is in the house or if it's a sensor on the fritz. You'll also need to know about battery backups, whether they have insurance in case they break something in your house during the installation and what their policies are concerning false alarms. It's common knowledge that most alarms can be circumvented by cutting phone lines so talk to them about "cloning" to a nearby phone line to prevent the system being rendered inoperable by someone with some wire cutters.

Delay/Deny

I'm going to lump these two together because they are part and parcel of the same part of the program. In other words, a good lock and a solid door will deny entry to an amateur level thief, but only delay the seasoned pro. So, assuming they're not deterred by your best efforts to live in the right part of town and instigate a neighborhood watch system etc., then the next layer in our defense is to delay or deny them. The longer it takes for them to pull off the crime the more inclined they're going to be to go find a softer target. In fact, most law enforcement officials will tell you if there's a thousand dollars in one house with locks and an alarm and ten dollars in the one next door with the window open, the crook will take the easy ten every time. You have to remember they're lazy – otherwise they'd have real jobs and work – and they're opportunists.

So, how is your yard? Do you have a fence? If you do, is it chain link, solid or flimsy and is it hooked up to an alarm system? A privacy fence can be a double-edged sword. It denies someone attempting to case the joint the chance to look in and see if you're in the yard or home or even what quality of home (and therefore what type of valuables are likely to be around) you have, but if they climb over and begin to work on a window, the neighbors can't see them and won't be able to alert the police.

Our next layer of defense is the house itself and specifically windows and doors. Are they good, is the frame solid, are you using quality locks and deadbolts? What about other entry points such as skylights, dog flaps and garages?

Doors should be solid and not the cheaper hollow core variety you find on a lot of houses. The only two versions worth getting are solid wood or metal. While the others might be cheaper the money you saved will be the last thing on your mind when someone kicks it in with one solid punt kick. Ensure the hinges are not on the outside of the house and eliminate doors that have glass paneling in them for obvious reasons. You'll also want a peep hole but please don't waste money on safety chains. Any eight-year-old can kick a door hard enough to render them useless. There are some products available that you can put into the floor behind the door that are aftermarket devices. They work very well but the problem becomes people become lackadaisical about their use and then they're of no value. If you do have one use it but if you want a really cheap viable alternative buy a two-dollar rubber door wedge and kick it under the door instead.

The frame of the door is often a weak spot. Burglars use a technique called "spreading" whereby they place a wedge between the doorframe and the wall and cause the frame to bow thus allowing them access. It's no good investing in a quality door if the frame it sits in can be defeated easily. Have it reinforced by using 3-4 inch screws and making sure they go all the way into the studs.

Before we give up on the subject of doors beware of several varieties that are inherently weak. The first is pet doors. Some teams use small members or even children to gain access this way. If you have one make sure the dog that uses it is big and intimidating enough to stop someone trying to gain entry this way.

The next is the glass sliding patio doors. Spend the money and invest in the factory lock (sometimes called Charlie Bars) that drop down and secure in place. The problem with the broomstick or dowel in the runner is that it can be circumvented easily.

Finally watch out for your garage doors. A lot of the older ones use a remote that only has five different possible combos. Enterprising thieves would drive down neighborhood streets pushing the remote fob and watching for garage doors that would open. Upgrade yours to include the version with the roaming pin number that changes every time you use it. Consider using a padlock on yours when you're in the house if your garage is attached.

Aside from the door itself and the frame the next best item is going to be your locks. Invest in the best you can afford and make sure the bolts go at least one inch into the door frame. The absolute best, inarguably, is a double cylinder dead bolt. That means it requires a key on the outside to

174

open and one on the inside as well. If you have one with only a key on the outside a burglar can cut a hole in the door, break a pane of glass etc., and reach in and turn the latch. If it's the version that requires a key on the inside as well he's limited to taking any of your belongings out by the windows because he won't be able to open the door.

You're going to have to ensure that a key is conveniently located near such locks in the event of a fire in the house. If you must escape in a hurry you don't want to be trying to remember where you left your keys during the fog of waking up and the stress of dealing with a house fire.

Along with the lock make sure you install a strike plate. It will prevent a crook from jimmying the door and a competent locksmith can put one on in short order. One final tidbit, if you're buying a home from someone (or renting) have all the locks re-keyed. You have absolutely no idea how many people have had keys given to them by the previous owner/tenant so to ensure your safety cut new ones. Don't worry, it's cheap and the locksmith doesn't even have to charge you for new locks. All they do is change the pins on the inside of the tumbler and give you new keys that work with them.

Remember not to hide a key outside. Any professional criminal worth his salt can find your hiding place – no matter how clever you think you've been – in about five minutes. I was bodyguarding a client in Florida and he had a two-story penthouse on the top floor in Boca Raton. One day I had cause to go down to the floor below and I noticed one of those fake rocks that you hide your key in was in the hallway outside one of the condos??? I knocked on the door and a sweet little eighty-year-old lady emerged and asked how she could help. I asked her about the rock and she very proudly explained that she'd seen it a store and bought it so the bad guys wouldn't know where she kept her spare key. (As an aside I assumed that's something I'd only see once in my life but a few months ago a lady of similar age had one outside her door in my apartment building. The mind boggles.)

How about the windows, are they double glazed and excellent quality or cheap? If they were broken, is access to the house then easy? My trick is to keep glass coffee tables or large fish tanks behind windows on the ground floor. Imagine breaking or forcing a window thinking you're going to climb in to the house and discovering a glass coffee table. Just how do you navigate your way around that? If you don't have the budget the coffee table trick is great. If you do, seriously consider replacing the glass with better quality stuff. Ask a glazier but they make glass now that's virtually indestructible. You can also apply a shatter proof sheet to it that will hold the glass together if someone attempts to smash it. You may hear mention of ornamental grillwork over windows but the problem is there's no way to escape via the windows if you're caught in a house fire. Yes, there are fancy versions that are hinged and held in place by a key, but they're fairly pricey and you're probably better off going for the upgraded glass and adding some locks. Again, a competent locksmith is worth his weight in gold with what he can advise you on with regards to locking stuff and the latest and greatest counter measures.

Finally, play the part of a bad guy. Think outside the box a little and figure out how you'd get in without a key if that was your goal. If you can get into your house after losing your key – and most homeowners can – then a bad guy can get in just as easily.

What follows is a personal story about my time in the French Foreign Legion which will illustrate how a little creative thinking got me past all sorts of security. In fact, it used their very good security against them and should educate the astute reader on some other measures to take regarding their home security.

While I was a member of the military police at Legion HQ in Aubagne we received orders to go test the security on the General's personal residence. This was an annual event to make sure everything worked and to test some recent security upgrades due to threats against military personnel in France. I was assigned the task by my Sgt. and given command of a group of four other MPs to conduct the test. Of course the security team in the house was told which week we'd be coming as one can't have us being successful and embarrassing the powers that be. I took my team over and began by tripping the alarm at about 2210 hours and then running away. I left with them as all the lights were being turned on and armed guards were flooding the yard. A few hours later we went back and did it again. Then another hour or so and then again. Then a while later and again. By about the seventh time – now about 0430 in the morning – they finally assumed it was the alarm going haywire and turned the system off at which point we got in and "killed" everyone.

On a commando course I did a similar trick and entered through the roof of the house by lifting some tiles and going in that way. I assumed, correctly it turned out, that the attic and the attic trapdoor wouldn't be alarmed and they weren't. Like most people they'd only bothered alarming the windows and doors.

Lastly, seriously considering buying a dog. Even an untrained one, or one not particularly suited to man-stopping, will still bark and give you advance warning of someone creeping round outside. With their superior hearing and sense of smell they are twenty-four hour a day furry burglar alarms. Just don't make the mistake one high powered woman did in California. She'd been raped once, and determined to stop it happening again, purchased two attack trained German Shepherds. The next time the bad guys came, the dogs were outside locked in the cages she'd bought for them barking their heads off.

Some people think you need attack trained dogs or dogs of a certain breed known for their man-stopping qualities such as Rottweilers, German Shepherds, Dobermans, et al. In reality you don't and you might even be better off without ones of that ilk. To begin with, some insurance policies exclude certain breeds and secondly, there is always the risk of being sued by some neighbor who steps in to the yard to recover a football or similar and ends up being mauled. I personally would rather have a dog that makes enough noise to wake me and has a deep enough bark to deter someone listening to him do so from the other side of the door. If you can't deal with the dog consider purchasing the biggest dog food bowl you can find and marking it with "Killer" and leaving it on the front porch. Just like the warning signs that alert people to the fact that you have an alarm system even though you may not, the dog food bowl creates the impression you own a huge dog. They even make alarms that make the sound of a large dog barking[15].

Defend

Despite our best intentions the bad guys have made it inside the house and now it's time to defend the castle and family. Inside the house, our next layer if you will, is where are you sleeping? Are you away from the main door to buy time or on the ground floor next to a big window?

Safe Rooms: Many millionaires now are having safe rooms built into their mansions. These are heavily fortified rooms designed to withstand serious assault and come complete with their own air and food supply, communication links to the outside world, panic alarms and so on. You can make your own for a lot less than a millionaire will pay. Is there a room that has no direct access to outside? Can you put a heavy locking door on it and put some extra locks on the door? Is your cell phone in that room? Are there any weapons in there? It's no good owning a firearm for home defense if it's in the gun safe downstairs and you're upstairs in your improvised safe room. Consider putting some protein bars in there with some bottles of water, blankets, a first aid kit, a fire extinguisher, and perhaps most importantly, a flashlight. In the event of an attack, providing you have enough warning, you simply bolt yourself in the room, alert the authorities and wait the bad guys out.

I'm aware of one woman in Westerville OH who saw that guys were breaking into the house, so she locked herself in her car in the garage and called police from there.

Ok, we've tried to deter them before they even get near the house and detect them if they do. The last line of defense is to defeat them if it becomes necessary. Remember, if your safe room is good, the safer course of action is to hunker down and await the arrival of the police.

---

[15] In the same poll of burglars that revealed their concern about a car in the drive, they also stated that, for the most part, they were not fazed by little dogs at all.

Arcs of Fire: If, for whatever reason though, you do need to go out and confront the bad guys you must have a plan. Perhaps most important is what are your arcs of fire. The interior walls of most homes in America are sheetrock which will not stop bullets. If you fire and miss, and your round goes through the wall behind the bad guy, who's it going to hit? Your family members or your neighbors? Remember, rounds can and do travel a long way. A woman was hit years ago in the UK by a round from a military rifle range just over three miles away!! One of my students, officer Joseph, responded to a call of a negligent discharge in an apartment block. The idiot who'd screwed up had negligently fired his pistol and the bullet went through the walls of six apartments in total, miraculously hitting nobody.

Firearms: Many people have been told the shotgun is the ultimate for home defense based on the erroneous belief that you don't have to aim it to hit things. Is it? I would submit it's a myth. To begin with you need two hands to hold it so how easy it going to be to hold an intruder at gun point while you dial the police with the other hand? What about navigating through the house with a shotgun? Unless you're highly trained and know the tricks of SWAT and HRU teams the first thing around the corner is going to be the barrel of your weapon which the bad guy can easily grab. Then there's the kick of that weapon if you do need to discharge it and it can make big men flinch. Back to the fallacy that you don't have to aim. While it's true that there is some spread to the multiple projectiles coming out of a barrel, that generally doesn't happen till the round has traveled some distance, typically a longer distance than inside the average home. A better bet in my opinion is a handgun. It's lighter if you must hold an intruder at gun point for a long time, it's less intimidating to fire, and it's strategically easier to maneuver through the house with one held close to the body. Husbands and wives can both use one if necessary and holding it with one hand while dialing emergency services with the other is relatively easy as is pushing open doors while clearing the house. Just don't buy one and stick it in the drawer next to the bed assuming it will save you when the time comes. You must practice with it, and you should ask yourself how good you'll be with it, if you've just come out of a deep sleep after a few drinks to the noise of a gang running through the house heading for the bedroom. I thoroughly recommend buying an Airsoft gun, (a battery powered pistol that fires tiny plastic pellets) and practicing inside your own dwelling. Equip your friend(s) with one and have him/them play the role of bad guys busting into your house and engage them as if you would in the real world. It will be a complete revelation.

Another advantage of the handgun is that you can also carry a flashlight in the other hand. Yes, I'm well aware that there are lights that mount to the pistol, but given that the majority of all of these bumps in the night will be non-threatening targets, I'd rather have a separate light to illuminate whatever's making the noise than pointing my weapon at them. Naturally this will enrage some of the tactical crowd, but they neglect that the average person isn't going to have their level of training, and will be half asleep when doing this. You only need to do a little research to find stories like the Sheriff who shot his daughter who was

Sheriff Shoots Daughter

A Virginia Sheriff's deputy mistook his 16-year-old daughter for an intruder early Tue and shot her as she snuck back into their home, authorities say.

The teen was shot once in the torso and was listed in stable condition Thur.

The shooting happened about 3:30 a.m. Tue while McDonald, a 13-year veteran, was getting ready for work, said Capt. Donnie Lang. The home's alarm system indicated a door of the attached garage had been opened, and McDonald grabbed his personal handgun to investigate. Seeing a dark figure approaching him, he fired.

sneaking back into the house after slipping out to see her boyfriend. (see table)

With regard to the selection of a handgun for home defense think about having a caliber that both husband and wife are comfortable using. I know tons of men who argue the benefits of the .45 caliber round but there aren't many women who are comfortable firing a weapon of that size. If the jolt from the recoil doesn't faze them, wrapping their hands around the large grip can be almost impossible. Why not opt for the 9mm and then you can interchange ammo and weapons without any problems. Shot placement is inarguably more important than the size of the round especially in the 9 mil versus .45 debate as both rounds have killed plenty of people over the years. Also, as I'm doing this re-write a multi-year study has just been released by the FBI advocating the use of the 9mm as being more effective. What a lot of people forget when making these arguments is that the science has come a long way since the original 9mm. Their findings showed the modern day 9mm is as effective as the older .45s were.

If You Are Not Home For Any Extended Period: Consider timers that turn lights on and off (stagger them so they don't come on at the same time)

- Don't leave notes on the door saying you're out.
- Arrange for lawn care
- Stop your mail
- Arrange for a family member to drop by occasionally and make sure everything is ok
- There is a home security check list in the appendix. Grab it and see how many boxes you can check off.

22

TRAVEL SECURITY

For many people, traveling is the only time they think about security. When they're home or driving around it's the last thing on their mind, largely because they're in their comfort zone, and victims of the old "it never happens here mind-set." Taking this into account, this next section will tackle the best ways to protect yourself, and your property, when you're on the road, whether it be national or international. Never lose sight of the fact that bad guys love tourists for the following reasons: They're usually carrying cash or credit cards, they're usually lugging cameras, watches, and in the case of business travel, laptops, etc. More often than not, they're task fixated studying maps, looking for landmarks, lost, or gawking at a particular tourist attraction. They're not likely to spend thousands coming back to identify a thief who stole their nine-hundred-dollar camera. They're also potential kidnap victims (especially in third world countries) and/or victims of terrorism where security standards overseas are a pale shadow of what they are here in the States and other developed nations.

This section has been set up to work in a logical sequence. We've just taken care of our house before we leave on a trip in the section on "Home Security" and now we're going to go over airport security, hotel security, and taxis, as well as being out and about on foot. Before we break it down into various modes of travel, we'll go over some general rules that apply across the board.

General Travel Tips

Gather information about where you're going: (See resource section for exact sources): This comes under the heading of intelligence gathering, and one thing that was hammered into us in Special Forces during my time with the Legion, and later on bodyguard courses, is that time spent gathering intelligence is never wasted. Too many people spend more time studying the weather of wherever they're planning to go than local crime trends. You have no body to blame but yourself if you land in your dream vacation spot to find yourself in the middle of a coup and held by the local brigand and his henchmen.

It doesn't have to be as dramatic as that. What about the late eighties and early nineties when Florida experienced a spate of car jackings in which local criminals were specifically targeting rental cars (identified by their advertising stickers). A German tourist was dragged from her car during a bump and rob and had her skull crushed when the bad guys sped off in her car and ran her over in the process. To make matters worse, the whole event took place in front of her mother and her children. If you were intending to travel to Florida during that period and rent a car, and you bothered to do your homework by researching local crime stats, you'd have cottoned on to the bump and rob tactics and the targeting of rental vehicles. Advance knowledge such as that would have led you to pick somewhere else, drive your own car, remove the rental company stickers, and not to stop during a fender bender, but rather to drive somewhere public or call law enforcement on your cell phone from inside your (locked) car.

Document Safety

It's always a good practice to make copies of all your documentation and keep them separate. U.S. passports are particularly coveted in certain countries, and in the event yours is stolen, it will expedite the renewal at your local embassy if you have copies of all the paperwork. It's also safer when a bank or local business demands your passport to complete a transaction as you can hand over the photocopy and jealously guard the real thing. Similarly take a couple of passport photos with you as well, as they can also expedite acquiring a local visa for example. Another idea is to take a thumb drive that has copies of all your documentation with you. It then becomes a simple matter to plug it in to a local computer and print off what you need.

Leave An Itinerary

Always make sure you leave an itinerary with family members or a trusted friend. In the event you're kidnapped, or are injured and out of circulation in a local hospital, the itinerary at home will make the search for you so much easier than having to tell law enforcement agents *"Well, we knew he was planning to go to South America."*

Emergency Contact Numbers

Take a list of emergency contact numbers with you and include in that numbers for the local consulate or embassy as well as contacts at the airline, hotel, rental car company and so on.

Plan In Advance

There's a lot to be said for the adventure involved in not planning a trip and rolling with the punches as you explore the local countryside. From a self-protection viewpoint though it can be a nightmare and it makes leaving the aforementioned itinerary a problem. By planning, you have read up on local crime trends, customs, know how much money you'll need, what the weather will be like, places to avoid, and places to see. I learned for example, when accompanying the celebrated American artist Peter Max and his exhibition to Russia, that toilet paper, toothpaste, and soap would be in short supply. I also found out that Marlboro cigarettes could be used as currency at the time. All you had to do was stand on the side of the road and hold up a carton and locals would stop and take you wherever you wanted to go. I found out too that Levi jeans were worth their weight in gold and small tokens of things like soap and TP would be very welcome by locals. Knowledge such as that is priceless when visiting other countries.

Don't Be An Obvious Tourist

We've all heard about the ugly American tourist in their loud floral shirts, cameras around necks and flashing their cash like it grows on trees. Unfortunately it's all too true. I'll never forget the day I was on the tube in London and overheard (along with the rest of the carriage), one American gentleman who'd just discovered a fellow Yank on the train. They were about eight seats apart which didn't stop them from having their conversation. One of them was telling the other he was thinking of going to see Stonehenge. His newfound friend, at full volume, told him *"Aw hell, don't bother, it's just a pile of rocks."*

Remember, bad guys target tourists so don't identify yourself as one. An old trick from my bodyguarding days was to carry a local newspaper and stick a pack of local brand cigarettes in my pocket. Now, I don't smoke, and I sure couldn't read most of the papers, but any local criminal element looking for a potential victim assumed that I was either a local, or familiar enough with their country that I could speak the lingo and knew my way round.

If you're going to need a map to get around study it in your hotel room before you go out or consider hiring a local guide. Using a taxi driver to take you to where you want to go is another viable option. Just don't stand around in the middle of a crowded side walk studying your map. Not only are you identifying yourself as an out-of-towner but you're also task fixated again which will give the bad guy ample opportunity to make his approach undetected. Another thing that gives Americans away are backpacks. Watch what locals use and copy them.

Be Aware Of Your Clothing

There's a well-known story in the UK about a group of teenagers who were on a budget trip to Africa. To save money they bought all their clothing from the local Army Navy store figuring it would be cheap and hard wearing as well as full of pockets. Unfortunately, they were mistaken for mercenaries by the local militia, who lined them all up and shot them.

Clothing can also identify you as an out of towner again. Just how many cowboy hats do you think you'll see in Hawaii? And how many white shoes and floral shirts will be spotted in downtown Manhattan? Research your intended destination again and dress like the locals do as far as conveniently possible.

I was bodyguarding the band Warrant during their heyday and at the time was in LA with them. It was a day off so the other bodyguard and I decided to work out at Gold's Gym in Venice Beach. I normally wore a red bandana when I trained and was going to get a run in before lifting. Fortunately for me, one of the local gym rats pointed out that two notorious street gangs lived a few blocks behind the gym, and one of those gangs was identified by the wearing of a red bandana. He was certain I'd be mistaken for one and shot by the other if I'd gone for my run wearing it.

The same can be said for t-shirts that might either deliberately or inadvertently insult locals. Your Ku Klux Klan t-shirt might be all the rage in the deep south at a trailer park, but I'd submit it might get you some unwarranted attention in Harlem in New York, NY.

Be Aware Of Your Haircut

Just as your clothing can get you killed so can your haircut. Go to any local mall in the States and you can spot the cops and military guys a mile away with their screaming eagle haircuts (extremely short sides and a tuft of longer hair on the top). Wear something like that on a flight to the mideast that is taken by terrorists and you're going to be in a world of hurt. As the old spy novels said, try and be the "gray man", or in other words, the guy that goes to the party that nobody remembers or can describe afterwards. There have been plenty of stories of off-duty police officers out with their families, being targeted by gang members who've spotted the haircut and know exactly what it is the off-duty cop does. This is more important than ever due to the recent spate of attacks on law enforcement officers around the country.

Sanitize Your Passport

If you're going to certain countries you're going to want to sanitize your passport. For example, it's not kosher to go to some Middle Eastern countries with an Israeli visa in your passport. The same used to be true of South African visas discovered during visits to other African nations. When I worked as a bodyguard in London I had the Australian embassy issue me a second passport. They don't like doing it, but if you explain the reason, and back it up with documentation and tickets to the offending country, they'll usually issue you with one. When I went to Russia with Peter Max they didn't actually stamp the passport. They stapled the entry/exit visa into the passport to be removed later should it become necessary.

Put Personal Affairs In Order

One of the things we've learned over the years from de-briefing kidnap victims is that there is great peace of mind in knowing that all your personal affairs such as wills and bills have been updated and paid, etc. Don't put it off until your return because if there is an unnecessary delay – and remember it may be something as innocuous as a hospital stay due to an injury while on vacation – you might find yourself in financial trouble upon your return. Good travel is stress free travel.

A Doctor's Letter For Meds

You'll absolutely want to take a letter from your medico when you travel with prescription drugs to prove that you're in need of the meds in question and not a drug smuggler. This is absolutely no joke as certain countries treat drug smuggling very seriously and execute almost immediately anyone convicted of trafficking. Also, keep in mind that what might be considered over the counter stuff here might be prescription somewhere else. Motrin, for example, is a prescription only drug in the UK but available here over the counter and let's not forget what happened to Sylvester Stallone when he visited Australia with his "supplements" that got him in hot water down there. Indeed, As I write this, Laura Plummer, 33, has been arrested in Egypt bringing her husband's pain pills into the country and is facing the death penalty without a letter from a doctor stating they were ordered by him

On the subject of medicine, consider carrying extra if you're traveling for any length of time. Trying to renew a prescription overseas can be almost impossible and in some cases the same drugs don't even exist. The same can be said for prescription eye glasses and/or contacts. Nothing can be worse than losing your last pair of contacts in some foreign hell hole and facing the dilemma of traveling without them.

23

AIRLINE SECURITY

From the plane hijackings of the seventies, to the Lockerbie disaster and 9/11, it doesn't take a rocket scientist to figure out security on aircraft is something we all need to be concerned with and prepared for. Here are some simple tips to mitigate your risks of ever becoming a victim.

Airline Selection

It doesn't take a genius to figure out that American carriers are going to be the prime target for terrorists intent on making a statement. Neutral carriers such as SAS and KLM etc., are far better bets if you want to reduce your chances of not ending up the victim of a terrorist attack/hijacking.

Avoid Stopovers

Stopovers are a security nightmare. This is how the bad guys got the bomb on the Pan Am flight that was blown up over Lockerbie. They checked the bomb with their luggage when they got on the flight in Athens and then they left the flight in Frankfurt Germany leaving their bags, with the bomb inside, on board. On a long international flight it's not always going to be possible but try and keep them to a minimum. An added bonus of flying direct is that you reduce the risk of lost luggage and missed connecting flights.

Airline Clubs

Airline clubs cost on average a couple of hundred dollars to join but give you an extra layer of security when you travel. When you join you get to hang out in their private lounge away from the hoi polloi (not to mention the added bonus of wi-fi access points, snacks and conference rooms etc.) They're usually discreetly tucked away in some quiet corner of the airport, and should there be an incident, you'll be far away from the center of attention.

Double Check Departure Times

The reason for this is that the longer you hang round an airport the greater the risk. Double checking departure times before leaving the house can save you the inconvenience of sitting round an airport bored out of your skull for six to eight hours.

Check In Early

If you know you're going to be traveling at peak travel times, or if your flight is going to be fully booked, get to the airport early to avoid waiting in long lines. As soon as you're through security get into the airport club mentioned earlier. Another trick to expedite your time waiting around at airports is to have your tickets mailed in advance or to use e-tickets.

Be Aware Of Surfing

Surfing is the name given to the technique used by criminals who look over someone's shoulder and garner personal information. On one episode of Oprah she interviewed an "on the ball" airport police officer who'd spotted a family taking videos of each other two days in a row. His suspicions aroused, they impounded the camera and discovered "dad" had a zoom lens on it and would pose the wife and kid near people using their credit cards and he'd film the info on the card and use it to go shopping with.

Another common method is for burglars to go to airports and wait in the line behind travelers with their names and addresses on their luggage.

They memorize the info and then go stand behind someone else, and do that all day. After a few hours, they have a list of people and their addresses who they knew would be out of town on travel. If you do use a luggage label put it inside your luggage and not on the outside. Alternatively, buy one of the labels that come with a flap that keeps your info safe from prying eyes. Surfing can also be done anytime you access your credit cards, ATM cards, debit cards, driver's license, and passport to name but a few. Be very aware of people standing very close behind you or in your personal space when you're pulling anything like that out.

Get Through Security Fast

This, at first blush, might sound impossible. After all, what control do you have over how fast security moves? Actually, more than you think, at least as far as you're concerned. To begin with err on the side of caution and remove absolutely everything that might set the metal detectors off. Too many times people assume their belt buckle or watch probably won't trip the sensors, but every time it does, it's back for another trip through the detector. Your travel agent, the airline's website and the TSA (or your country's equivalent), will have a list of items that you're not allowed to travel with. Do yourself, and your fellow travelers, a favor and leave all that stuff at home. If they say no lighters, don't pack one. If they say no liquid in containers over a certain size don't try and get away with it. Pack light and move fast.

Watch Our For Scams

Thieves and criminals are constantly coming up with new versions of old scams but here's a couple to be aware of that are used at airports all the time. The first is done when someone covets your laptop (the most frequently stolen item from airports by the way). Right as you arrive at the security conveyor belt and metal detector and just after you've placed your laptop on the belt a traveler in a rush will jump in front of you ostensibly in a hurry for a departing flight. His pockets will be full of objects that will trigger the metal detector and he'll apologize profusely as he removes them and goes through again. Once again something will trigger the detector until finally he goes through. By the time you get through your laptop has been picked up by his accomplice who was already inside ahead of him waiting to snag your bag.

Another involves the rest room. Most travelers will hang their jackets on the cubicle door while they go about their business. The thief waits a few seconds for you to get settled and then reach over the door to remove your jacket and whatever you're carrying in the pockets at the time. Either keep your jacket on or put it on your luggage which will be in the stall with you, right?

Avoid 1st Class

I like first class as much as the next person, but in the event the plane is taken by terrorists, the first-class passengers are the first ones targeted because they're generally thought to be wealthy, influential, and connected. Once again we're reminded of the need to be the gray man who blends in. Another reason, perhaps a little morbid, but certainly true, is that statistically the greatest chance of survival in a plane crash is the last third of the plane.

Listen To The Safety Lecture

Too many people take the security lecture for granted. Don't! You need to know where the exits are, identify how many seats they are away from yours and learn any idiosyncrasies of the aircraft you're on. The mass confusion and hysteria during a plane crash cannot be underestimated. People will be climbing over one another and chances are the craft will be filled with smoke which will make simply looking for the exit almost impossible. Any advance knowledge you have is going to expedite your chances at safely evacuating the aircraft...and in a crash where smoke is present, seconds count.

Check Out Fellow Passengers

Some readers will no doubt remember the furor caused when some passengers complained about a group of Arabs traveling here in the States who insisted on praying in the departure lounge right before boarding. The Arab travelers also requested seat belt extenders (great improvised weapon), despite not being overweight, as well as a few other oddities. I don't care what the lawyers are saying, or the politically correct crowd are wailing about, those people absolutely did the right thing. Trust your gut, and if someone makes you nervous, scrutinize them or point it out to the relevant authorities. Neighbors of the couple who went on a shooting spree in San Bernardino suspected the couple were up to no good, but remained silent because they were afraid of being labeled racists.

Inflammatory Reading

This tip dovetails with being careful about the type of clothing you carry. In some Middle Eastern countries pornographic material will get you a prison sentence. In what is undoubtedly an extreme case, two priests were executed in Saudi Arabia for having bibles in their luggage. What makes that case even more outrageous is that Saudi Arabia wasn't their intended destination. Their plane was diverted due to a mechanical problem and during the re-boarding of a replacement aircraft their luggage was searched and the bibles were found.

No Politics Or Religion

At home, feel free to let rip about whatever political or religious affiliation you may have. That's one of the great things about living in somewhere like the US. Overseas, however, they take this stuff far more seriously than we do, and again, a discussion of either can see you imprisoned or worse. Many Middle Eastern countries, for example, have religious police whose job it is to listen for anything considered blasphemous and proceed accordingly. Some of my colleagues on team jobs overseas have even avoided mentioning that they were U.S. citizens and instead claimed to be Canadians or from New Zealand just to avoid any hassle.

Check Out Your Seat

Dennis Martin, president of the UKs first ever bodyguard school for the public, and a revered trainer, sat in a seat once and found a bullet down behind the cushion. It turns out the plane had been used by a law enforcement group for hostage rescue training and a stray round had ended up there. Planes fly all over the world and some airports have almost no security. One of the methods favored by terrorists to get weapons and explosives on board is to have a sympathetic member of the ground crew stash the contraband in a pre-arranged location during their work on the craft. If that's been done in Athens Greece for example and you're boarding the plane in Germany it would be a good idea to check at least the parts you can.

Shoes And Seat Belts

If there's a crash that you can walk or run away from, it's going to be on the ground during take-off or landing. Trying to run from a burning plane, across debris, and probably wooded areas that generally surround airports, is no fun in bare feet. I always insisted my clients leave their shoes on and seat belts buckled until reaching cruising altitude and replace both when we were beginning our descent.

Smoke Hoods

I always packed two of these. One for me and one for my client. I got grief about this from friends (not fellow professionals) but scanning the NTSB database is eye-opening.

In 1973, a Boeing 707 landed in Paris only eight minutes after a fire broke out in the lavatory. 124 passengers and crew died from smoke inhalation.

In 1980, a Saudi plane was climbing out of Riyadh and reported smoke in the cargo department. The plane returned to Riyadh, but by the time they got the doors open, all 301 on board were dead from smoke inhalation.

In 1985 a British 737 declined to take off due to an engine fire and smoke in the cabin. The air crew attempted to evacuate the plane but were hampered by panic amongst the passengers. 55 people died – 48 from smoke inhalation.

I used to like the one called Evac-u8 but they're now defunct. Shop around on line and you'll find them for under $100. They're not just good for aircraft either...home and hotel fires are just as dangerous and these will typically buy you about 15 minutes of air time.

Avoid Excessive Drinking

This should be a no-brainer, but don't be so out of it that if something does happen you're incapable of functioning properly. Keep in mind also that every week it seems there's some fool being hauled off a plane to face Federal charges due to being inebriated and causing trouble.

Air Crew As A Resource

If you're flying into a new city on business (or on vacation), the air crew who regularly fly the route are a great resource for cheap hotels, safe parts of town and not to be missed restaurants, etc. Unlike embassy personnel, who either won't have time or will be very cautious about saying anything derogatory about their host country, air crew aren't so restricted.

24

LUGGAGE SECURITY

Luggage Labels

We've already mentioned this one under travel tips, but again, don't put your name and address on the outside of your luggage where it's visible to anyone attempting to surf. Place it inside or buy a label that has a security flap over it that conceals your information.

Use Your Office Or A P.O. Box Address

Consider using your post office box number or the address of your workplace on the luggage instead of your house. That way, if someone gets to read the info, or steals your bag, they don't have a handle on where you live. It will still get back to you in the event it's lost by the airline, (hopefully), but you don't have to worry that some miscreant has it and is now aware of where you live and the fact you're out of town if it goes missing.

Remove Labels ASAP

Remove labels and tickets that mark destinations from your luggage as soon as you can. They give away far too much information to predators and identify you as well.

Dress Up Your Wallet

Imagine for a minute you're in a plane taken over by terrorists. The first thing they're going to do is confiscate everyone's wallet for the information, etc., that they carry. Many terrorists come from countries where families are paramount so carrying pictures of your non-existent family with a bushel full of kids etc., can mean the difference between life and death. By the same token, don't carry anything in your wallet that may get you in trouble. Again, assuming a worst-case scenario with terrorists taking over, get rid of anything in your wallet that could in anyway be incriminating. Membership cards to certain organizations, military I.D, religious icons, political stuff and so on.

Check Your Luggage Fast

The sooner you check your luggage the less likely it is to be stolen and the more chance it has to make the flight you're supposed to be on. It also beats lugging around heavy luggage longer than you have to.

Avoid Expensive Luggage

I hate tips like this one because I'm a sucker for designer labels, being a firm believer that if you've worked hard for your money you should be able to flaunt it by buying something nice. Having said that, designer label luggage screams wealth so any thief worth his salt is going to go after the high-end stuff before he grabs some generic brand gear. Leave the Hartmann and Luis Vuiton behind, unless you have a private jet, and opt for something cheap and nasty instead.

Be Careful Of What You Grab

Many bags look alike, especially when you're tired. Unless you want to spend hours in an airport lock up explaining to the nice officer why you were trying to take someone's bag that didn't belong to you, be very careful that the bag you grab is indeed yours. Consider putting some clearly identifiable mark on it such as a piece of duct tape or a certain color ribbon round the handle, etc.

Be Aware Of Laptop Theft

As previously mentioned, laptops are the most stolen items at airports worldwide so consider one of the many security measures made for keeping them safe. One of the better ones is a proximity alarm. If your laptop is moved more than a certain range from you an ear-piercing alarm goes off that alerts you, and everyone else, that your laptop is being swiped. At last count these devices were available for under $100. There are a slew of other methods available from tracking devices and cables to passwords and special tags that identify the user etc. Whichever method you use, use something. The British Ministry of Defense disclosed recently that it had 67 laptops lost or stolen during the last three years.

Bathroom Stall Safety

Using the end stall in the bathroom will cut down by half the risk of someone reaching under the gap and swiping your luggage. If you can, use the end stall and place your bags etc., up against the wall away from the cubicle next door. I try and use the ones with the baby changing table in them. This allows me to keep the luggage and personal belongings away from both the gap on the floor and the reach over the door trick.

Don't Mind Anyone Else's Bags For Them

You'd think most people would be aware of this one by now but every year some idiot in Thailand or Singapore is asked to mind someone's bag which invariably turns out to have drugs in it. While they're being surrounded by law enforcement the real smuggler slips through with his load. Alternatively he uses the unsuspecting mule in the hope they make it through with the goods knowing if someone does get caught it won't be him. In the UK the fear is that someone will plant a bomb in the bag and have you inadvertently carry it on board or into the terminal.

Undoubtedly, the worst example of this was Ann Murphy. In 1986, Ann Murphy met a Jordanian Nezar Hindawi who got her pregnant and then arranged for her to fly to the Middle East to meet him where they would be married. Hindawi had packed Anne's bag with explosives in a hidden compartment which would, if it had detonated, killed her, their unborn child and 380 other passengers. Fortunately Hindawi's plot was thwarted by an alert El Al security guard and Hindawi was arrested and sentenced to one of the longest prison sentences ever handed down by the UK judicial system. He received a sentence of forty-five years. No doubt that's an extreme example, but the bottom line is to be very careful of what goes in your luggage and whose luggage you're carrying.

Never Let Your Bags Out Of Your Sight

This dovetails with the preceding rule. If you let your bags out of your sight, even for a minute, someone can slip something inside. Alternatively, they can steal them, or airport authorities may remove them and blow them up. Keep them with you, always.

Luggage And Taxis

If you have enough luggage that it requires placing it in the trunk of the cab make sure that you load it in yourself. An old ploy was that the driver would put it in for you but "accidentally" forget to put one bag in. His accomplice waiting just nearby would steal your bag. Later, upon arriving at your destination and realizing you're a bag short, your driver would apologize profusely claiming it was an honest mistake, an airline error, or that you only gave him two bags, etc. Either way some of your luggage was gone.

25

HOTEL SECURITY

Hotels have always been a hotbed of trouble for tourists. Some of the most famous attacks have been against celebrities; Connie Francis, the famous singer from the fifties and sixties, was robbed and raped while her manager and husband were both in an adjoining room of her hotel. Sophia Loren was yanked out of bed at gunpoint in the Hampshire House Hotel in NY and made to hand over $700,000 worth of jewelry which was uninsured. Zsa Zsa Gabor was robbed of $625,000 worth of jewelry in the elevator of the Waldorf Astoria, again in New York. Most recently we had one of the Kardashians robbed in a hotel in Paris which made international news.

The essential point is that criminals love targeting tourists, and tourists hang out at hotels. Tourists are a favorite because they're preoccupied – read "task fixated" – with taking in the sights, generally have spending money, don't know their way around, and are unlikely to come back for any subsequent court case due to the fact it will cost them more in travel expenses than whatever it is they've lost.

Hotel Choice

Hotel security begins with your choice of hotels. Always spend the most you can and book a hotel in a nice part of town that's part of a recognizable chain, if possible. Hotels of that ilk are more likely to be concerned about security and their reputation and therefore will have spent money on various security measures.

Room Choice

Next decision to make will typically be which room you opt to stay in. As a bodyguard I advised my clients to stay in a room between the second and seventh floors (The tenth at the extreme). The ground floor room is particularly susceptible to break ins as crooks can make a quick getaway. Also, consider that there's always a slew of people walking up and down the ground floor hallways, on the way to and from various seminars and functions, so it's hard to keep track of everyone. Rooms above the seventh floor – and in extreme cases the tenth – can't be reached by fire truck ladders in the event of a hotel fire. That means, in the event of an extreme fire, that prevents access to the fire escapes, your only option is going to be to jump. It might sound like that would never happen but hotel fires are more common than people think, and it wasn't that long ago, we were faced with the chilling

Hotel Fire Kills 85

The second-largest loss of life hotel fire in US history took place 20 years ago this week at the MGM Grand Hotel/Casino in Las Vegas, Nevada.

As smoke filled the 26-story high rise, 85 people lost their lives and hundreds of others were injured.

The November 21, 1980 fire scene was a grim sight, unlike anything else he had ever seen, said Deputy Chief Ralph King of the Clarke County Fire Department.

stories of people jumping from the upper floors of the twin towers during 9/11 because emergency services couldn't reach them.

Checking In

Let's start with the checking in process and walk through the typical hotel stay, and deal with security. To begin with, don't permit the desk clerk to announce to the world what room you're in. Have them write it on the envelope that your key goes in and be very aware of people lurking when you're checking in. This is especially important if you're a woman traveling alone. Predators who target the lone female traveler will learn what room the woman is staying in by "surfing" (hanging about just behind someone and looking over their shoulder to read or overhear information) unless you remain vigilant.

Lone Female

In the event you are a lone female, try and get a hotel employee to accompany you to your room and have them go in and check it before you go in on your own. There have been many cases where the perpetrator has been waiting in the room, hidden, who pops out of hiding once the woman is inside and the door is locked.

Room Placement

Make sure the room isn't too close to the elevator for a couple of reasons. One; it will be noisy as the elevator carries guests up and down all night long, and two; it gives bad guys an excuse to be hanging around without causing undue suspicion. The other thing you want to avoid is a room directly opposite a fire escape or utility room door. A common trick is for bad guys to lurk behind the door, and when you roll up to open yours, they rush you from across the hall and are inside your room before you, (or anyone else) realize what's happened.

Recce Time

Once you've placed your luggage in the room and verified the windows, etc., are locked go out and count the doors between your room and the fire escapes. If there's a fire and you must leave your room, (more on that in a minute), the smoke will fill the top two thirds of the hallway making viewing the EXIT signs almost impossible. The only way you're going to be able to determine which door is the door to the fire escape is if you know in advance and then count them off while crawling on your hands and knees. I also make a point of checking the fire extinguisher's location on the floor and verifying the last time it was serviced and whether it's charged. In a lot of third world countries the extinguisher, if it hasn't been stolen, will never have been serviced since the day it left the factory. Now, go down the fire escape and make sure it's clear of obstacles and figure out whether the door at the bottom opens inwards or outwards, and it too is clear. Be careful doing this as some doors don't allow you access back inside once it's closed behind you.

Room Security

Once you're in your room lock your door immediately and review the security notice that's usually affixed behind the door. There'll be advice on here concerning security and safety and it's always worth perusing. A good idea is to take a picture of it with your cell phone. That way you have all the info to hand if you're forced to leave the room due to a fire.

Just because the door is locked don't assume you're safe. Too many hotels are guilty of employing cheap labor to service the rooms. A lot of these employees have, in the past, been busted passing copies of their pass keys to their boyfriends (often gang members), who rob valuables from any available room and/or attack people inside. I always carried two cheap rubber door wedges (usually less than $2 at your local home store), one for me and one for the client. Kick those under the door when you're in your room and even if the bad guy has a key it won't do them any good. Another great option here, that I stole from Dr. John Giduck, is using bubble wrap right inside your door. Also, ensure you've locked the windows and doors to any existing balcony. Another common trick was

203

for people in the adjoining room to hop from their balcony to yours and slip in that way. People mistakenly thought, just because they were on the fifth floor, it would be safe to leave the balcony door open and enjoy the breeze etc., only to find some bad guy was in the room, having hopped across from a floor above, below, or beside.

Leaving The Room

If you leave the room leave the television on and hang the "do not disturb sign on the door." The idea here is to create the impression that the room is, of course, occupied which will give pause to someone thinking of slipping in during your absence. Before you leave make sure you hide your valuables. I always tip the maids on arrival, tell them my room will be fine, and I'll come and see them if I need a towel or something similar. There's no need therefore, for them, or anyone else for that matter, to go in my room. I never use the hotel room safe even if there is one as they're about as secure as a shoebox and again, an obvious target. Instead I hide valuables in all sorts of places.

Phone Call Scams

If someone comes to your room and you're not expecting anyone, don't open the door. Ask first who it is, and if they claim they're from management, call downstairs and verify with the front desk that someone was sent up. The same goes if someone claiming to be from management calls you on the phone and tells you they need to see you downstairs in the lobby. Thank them and then immediately call the front desk and confirm management just called. One executive I'm aware of was kidnapped in India when he fell for this ruse. He went downstairs at what he thought was the behest of management and was snatched by a team of bad guys waiting in the lobby.

Another ruse to be aware of works like this. The bad guys lurk in the lobby where people are checking in. They glean your room number, either by overhearing the clerk tell you what room it is, or reading it off the key card. They give you a few moments to get settled and then call you from the parking lot on a cell phone claiming they're from the front desk. The message will be along the lines of their not being able to process your credit card properly and could you please give them the number again. Most people, tired from the trip, dealing possibly with jet lag, and having only just checked in, assume it's a legitimate query and give out the number only to discover later their card has been maxed out by the bad guys. Once again, the defense is to tell them you'll find the card in a minute and call back down to the desk to make sure the enquiry was legit.

Name Tags

Assuming you're attending the hotel for a convention make sure you remove your name tag when you're out of the lecture room or convention hall. It's too easy for a predator to read your name and then knock on your door and address you by name, which will make you think you know them and they know you.

Hotel Fires

Lastly, but certainly not least, in the event of a fire in the hotel the safest place is to stay in your room and place wet towels along the bottom of the door and remain near the windows. The fire mentioned earlier in this section involved a horrifying account of people carbonized in an elevator discovered later by firemen. Never ever use elevators during a fire. Another elevator in that same conflagration had its cable burn through due to the extreme heat and it plummeted to the bottom of the shaft. You must also be extremely careful opening the door. If the fire is on the other side it will rush in to your room in a bid to engulf all the oxygen and it will kill or burn you if you're in its path. If you must exit your room via the door make sure there's no fire on the other side (the handle will be hot if there is and there will probably be smoke sneaking in under the door) and then crawl on the floor to the fire exit and go down the stairs. Consider traveling with the smoke hood mentioned under the Airline Security section. Simple to use and very affordable so there's no excuse not to have one.

The other alternative is to go out the window using bedding for ropes. Here are a couple of tips to do that safely – or as safely as humanly possible.

Don't use towels as ropes as they're too thick to stay tied together

Use sheets and tear them into strips lengthwise approximately fifteen to twenty inches wide. Wet them by soaking them in the tub or under the shower. Wetting them does several things. It makes them stronger, less likely to burn, less likely to cause rope burn if you start sliding too quickly, and helps them stay twisted up which is what you want.

Make sure you know how to tie a sheet bend or a reef knot, as anything else will probably come undone as you're climbing down. Depending upon the height from which you fall, this could kill you.

Put a coat, door mat, or pillow on the window sill under the rope so it doesn't chaff and/or tear on the sharp edge.

Make sure your improvised rope is tied to something solid that will bear your weight.

One final tip. I've heard some people suggest lying in the bath tub which should be filled with water. Seriously people…isn't this how they cook vegetables? Stay in your room near the windows until help arrives, and if it doesn't, exit via the window or the hallway if it's safe to do so.

26

ACTIVE SHOOTER/KILLER SURVIVAL

In this updated version of the book I'm adding some new sections based on what's been happening recently around the country and around the world. There will be this section on Active Shooters/Killers, one on surviving a riot or flash mob, and another on what to do if you drive your car into a mob of protestors blocking the road.

Active shooters come under the section "soft skills" because, unless you've got a weapon handy and/or you're officially employed to go hunt them down, surviving an event like this is a soft skill.

The Basics

According to most law enforcement officials called upon to come up with a plan for civilians in the work place to survive an attack of this kind, it's RUN, HIDE, FIGHT. We're going to learn here why that might not be your best option. Keep in mind that it's still a better option than the truly lamentable, limp wristed, milquetoast advice given by UK law enforcement and government which is to "RUN, HIDE, & TELL".

The official definition of an active shooter event – hitherto known as an ASE. – agreed upon by US government agencies (including the White House, US Department of Justice, FBI, US Department of Education, US Department of Homeland Security and Federal Emergency Management) is *"an individual actively engaged in killing, or attempting to kill, people in a confined and/or populated area."* Personally, I think they've got it wrong, as they so often do. What about an incident like the shooting in San Bernardino in 2015, by Farook and Malik? While most would label that a terrorist attack, as far as the victims were concerned, it was an active shooter event, but they weren't dealing with an individual. The same goes for the Kenyan Mall shooting in September of 2013. A team of at least four individuals entered the Westgate Mall and killed 67 people and I don't think anyone would argue it was an active shooting event. It would also be hard to refute the recent terrorist attacks in France, at both Charlie Hebdo (2 attackers) and Paris early 2016 (multiple teams), were ASEs.

They (the government), then go on to say *"In most cases active shooters use firearms and there is no pattern or method to their selection of victims."*

Be careful that the terms and definitions used by the "gub'mint" don't throw you. Notice they say "most" used guns, but a truer name would be "Active Killer" because some of them have used axes, knives, machetes, and/or explosives. One example was at Franklin Regional High School in 2014 where 21 students were stabbed, and lest you think that was an anomaly, there was the Somalian in the mall in Minnesota in 2016 who stabbed nine people. It's for reasons like these that some more progressive agencies are now using the more accurate terms of "Active Killer" or "Violent Intruder." As for the government's claim there is *"no pattern or method to their selection of victims"*, again, I beg to differ. The Columbine school shooting had victims that were specifically chosen by Harris & Klebold, and Charlie Hebdo was targeted because of their satirical attacks on Islam. Many of the workplace violence incidents are aimed at individuals that the killer thinks are responsible for his being fired, or other perceived transgressions.

Be careful also with statistics which claim most are over within ten to fifteen minutes. These times are skewed due to events like the Mall in

Kenya which lasted for approximately 3 days[16] and Norway where Anders Brevik went on a killing spree at a religious retreat which went on for hours. The average event in the US is over in four minutes.

Regardless of how long it takes, ASEs are unpredictable and evolve quickly. Because they are over so fast you must be prepared both physically and mentally to deal with such an event on your own because help will almost always arrive after the situation is over.

Something else to keep in mind which the government description seems to ignore is that they're not all workplace violence incidents. Some are but others occur in schools, shopping centers, and others are categorized as terrorist incidents. Don't, therefore, get faked out by descriptions and semantics. Any time an individual, or group, is on a rampage attacking people, with any type of weapon, you need to have a plan of action to deal with it or risk becoming one of the victims.

Statistics

Active Shooter Events are increasing: Over 160 between 2000 and 2013 according to FBI statistics. (Others place that number at 110).

The first seven years of the study show an average of 6.4 incidents annually, while the last seven years show 16.4 incidents per annum.

Almost every incident has occurred in a gun free zone!

These incidents resulted in a total of 1,043 casualties (486 killed, 557 wounded – excluding the shooters themselves.

More than half the incidents – 90 shootings – ended on the shooter's initiative (i.e. suicide, fleeing the scene), while 21 ended after unarmed citizens successfully restrained the shooter.

Most are over before law enforcement members arrive on scene.

The highest death tolls occur in educational facilities.

---

[16] The attack began at noon on Saturday the 21st and the mall was finally declared secure on the 24th.

Attacks have happened in Malls and other places of commerce, places of education, theaters, places of worship, military bases and work places, open spaces and residences. In other words, pretty much everywhere.

- Roughly half have occurred at places of commerce
- 22 out of 23 shooters in non-pedestrian commerce (business offices, etc.) were former employees.
- Most dangerous day of the week is Wednesday.
- Second most common are educational facilities.
- Motives are usually anger, revenge, ideology, or mental illness.
- Six of the incidents were perpetrated by females.
- Two involved more than one shooter, but this is expected to increase. (Kenyan Mall, Paris, San Bernardino, etc.)
- Attacks vary between poorly thought out to carefully planned and coordinated
- 2/3 of the ASEs that were stopped by intervention, were stopped by civilians who were armed.

WHAT DO THE STATISTICS TEACH US? That ASE's are on the rise (one every 3 weeks), places of work are the most often hit target, and that civilians i.e. you, are going to have to stop it, not law enforcement. Also, gun free zones are extremely dangerous, as are Wednesdays.

Your Defensive Plan

Mindset: Your plan begins with mindset, as it so often does, and the doing away with the *"it can never happen here"*, or *"it only happens to other people"* mentality. It absolutely can happen, anytime, anywhere and you need to be ready to deal with it. By having a plan and by thinking about various options the idea is that you won't be floundering when the time for action comes.

It's fairly easy to grasp this concept, or it should be, and that is panic sets in when the brain searches for answers and can't find any, and people who panic tend to make lamentable choices.

Mindset Part II: Are you willing to inflict injury and death on someone to save lives? This is not a question you need to begin wrestling with during an ASE. Understand that you may have to take a life to preserve the lives of innocent victims and act accordingly. Are you willing? Again, the more of this decision-making process that can be figured out ahead of time, the greater your chance of prevailing. Instead of running around like the proverbial chicken with its head cut off, you are following a preordained plan of action and that can easily mean the difference between life and death.

Situational Awareness

"Who's around me and what are they doing?" That's situational awareness summed up in one sentence and is the bedrock of anyone's self-protection plan. When it comes to ASEs however, we must go a couple of steps further, and one integral part of situational awareness that applies to ASEs is knowing what gunfire sounds like. Many victims have reported *"it sounded like firecrackers",* and in the cinema in Aurora Colorado, when James Holmes went on his rampage, survivors said that they thought it was part of the movie. By the time a lot of people realize what they're actually hearing, it's often too late.

That means, if you live in an environment where it's possible, getting to a gun range and exposing yourself to the noise of gunfire so you can recognize it. Failing that, I would recommend going with the assumption that anytime you hear firecracker type noises or what may sound like a car backfiring – and it's not the 4th of July – factor in the possibility that it's gunfire. I'd rather make that assumption and be wrong than not make it and get caught out.

Another factor of situational awareness is establishing baselines wherever you are. What does that mean? A baseline is something we establish in advance to use as a comparison to something else. The baseline in a library for example is quiet while the baseline at a rock concert is noise and people holding up cigarette lighters and waving them back and forth. You must watch for anomalies to baselines and switch

211

your awareness levels up a notch. An example is that of the aforementioned cinema massacre in Colorado. Holmes was dressed as the joker, left the movie after 20 minutes, propped the back door open, came back in wearing tactical gear, carrying weapons, and throwing gas and smoke grenades. None of this would be deemed baseline behavior for a night at the movies. (This is not a criticism of the victims by the way. Many others in the theater had dressed up for the movie and patrons thought it might have been part of a special effects publicity stunt which is understandable).

A more personal occurrence, illustrating the same thing, happened while the author was stationed in Djibouti while serving with the 13th demi-brigade of the Foreign Legion. In 1987, agents of Gaddafi, hired by Al Quaeda, planted a briefcase bomb in a club called "Café Historil" which was frequented by members of the military. Normally – baseline remember – when you step one foot outside of a club in Djibouti you are immediately besieged by taxi drivers who surge forward in their ubiquitous green Nissans and hassle you about being your driver for the trip back to the base. They all scream at once *"warrior, warrior, venez avec moi"* etc., in a bid to win your business.

On the night of the bombing, as pointed out by a fellow Legionnaire the next day, there wasn't a taxi in sight nor within several miles of the club in question which is simply unheard of. In other words, this was a baseline anomaly and it should have raised his suspicions. Sadly it did not and he walked off to try and find a cab elsewhere. They, the cab drivers, had all been tipped off about the bomb through their local mosque and stayed well away. Had he recognized the anomaly and what it might represent, chances are he could have run back inside and told everyone something was up, but instead nine people, including some marine biologists from Germany, were blown up.

Cover/Concealment & Exits

Another major part of situational awareness is not only being aware of who is around you but also your environment. Where are the exits? (work managers need to ensure that there are at least two, everywhere), what improvised weapons are available, what cover[17] is available, and what concealment. Not a lot of stuff in commercial workplaces and/or schools will stop rifle bullets.

Behavioral Traits

Workplace violence, etc., and signs that you need to be on the lookout for include some of these behavioral traits demonstrated by active shooters in days leading up to the event:

- Depression
- Violation of Work Place Rules
- Explosive Outbursts
- Paranoia
- Talk of Problems (seemingly insurmountable)
- Talk of Suicide
- Previous History of Violent Behavior
- Lack of Attention to Personal Hygiene and Personal Appearance
- Fascination With Violence
- Empathy With Other Killers
- Socially Inept
- Loners
- Bowl Haircuts
- Living in Mom's Basement*

* The last two are mine but there seems to be a propensity for these guys to have really crappy haircuts and to be living alone with their Mom.

---

[17] Don't mistake cover and concealment as the same thing as many do. Concealment is anything that will hide you from view whereas cover will actually stop bullets. Priority therefore should be getting behind the latter.

Game Day

EVADE, DENY, ATTACK (OR WHY RUN, HIDE & FIGHT ISN'T
ADVISED)

Evade

Running is the first part of the generally accepted *"Run, Hide, Fight"* stratagem. While getting away has definitely saved lots of lives, there are other issues that need to be considered before one just blindly starts running from wherever they happen to be when the attack starts.

Where is/are the shooter(s)? It's no good running if you're running towards him, and determining where they are by the noise of gunfire can be very difficult indoors with echoing off walls and acoustics, etc. What about the teams of shooters we saw in Paris in 2016? Are you running straight from one into the sights of another? There was an incident recently, where a guy opened fire on a party and had his friend waiting around the back in the neighbor's yard as a sniper overwatch, dropping people as they ran to what they thought was safety.

Are you capable of running at full speed out of a mall/theater/place of work, etc? People have heart attacks and babies during shootings because of the undue stress placed upon them while the attack is going down. Look at some of the pictures and physical stature of the average active shooter/killer and compare it to the typical overweight sedentary office worker. In the recent attack in the mall in the state of Washington, one victim was 95 years old.

Are you dragging children with you? Do you have friends, family, or co-workers that are wounded that you're running with or trying to save? What distance are you from the shooter? What environment are you in? Remember the attack on the train in France that was thwarted by 3 American service men? Had they not been there to intervene where would anyone have run to on a speeding train? How about the club in Paris where 110 patrons were killed by active shooters (labelled terrorists). Where were they supposed to run to exactly? The term "evade" is a far better concept because it's not just blindly running which tends to be associated with panic. If you can evade the shooter(s), do so. If that means evacuation, remember to move fast, stay low, leave valuables, leave the wounded, and leave the indecisive. If you're at work, have a designated rendezvous point[18] away from the building and don't just stand around in the parking lot like a herd of sheep.

Deny

Hiding has gotten a lot of people killed. In the Virginia Tech shooting the killer shot students hiding amongst the dead and he went back and shot wounded students ensuring they were dead. As an FYI they discovered later that he practiced against targets hiding under desks at his local shooting range. (Pre-attack cue anyone?). The Norwegian mass killer also shot children hiding amongst other victims as did the shooter at Columbine and the guy at the gay club in Florida in 2016. Incidentally, it's standard operating procedure, in Hostage Rescue Teams, to shoot any terrorist who appears to be dead as you run past them in case they're playing possum and planning to jump up and shoot you in the back as you do so.

Here's another major problem that I have with hiding, and that's the inane advice to lock your door, turn off the lights, and silence your cell phones. Given the large amount of workplace violence incidents (remember that 22 of 23 were former disgruntled employees) do you think that maybe they won't be fooled by the fact that the doors are locked and the lights are off to everyone's office? I can just see the shooter now as he walks down the hallway confronted by a bunch of locked doors and dark offices saying to himself *"Gee, I sure picked the wrong day to come kill*

---

[18] I was always amazed at bouncers in the US who have very little training at all. We all had a rendezvous point away from the club so, in the event of fire for example, we would know where to go. If a fire chief walked up to security he could tell him whether or not all the staff got out based on whether everyone was at the rendezvous point .

everyone. I guess they're all on vacation." (this of course would be despite the fact all their cars are in the parking lot). The other major problem with this particular gem is that nobody seems to consider that the employee in question probably went through the same training that advised hiding, locking doors, and turning off lights. Denying is a far better strategy because he has no idea when he turns up what that might entail whether he's been through the training or not. What he does know is that the people on the other side of the door have planned a nasty surprise for him and will be trying to stop him and not just hiding under a desk pissing their pants and hoping he doesn't come in and shoot them all.

Something else you need to take into consideration is that buildings, especially modern ones, are not designed to stop incoming rifle rounds. One stray round in a Charlotte North Carolina SWAT shooting went through 2 houses, 4 fences, and ended up in the headboard of a woman's bed (while she was in the bed reading a book). So, all these gimmicks you see coming out on social media to lock the door are about as effective as a chocolate coffee cup.

Yet another issue with hiding is that it's passive in nature, i.e. let's just sit here, do nothing, and wait till it's all over...hopefully we'll survive. Deny, on the contrary, is active and involves being ready to take the fight to the guy should the area you're in be breached.

If you are opting to stay where you are and deny entry, maybe because evasion isn't viable, pile furniture and anything else heavy up against the doors, turn lights off (so you're harder to see and not backlit when he/they enter), and then get ready to execute your attack plan should a breach occur.

Whether you'll be on your own during this phase or have assistance, is open to a slew of variables. I personally have a problem with active shooter training that play acts with a mob of people throwing stuff at the guy wielding a cap gun while a group of stalwart co-workers tackle him to the floor. Real gun fire, especially in confined spaces, is incredibly loud and causes people, even trained ones, to freeze in their tracks. A good friend of mine, Keith Childers, used to be the SWAT trainer for his police dept. and one of the heads of the North Carolina Tactical Officer's Association and he talks about times in training where big burly State Troopers, upon hearing real gunfire during training inside a building, grabbed female officers and hid behind them due to the shock of the noise. The destructive force of those rounds on a human target is gory and terrifying to the uninitiated. Expecting your co-workers to charge him with you is, in my opinion, wishful thinking at best. A better plan is to assume that it's going to be you, on your own. Find a place of ambush, and launch as he goes past. As I write this, the attack in London by the three Islamic extremists has just happened. Despite large mobs throwing chairs, bottles, and glasses, it lasted eight minutes until armed police arrived and shot them dead. The crowd throwing things didn't deter them at all.

Attack

"If you knew you were going to be fighting a gunman for your life tomorrow what would you be doing to prepare for it today? Another way to look at this is *"If the time to perform has arrived, the time to prepare has passed."*

If you're serious about your self-protection training – and you should be – it's important to familiarize yourself with weapons so you know what a malfunctioning one looks like and what reloading looks like. This is easily your best chance to attempt a counter-attack. (Remember 2 out of 3 ASEs are stopped by unarmed civilians). The French train attack that was stopped by three young American men (two of whom were in the US military) was during a malfunction of the attacker's AK-47 in which they were able to take advantage of his malfunctioning weapon to charge him and take him to the ground. There's no doubt that their exposure to weapons during basic training gave them the knowledge to recognize that moment and capitalize on it.

Whether it's during the "DENIAL" phase of "EVADE, DENY, ATTACK" or the "ATTACK" phase, if it becomes necessary to go after the gunman, your best bet is to hide and ambush them. It's also highly advisable to get some form of unarmed combat training (check out the author's upcoming book on hard skills or Udemy course) from a reputable instructor (see appendix) on exactly how to attack and disarm a gunman so you don't get killed in the process. Again, a considerable number of shooters who have been stopped, have been stopped by unarmed civilians who had a go.

Also, keep in mind it will be easier to take a rifle away from someone during this process than a handgun, but regardless of whichever one you encounter, keep away from the bit where the bullets come out. Also, keep in mind that a firearm is designed to give the user an ergonomic advantage during a struggle, hence my suggestion to seek out competent training. Finally, remember that there are some people teaching to grab hold of the rifle barrel to do a disarm which is more proof that a lot of instructors don't have much real life experience. Barrels get white hot during repeated shooting and will pretty much burn a hole through your hand if you attempt to grab one. Tackling the man holding it is better advice.

Considerations If You're Armed

If you're fortunate enough to live in a country or state that allows you to have a weapon for personal defense, you need to consider the following with regards to intervening in an ASE type of event.

A lot of the people licensed to carry a concealed weapon have no doubt thought about being able to prevent a crime by the brandishing and/or use of their weapon. Indeed, there are countless examples of that very thing occurring, but it would be naïve to ignore the times when it hasn't worked out to the concealed carrier's advantage. Evading and Denial are probably always going to be your go-to options first, armed or not. Consider; law enforcement is arriving after receiving reports of an armed man shooting people. They roll in to see you standing over the bad guy with your weapon out having just shot him. What do you think they're likely to do? What you do if you were one of them and rolled up on scene to see a guy there with a gun standing over a dead body?

Imagine you were in the Aurora Colorado movie theater, and armed. Are you honestly confident that, with people running everywhere, in a room full of smoke and gas, in the dark you could have surgically taken out the killer without hitting anyone innocent as they ran around terrified in front of you?

In Jakarta in 2016 the team that hit the city had something called sniper overwatch[19] and police officers were killed as they attempted to take out the bad guys.

How about the Walmart in Las Vegas in 2014 after a couple starting a "revolution", executed two police officers at a pizza restaurant, and ran across the street into the Walmart. A CCW (concealed carry weapon permit) holder tried valiantly to stop who he assumed was the killer, i.e. the man, and ignored the female accomplice who shot and killed him.

What about what you're carrying. Most concealed carriers tote something small because it's easier to conceal and lighter to carry all day. If that ends up being a .380 or any other "mouse gun" good luck over any significant distance. Some carry rifles in their cars and full "battle rattle" in preparation for such events. Given the average ASE is over in 4 minutes, are you going to have time to run to your car, get kitted out, grab your weapon and run back to take care of business before it's all over? Not if you're honest with yourself.

People will be running both towards and away from the shooter, usually in a blind panic, and you're planning on running towards him/her...just how is your ability to perform a head shot on a moving target with a backdrop of running innocents? Can you be certain another CCW holder won't see you with your weapon and assume you're one of the bad guys and shoot you first?

---

[19] A term used to describe when a sharp shooter takes the high ground and watches over his team mates doing the killing. If he sees anyone running in to intervene he takes them out.

If you decide to intervene (and there have been incidents where it's viable), make sure after you've dropped the bad guy(s) that you keep your weapon discretely out of sight. The second you're aware of law enforcement officers arriving, drop your weapon, show your hands, and comply with every direction you're given. They do not know, and have no way of knowing, if you're one of the good guys, and will assume that anyone who is armed is a threat.

If you have intervened and someone you know is on the phone with emergency services (or you are), make sure that they make them understand you have intervened and that they describe you and what you're wearing as well as a physical description to reduce the chances of you being shot by a good guy.

Even undercover police officers with badges get shot. In a recent study conducted by LAPD, a staggering 98% of undercover police officers were "killed" during scenario based training with simulated ammunition (called SIMS). Responding officers failed to notice the undercover officer's badges hanging around their necks on a lanyard or clipped to their belts.

In essence, you're going to have to be very careful, extremely so, of drawing and/or attempting to use your personal weapon during an ASE (or any serious crime), lest you end up on the receiving end of a fellow CCW holder or law enforcement officer's shot. Most important of all is to keep in mind that you **DO NOT** have a legal duty to engage if you're a civilian CCW holder. Sometimes, the best option is going to be to protect you and your family, and leave it at that.

Basic Medical Considerations

A few final thoughts on the ASE issue with regards to medical necessities.

Paramedics will NOT be allowed into the facility until law enforcement officials have deemed it safe.

Police officers responding will NOT stop to render first aid to victims right away as their primary mission is to locate and stop the killer before he racks up an even bigger body count. Only after that mission is accomplished will first aid be rendered.

Given the average law enforcement response time, you would therefore be wise to learn some basic first aid for knife and gunshot wounds. There have been several episodes where victims have bled out before paramedics could intervene that would have been saved with such knowledge (check the resources for a list of schools/individuals who offer this sort of specialized training).

Tourniquets, whether improvised or designed for the job, have been saving bunches of lives on battlefields in recent years. Once thought to be dangerous, they have now come back into favor and their application is being taught to most first responders as part of their standard training. As an FYI twenty-seven of them were applied during the aftermath of the Boston Marathon bombing, which undoubtedly saved lives, and not one of them was designed specifically for that purpose, i.e. they used belts, lanyards, clothing, etc. Make sure what you use is at least 1.5 inches wide and cinch it down tight enough that you can't get two fingers underneath it. On a tac-med course the author attended in Florida, taught by an active SF medic with battlefield experience, getting them on within eighteen seconds or less was stressed. How many cops or paramedics do you think will be on scene within 18 seconds of you being shot by an active shooter?

Training designed for this type of event is different from your regular Red Cross Basic First Aid course. See Resource section.

If your organization would like training in dealing with an Active Shooter/Killer, other than the quick fix public service announcement favored by lazy management, you can arrange to do so through www.H2BG.com.
You'll find it on the Training Page under resources on the site.

27

ASSESSMENT

Situational Awareness Part III: As previously mentioned, the term situational awareness can be summed up as *"who's around me and what are they doing?"* With that in mind it makes sense to learn how to size people up. As a bouncer, I had the time from when they got out of the cab until they crossed the sidewalk to determine whether they were a good fit for the club or not.

Whether you're a bouncer or not makes little difference. A lot of maniacs will give off a certain vibe before they attack and Israeli security forces spend a lot of time on how to spot these signs on passengers waiting in line to board one of their planes. How about the footage of the Boston bombers? When you look at it later, you could see that they did not fit the baseline performance of all the other spectators.

Here then is a partial list of some of the stuff you'll want to be looking for when sizing people up. This also works if you're in an argument with someone and trying to learn as much as you can about them before the fight.

Size

Should be obvious because despite the old nonsense about *"the bigger they are the harder they fall"* bigger stronger opponents are harder to handle as a rule. They don't have weight classes in sport combat to protect the heavyweights from the lightweights.

222

Fat Or Muscle

He might be bigger but is it muscle and does he work out or is he just big and fat? Don't make the mistake of assuming that fat guys are slow. Speed is based on genetics, i.e. how much speed twitch muscle fiber was he born with.

Clothing

Clothing can tell us a lot. Is he wearing something like the previously mentioned bandana which would indicate gang affiliation? What about a t-shirt with a logo for a martial art school or boxing gym? How about outlaw biker gear? Is he wearing heavy boots or flip-flops? Is his clothing right for the weather? Why would someone be wearing a big heavy coat for example on a hot day? What about back packs in an environment where you don't typically see them (the latter is how the Boston bombers and the suicide bomber in Manchester got their explosives to ground zero). I typically don't worry about someone in a Tap Out shirt as I've found when you fight them that's what they like to do i.e. tap out.

His Watch

Less people are wearing them now (sadly) but which wrist he's wearing it on will tell you whether he's a righty or a lefty (right handed people typically wear theirs on their left wrist and vice versa). Why is that important? Because it will tell you which hand he's likely to throw first, especially if he's untrained.

Tattoos

Like clothing, tattoos can tell us whether he's affiliated with a gang, been in prison, and in some cultures, whether he's done time for killing someone. Certain Filipino martial arts clubs have 3 small dots tattooed on their thumb knuckles.

Jewelry

Again, jewelry can be a giveaway. Many boxers sport a small pair of boxing gloves on a chain around their neck. All the black belts in a certain karate organization in Australia wear a distinctive cross. Rings across all the fingers is typical in the outlaw biker world. A wedding ring might mean he's got more to lose and therefore be less likely to fight. Earrings, if they're big enough, can be great handles to yank someone around with.

Missing Arm Hair

One trick of people who really work with knives a lot is to test their sharpness by shaving a small piece of hair on their forearm. If you notice a knife clip in their pocket and a patch of hair missing that knife is undoubtedly razor sharp and the guy spends a lot of time with it.

Weapons

Learn what a weapon under a t-shirt looks like. Study ones under the shirt on the right hip and the harder to spot appendix carry. Look for knife clips in pockets. Bulges around the ankles can tell you if someone is wearing an ankle holster.

Scarring

If someone has a flattened nose and a lot of scarification around his eyes it might be a sign of a boxer or MMA practitioner. Calloused knuckles (the big two) are typical with someone who's heavily into karate I never worried much about guys with heavily scarred faces as this just means they get hit a lot. The ones with scars on their fists and pretty boy looks were the ones you had to be careful of. Also be aware of cauliflower ears. This signifies a grappling background so watch out, in a fight, for the guy to attempt to shoot in on you.

Demeanor

Is he calm and sober, or erratic and possibly on mind altering drugs? Calm guys can be very experienced and therefore dangerous. People on drugs can be a) unpredictable; and b) impervious to pain and therefore harder to stop.

Is he doing any of the four pre-fight cues? (grooming, looking around, hiding hands, weight shifting).

Stance

If the fight is imminent his stance can tell you a lot. It's pretty easy to spot a boxer and a wrestler, for example, which in turn will tell you what sort of an attack you should be preparing for.

Alone Or Not

Does he have any friends or is he on his own. His friends might not be readily apparent. You can often get in a fight against one guy to quickly find out there's a lot of his mates in the vicinity.

28

FLASH MOBS AND RIOT
SURVIVAL

In the original print of this book I didn't cover flash mobs and riots, but now, given the current political climate and shift in this country, and in Europe, they're undoubtedly becoming more common. In the last few years here in the States alone we've had serious riots in Baltimore MD, Ferguson MO, Pennsylvania State University, Flatbush NY, Anaheim CA, Baton Rouge LA, Charlotte NC, Milwaukee WI, North Dakota Pipeline, Washington D.C., Berkeley CA, et alia.

Flash mobs are also on the rise. Temple University in Philadelphia, Chicago, Washington D.C., Boston, and most recently on a train in Seattle when dozens of juveniles attacked and robbed passengers on the BART.

In keeping with the general theme of the book, i.e. soft skills being the art of awareness and avoidance, I've decided to talk about some strategies to keep you safe and out of harm's way should you happen to find yourself in one. Obviously, you're hardly going to try and fight your way out, so soft skills are about all you have going for you.

At first blush that sounds odd. How do you just find yourself in a riot, and yet, that's exactly what's happened to a bunch of people recently in the US and overseas.

How about the motorists who've driven into "black lives matter" protestors forming road blocks across the highway? What about people who went to work in Baltimore in the morning only to come out of work later in the evening to find themselves in the middle of a full-scale riot replete with burning buildings, destruction of property, and vandalized vehicles, etc? What about the folks in Germany who went to their annual New Year's Eve celebration to find themselves under attack in the Cologne train station by a pack of approximately 1,000 middle eastern refugees?

Stay Put

First, it might be safest to stay put in your place of work until management hires security to get you out, comes up with an alternative exit strategy, or the rioters move, or have moved on. With regards to rioters moving, sometimes they can be fairly static (outside an embassy for example) while other times it's a fluid event that moves from a gathering point to somewhere else. If it's the type that moves you probably won't have to wait long before the bulk of the crowd has gone and then you can move on out.

Stay Away

If you do decide to leave or walk around the corner to find yourself caught up in one, do not be a spectator. That also goes for watching one on TV and deciding to go down and check it out. Either way, you can end up, very easily, caught in the violence either at the hands of the rioters, or the counter-attack by the cops, who will have little time to listen to pleas of *"I'm only here looking."* You might also want to consider, if your caught on the local news on the periphery of one, whether as a participant or spectator, the fallout if your boss or important clients happen to see the broadcast. Will you have a job tomorrow? What about a criminal record or even the cost of defending yourself if you're caught up in the sweep and arrested? Stay away.

One of our Kansas City students, Megan, was walking along the sidewalk in the city going to a restaurant for lunch surrounded by a mob of anti-Trump protestors. Someone in the group near her threw a bottle and a cop immediately thought it was her. Now she's embroiled in a pending trial attempting to prove her innocence which will cost both time and money, and a possible criminal record.

Not only does the "stay away" advice apply to local riots where you live, but keep that in mind for places you might be going to visit. We've already addressed the importance of doing some research on the safety of wherever it is you might be visiting for vacation, and whether that's in the States or overseas, make sure you do your homework and check on the political scene and potential for unrest before you go. If it looks in the least bit dicey, again, stay the hell away.

In One, What Next?

Alright, despite your best intentions, you've been caught in a riot or flash mob. What should you do next? First, get to the fringes as fast as you can and get your back to a wall. If you have a backpack or laptop case hold that up in front, or, in the case of the backpack wear it like a chest rig. (Flip it around and wear it on your front instead of on your back.) This will make it harder for someone to grab you by the pack from behind and drag you to the ground, make it harder to steal stuff from it in the confusion, and act as somewhat of a shield against missiles, be they human or foreign objects.

Is there an open store front you can run into or an alley you can scoot down? If so, take the escape route and get the hell out of there. This will be obvious to some, but if the storefront is open because looters have broken the windows or kicked the doors in, do NOT enter in a bid to cut through to safety. Again, you run the risk of being arrested as a looter or being caught on camera running out of the store. Good luck trying to convince the judge or jury that you were only using it as a shortcut.

If you do have to try and get across the mob (and notice here we're in the process of going from bad to worst case scenario), you'll want to cross it in much the same way you swim across a rip tide and not against it. Trying to fight a rip will wear you out and before you know it you're drowning. Fighting against the surging of a crowd will exhaust you, (if it doesn't kill you), and is pretty much a losing proposition. I recommend going across them at a slightly forward angle, i.e. crossing but moving in the same direction they are as that won't draw too much attention to yourself.

One strategy you could possibly use here, and I'm aware of a mate who did it in Marseille when he walked out of the cinema into a protest on the Canebière by the local communists, is to pick up one of the discarded protest signs, as he worked his way out. By making them – the rioters – think you're one of them, you're far less likely to be attacked. Of course the obvious issue here is to be very aware of how close the mob is to the forces of law and order and what the relationship is between the two. Again, you'll have a hell of a time trying to convince judge and jury you weren't a willing participant.

Don't Fight

If you do find yourself singled out by the crowd do not try and engage them in a fight even if you're Jackie Chan, Bruce Lee and Chuck Norris rolled into one. Nor should you try and run, which will only activate their prey drive. Try instead to work your way around the side of the group and flank them or lose yourself in the crowd and confusion. Don't get me wrong, I'll fight if there's absolutely no other choice, but it's my last line of defense in a situation like this.

Get Away

Obviously, getting away to safety, at that point, will be your number one priority. However, it's also important to note that safety might not be the big line of police officers you see further down the street in a phalanx armed with riot shields and batons. Again, not the fault of law enforcement, but how would you feel if you were one of the cops, outnumbered a thousand to one, facing an angry mob threatening to rip you limb from limb, and you, a random person from the mob, come barreling up full-speed at them? What happens next could run the gamut of being flung to the ground and flexi-cuffed to being shot with a water cannon, a bean bag round, rubber bullet, tear gas or mace, or in some countries that don't "play" like they do here, shot and killed.

Tear Gas

On the subject of tear gas, which will certainly come into play at some point, a bandana is a great thing to have. While it won't eliminate the problem completely it will reduce the effect of smoke from burning vehicles and the burning associated with OC and tear gas. I recommend you hold it to your face and not wear it because wearing it wrapped round your face and knotted in the back makes you look an awful lot like one of the bad guys to law enforcement. Some say soaking it in soda, lemon juice or vinegar will help mitigate the effects of the various gases while others claim those tricks don't work. If you've never been exposed to it, (and this is why law enforcement and military members mostly have) it can cause panic even though it's really nothing but a nuisance unless you're an asthmatic. Some other things to keep in mind are, don't remove clothing as it causes a far worse burning sensation on exposed skin; don't wash your face with water as it can exacerbate the effects, (tear gas isn't a gas at all…it's a powder). Try not to swallow, and definitely don't rub your eyes. You will have to wash your clothing later, separately (probably several times) or throw it all away as it will stay contaminated for ages.

One final point regarding tear gas and other irritants is one I stole from my colleague and fellow trainer Greg Elifritz, and that is, if you wear contact lenses, get rid of them immediately. The gases can cause the lenses to melt which doesn't sound like a whole lot of fun. You should probably also carry spare contacts for that reason.

Clothing

If you paid attention to the chapter on the bug in bag you should have a solid pair of shoes on you. Wear those in lieu of any open toed sandals or high heels. You need to be able to run, kick, inflict damage, and get through broken glass and debris on the ground. Anything less than a good pair of shoes won't do that.

In your bug in bag, you will of course, have a first-aid kit which could come in very handy. Hospitals and paramedics are probably going to be overwhelmed in a situation like this, so anything that you can do to take care of yourself is going to be a godsend.

Cars & Vandals

A couple of other considerations; We've all seen images of rioters destroying vehicles. If one of them happens to be yours (parked outside when the riot begins, for example), do NOT confront the rioters or attempt to stop them. This could very easily get you a severe beating or result in you being killed.

As I previously mentioned, don't try to run out of a riot or mob. Keep your head down, avoid eye contact, and walk with a definite purpose. If you're unfortunate enough to be knocked to the ground during the melee, curl up into a ball, cross your ankles, keep your elbows tight to your ribs, tuck in your chin and keep your mitts up on either side of your head. Fetuses do this to protect their fragile bodies inside the womb and it works outside in just the same way. If you don't believe how dangerous this is, look up the story about the people trampled to death trying to get into one of the midnight sales at a Walmart a few years back.

When To Move

My last point to make is that if you have hidden out in a building while waiting for the crowds to disperse, they will usually do so after 3:00 a.m. That's a good time to make your move and walk out of the area. Make sure you know the area as well as you can because the mobile phone system could be down and/or overloaded, so using your mobile phones GPS may not be a viable option (check, because some phones and apps allow you to download maps to your phone so they can be opened at a later date without any service or GPS signal). Also, keep in mind while inside the building waiting that you resist the temptation to stick your head out the window and look at what's going on. Someone could easily spot you and lead an attack in to the building to get you, and law enforcement is not likely to be on call to come and save you.

Hands On

If all the above has failed, we're now going in to the realm of hard skills, i.e. physical fighting, which isn't really the purview of this tome. Having said that, I will touch on some brief points, because if we don't, and despite your best intentions, you may have no choice but to fight your way out.

If you're going to go hands on – let's assume a group of rioters have singled you out – you'll want to be as discrete as you possibly can. If you start jumping around like a squirrel on crack, you're going to draw attention to yourself and raise the ire of their colleagues and friends.

Weapons

Arming yourself at this point would be a good idea, as fighting a mob empty handed is not recommended unless you've had years of serious martial arts training. Even then, all the experts advise fighting empty handed as a last resort tactic.

What then is the weapon of choice? I would submit an impact weapon[20] is a good idea and much better than a gun even if you are carrying the latter. In the confusion of bodies running around, and movement everywhere ,as well as smoke, it's going to be too easy to miss your target and hit someone else, or, have your round go through the target and hit an innocent if you're using a firearm.

Another issue with firearms – and it's a major one – is that in many jurisdictions, police tactics will involve putting sharp shooters on roof tops to hold the high ground. If they look down and see you brandishing a weapon, again, they will have no idea that you're an honest citizen trying

---

[20] Impact weapons are ones that do damage by crushing unlike edged weapons which cut and poke and projectile weapons which are launched from a distance. Think bricks, rocks, clubs, baseball bats and batons etc.

232

to exercise your legal right to self-defense and will almost certainly shoot you.

A knife is another possibility but it would be my second choice behind the impact weapon. It's certainly low-key and discreet but the problem is that they rarely stop anyone in their tracks. Most stabbing victims never realize they've been tagged at all until way later. So, although you might be inflicting damage on the bad guys, they will almost certainly be oblivious to it while administering your beating.

The impact weapon, on the other hand, can be kept low and discreet along the side of the leg, and with very little effort be used to drop someone unconscious. Of course the ultimate impact weapon in one of these situations is a vehicle. Undoubtedly, if you're reading this book, you've seen images of cars driving through protestors trying to block highways and streets. Refer to the section on vehicle security if you should find yourself in this situation.

29

HARD SKILLS

Hard skills is the name we give to the actual fighting techniques that we'll use if our avoidance and awareness have failed us and we've ended up in a fight. They encompass everything from martial art techniques, to clawing and scratching, to improvised weapons, and tools specifically designed for the job.

Most people think about self-defense and immediately conjure up images of martial arts schools and people in uniforms wearing colored belts, jumping around like Jackie Chan on six cups of coffee, dispatching bad guys with a flick of the wrist. In truth, while there are martial art styles that are designed for that purpose, the majority are former shadows of themselves and are now redesigned as recreational activities to teach kids obedience, get adults in shape, and win trophies at tournaments. Real martial arts, the stuff designed at one point to kill someone on a battlefield when your primary weapon was unavailable, is sadly becoming harder and harder to find.

To help you in your quest to identify the real deal I've put together the following brief explanation of the major styles you can find in a search of your yellow page phone book or online.

Before I begin, it would make sense to explain the difference between a classical martial art and a traditional martial art. Credit for this brilliant definition goes to Gavin Mulholland in the UK who said *"Classical martial arts are the ones where the practitioners wear a particular costume, learn the lingo, and deviate not one iota from the original curriculum taught hundreds of years earlier in a bid to preserve the art form. A traditional stylist, on the other hand, is not concerned so much with the preservation of the style. Just as his forefathers "traditionally" used weapons to hand when fighting by grabbing farm tools such as nunchakus and tonfas, our modern traditionalist will pick up HIS weapons to hand such as a bar stool, a pool cue or a bottle."*

Does that mean that no classical style will suffice for surviving an altercation in the street? Not at all. There are some incredibly accomplished martial artists involved in such systems, but you'll usually find that they've had upwards of twenty years of training and a lot of cross training in other systems.

Will all traditional training prepare you then? Sadly, no. In fact, the majority will not for the reasons mentioned below.

To be effective there are three things someone must have to win a street fight. They must have technique, they must have tactics, and they must have the correct mind-set. The problem with a great deal of martial art schools is that they only teach techniques, but no tactics or mind-set. The student dutifully shows up, dons his practice uniform, learns a set of techniques that he must demonstrate proficiency in to obtain his next belt, and goes home. Nobody talks about tactics designed to survive outside against a human predator, nor do they discuss the necessary mind-set, or train it, to prevail in human combat.

The analogy I used earlier in the book explains why those three are so critical if you have any chance of prevailing in a fight. So, if you're going to begin training in a system, make sure it's geared towards self-defense and not sport, and make sure they don't only teach techniques. There should be a heavy emphasis on tactics and mind-set as well.

While there are myriad traditional arts to choose from, with hard versions and soft versions of almost every system, the following is a simple overview for neophytes to get an idea of what the various, most common, martial arts are.

Aikido

A Japanese art that was designed just after WWII to control and restrain adversaries rather than seriously injure them. It was derived from the far more violent art of Aiki-jujutsu. Due to its circular nature and complex techniques it is considered more of a polishing art for an experienced black belt from another art than a good art to start with. The other problem with Aikido is finding anyone who teaches a street practical version of it. There's also no ground work to speak of and no learning to get out of holds such as headlocks and full nelsons.

Pros: Can be practiced into your seventies and eighties. Doesn't train only to defeat people who train in the same system like almost every other martial art does.

Cons: No ground fighting, no getting out of holds and tending to lack in aggression or mind-set.

Karate

Karate is a generic term for a bunch of Okinawan and Japanese systems. The term itself means "empty hand" and is recognized primarily by its emphasis on striking and kicking. There is a broad array of schools ranging from the McDojo (a glorified child minding center designed to nickel and dime parents of small children to death) to hard styles that teach serious street effective systems. The latter are definitely in the minority. Goju tends to be one of the latter with very little emphasis on entering tournaments, almost no high kicks and close range elbows, knees and head butts. It also tends to have been less diluted as opposed to systems like Tae Kwan Do.

Pros: Learn to use all the weapons of the body from the head to the heels

236

Cons: Sporting versions tend to be too watered down to be effective as there is too much emphasis on looking technically perfect instead of efficacy of technique.

Judo

"The Gentle Art" Judo is an Olympic sport that focuses primarily on throwing an opponent cleanly for a point. While Judo players are tough, the use of a jacket for the majority of techniques can limit the efficacy of the art in the street, especially in a hot climate where adversaries typically wear t-shirts. If you live in a cooler climate though, where wearing a jacket is common for most of the year it can be very viable. Another great advantage is it teaches you to stay on your feet.

Pros: Tough training. Learn to stay on your feet. Learn to use clothing to your advantage.

Cons: No study of striking until higher ranks. Jacket required for a lot of techniques. No training for multiple adversaries.

Ju-Jutsu

Not to be confused with Brazilian Ju-jutsu, Jujutsu is the parent art of Judo. At one point it was going to disappear into obscurity when Jigaro Kano, Judo's founder, modified the techniques and made them safe for sporting competitions. Jujutsu is one of the most effective arts for real fighting because it incorporates striking techniques as well as throws and ground work. Once again, you do have to be careful and make sure you can find an authentic system and a good teacher.

Pros: Good all round art if you get the right style and teacher

Cons: Not many

Brazilian Jujutsu

Brazilian Jujutsu

or BJJ as it's often called, exploded on the scene a few years ago. It is a very effective ground fighting system (its focus) but puts practitioners in danger if they have to deal with multiple opponents. They also like to spout that *"95% of fights end up on the ground"* as a marketing ploy, but in reality, it's not true. The statistics came from a study of LAPD "use of force" reports which has little to do with the type of fighting you or I would do. The police are trained to take someone to the ground because it's easier to contain them while you put the handcuffs on a non-compliant subject. Also, they're not encouraged to punch and kick so it's more likely to see three officers crash tackle a suspect to the ground than to see them stand around striking a suspect.

It might also be fair to say that 90% of drunken red necks end up on the floor when they fight, but you must keep in mind that they're not trained and they're drunk. Bouncers I've known over the years, myself included, can usually count on one hand the amount of fights we've had that have gone to the ground.

Pros: Teaches you one of the most effective ground styles in the world today and is great exercise.

Cons: Doesn't do much good being on the ground if you're up against multiples. Pushes untruths such as 95% of fights end up on the floor and you can't beat multiple opponents.

Tae Kwan Do

Tae Kwan Do is commonly called Korean Karate. It is another relatively new art, stolen from Shotokan and then augmented with kicks. TKD's emphasis is almost exclusively on kicking which makes it ineffective in the street. It has also become an Olympic sport, which again, has removed a lot of the emphasis on the original, more military version taught to the Korean Army. Of course, as with any of these arts, there will always be exceptions to the rule, but for the most part TKD isn't the answer.

Pros: Like karate, learn to use all your body as a weapon

Cons: No sweeps or ground work. Too much emphasis on kicking and sport and not enough on punching.

Kung Fu

Kung Fu is another generic term like karate that applies across the board to most Chinese martial arts styles. Some are internal arts which take years of study to master and others are external arts that, while they're quicker to master than the internal, tend to be less effective than their Japanese counterparts due to their mimicry of animal's and their movements. Even Wing Chun, arguably the most scientific of the Chinese systems, lacks ground fighting and escapes from holds etc.

Pros: Like karate…learn to use every part of your body as weapon

Cons: Can be too esoteric and flamboyant for the real world

Tai Chi

A Chinese exercise system that focuses primarily on ultra-slow movements that are designed to increase agility, balance, and blood flow as opposed to training people to actually fight. Again, there are a couple of exceptions but I don't think it would be stretching it to say that 99.9% of all Tai Chi practitioners practice the version designed to make you healthy. The problem with the ultra-slow training is that it isn't anything like real combat speed. I've had practitioners argue that they can speed up when it's for real, but that would be like training for the Indianapolis 500 by driving round the track every day at 4mph claiming you'll just speed up race day.

Pros: Can be done for the rest of your life. Will promote health benefits such as lower blood pressure, flexibility, and stress relief. Harvard medical just got done with a ten-year study and backed up the claims.

Cons: Almost nobody teaches what the moves in the form are. No sparring with live resisting opponents. Too slow to be of much use in a real fight.

Krav Maga

Originally an unarmed combat system designed to be used by the Israeli Defense Forces, a lot of modern Krav Maga has become a watered-down version that focuses more on fitness than fighting. It can be good if you find the right instructor but the hyped-up marketing has had an impact on the system and finding good instructors now is hard.

Pros: Straight forward system utilizing boxing hand work and karate kicks plus basic groundwork and counter weapons work. Lots of emphasis on gun and knife defense.

Cons: Tends to be emphasizing more and more fitness in the workouts. Watch out for the schools that teach the simultaneous block and counterpunch knife defense nonsense.

Filipino Martial Arts

FMA is a generic term applying to all the Filipino martial arts which are most noted for their use of the stick and knife. Just like karate and kung fu, some of the systems are less interested in real fighting than they are about preserving an art form. Other systems are extremely street effective. One of the big advantages is that many of the movements are interchangeable whether you're wielding a stick, a knife, or your empty hands.

Pros: More and more fights tend to be with weapons nowadays (you may as well learn a system that utilizes them).

Cons: Can be too much emphasis on drilling rather than fighting. Not much time devoted to groundwork or escaping holds. Tend not to punch very hard because they're used to the stick or blade doing the work for them.

Jeet Kune Do

was the system that Bruce Lee developed and reluctantly labeled. It was an amalgamation of a bunch of different systems by Lee who was incredibly innovative. Once Lee passed away, the system fragmented amongst his original students and nowadays it is a crap shoot as to whether you'll get a good school or not. They tend to be jack of all trades and masters of none when it comes to actual fighting techniques, but once again, there are exceptions.

Pros: Good all round system which tends to study all aspects of fighting

Cons: What makes it good also makes it bad. Tends to try and cram too much stuff into their syllabus so, instead of being good at a few things, they're mediocre at a lot of them.

Boxing

The western art of boxing has some good things going for it. One, you'll learn if you can take a punch; two, you'll get in great shape; and three, you'll learn four punches and myriad combinations thereof. The problem with it is that it's usually going to be an art that's limited by who can train. I've seen eighty year old students on the mats in dojos...I've yet to see any eighty-year-old boxers. It also trains you to fight only one person at a time who is conveniently unarmed, the same weight as you and about the same skill level. To make matters worse it doesn't deal with what to do if you've been knocked down, are facing weapon wielding opponents, multiple opponents, or being grabbed from behind.

Pros: Only four punches to learn so relatively simple to pick up. Teaches you to take a punch and hit a fully resisting opponent and gets you in great shape.

Cons: Trains you to fight one man over ten rounds who weighs the same as you, who has no friends, and isn't carrying a weapon. Won't train you to deal with getting out of any hold except for a clinch and there's no weapons defenses or ground fighting.

Choosing A School

There are other arts and other systems out there, of course, but these tend to be the main players you're going to run across in your average city. If you are going to choose one of these to begin training, here are some simple guidelines to help you go some way towards not getting ripped off.

Ask around, look on forums, Google the school and instructor, and talk to some students and get their feedback.

Be very cautious if the instructor is grossly overweight and insists on being called Master or Grand Master. I've run into some exceptions but for the most part if they're overweight they're probably not any good and they certainly lack discipline.

Run away if they try and tell you fighting is easy or if they start talking about stuff that is too good to be true.

Ask if they cover mind set, stress inoculation, tactics and legal aspects of fighting. Leave if they don't.

Avoid anyone who tries to hit you with the hard sell. While there is nothing wrong with contracts per se, double check the exit policy. Some schools make you pay a cancellation fee or keep billing you for years after you've stopped training.

Watch the interaction between students and instructors. Do they respect each other and are they appearing to be in an environment that promotes learning.

What is the ratio of children to adults? You may not want to be the only adult in a class full of eight-year-olds.

It's very much a case of Caveat Emptor when you join a school, so do your homework and avoid wasting your hard-earned money and your time.

30

NATURAL WEAPONS

The actual striking techniques we learn are simple to apply and you've been doing most of them your entire life already. Push something and you've done a palm heel. Walk up bleachers or wade into surf and you've done knees. Reach into the cupboard and grab a can and you've done a cradle hand. They are;

Palm Heels

If you've ever pushed someone or pushed a door open you've performed a palm heel strike. It is used by drawing the fingers back as tightly as you can (almost as if you're trying to give yourself a wristlock), and then striking with the two fleshy pads on the base of the palm of the hand. There are many reasons why it's such a great strike and some are;

a) If given the choice between punching a brick wall or palm heeling it, everyone will choose palms for obvious reasons.

b) It's almost impossible to break so you can't be injured to the point where continuing to strike isn't possible.

c) It looks like you're pushing or slapping someone as opposed to punching them.

d) Because it looks defensive instead of offensive in nature it's far easier to use as a pre-emptive strike.

e) People tend to hit harder with a palm because there's less reticence about breaking the bones as there might be with a fist.

f) If you hit under the chin the fingers automatically find their way into the eyes giving you a one-two effect.

g) It looks inoffensive to the other guy so it helps to deescalate situations.

You can deliver the palm with the fingers pointing upwards, i.e. at the twelve o'clock position, with them pointing outwards, (3 o'clock position) and angling inwards, (9 o'clock position), depending on what target you're specifically trying to hit. For example, if someone's head is leaning slightly forward in the standard position, i.e. your fingers pointing up at 12 o'clock, your fingers will hit his forehead and fold backwards. It's exactly this situation that calls for the fingers to be rotated out to the 3 o'clock position.

Unlike a fist which requires some precision to land perfectly a palm heel can deliver a strike in the dark against a target that you can't see clearly. With the fist in that situation you might hit teeth or forehead and injure your hand, but with the palm it doesn't matter as you'll deliver the shock you need anyway.

Finally, the palm can be delivered at extremely close range in the same way a boxer delivers an uppercut. Called a chin-jab by fans of the WWII military unarmed combat manuals, this powerful shot snaps the chin back and causes massive brain splash.

Cradle Hand

If you've ever reached into a cupboard or the fridge for a can of something you've performed a cradle hand. You use the same motion only at full speed and imagine his throat is the can you're trying to snatch from the cupboard. Done hard enough this strike could, in theory, collapse the trachea. It can be used as a lightning fast strike to cause a gagging reflex or you can strike and then grab hold of the windpipe. In one fight I've been able to touch my finger and thumb together behind the assailant's windpipe. It can be hard to use once the fight has started as often the opponent will tuck his chin down and have his hands in the way. As a preemptive strike though, it is wickedly effective.

Fist

A lot of experts denigrate the closed fist saying you'll break your hand if you hit someone with it. In over 2,000 altercations, I've only broken my hand twice. Once was when I was young and inexperienced and he zigged when he should have zagged and I clipped his skull with the little finger knuckle, and the second was hitting a guy wearing a motorcycle helmet. Of course, a lot will depend on genetics and your bone structure, but if you hold the hand in the correct position and hit with the two large knuckles you should be ok. Understand also that I have trained in karate for over thirty-five years and that included years of pushups on my knuckles, makiwara training[21], hand conditioning, and so on. It's beyond the scope of this book to teach someone how to do that properly when there are simpler, easier methods available such as palm heels and hammer fists.

Another reason for striking with the fist is that it's instinctive, when mad, to ball your hands into that formation and get ready to do battle.

The fist should be thrown in as straight a line as possible (the shortest distance between two points is a straight line), and can be rotated as it's thrown. It must be squeezed as tight as humanly possible to avoid damage and the thumb must never be placed inside. It always provides support to the index and middle fingers and thus it supports the fingers of the two knuckles you should be hitting with.

There are some who argue that you should hit with the bottom three knuckles, but this is completely false. Advocates of this theory come from boxing where the proponent's hands are wrapped and strapped and then slipped into gloves for combat, or from Wing Chun who aren't particularly noted for being power punchers. I relied on my fists to earn a living and was averaging five fights a night at one point. If I'd damaged my hands I'd have been out of work, so, believe me when I say, the two big knuckles

---

[21] A device used by old style karate students to develop power in punches and condition their hands for striking.

are the only two worth hitting with if the fight is bare knuckles. This should be common sense, but if you're still not convinced go pull up a hand x-ray on the web and look at the size of the bones behind the big two knuckles vs the smaller ones.

Hammer Fist

So called because it's the same motion you'd use to hammer something. It's formed by making a fist and striking with the fleshy part of the hand between the base of the little finger and the wrist. It's another good simple strike like the palm heel that lends itself to hitting hard with little or no hand damage. The strike is a very versatile one as it can be done in a vertical manner, downward (like a small hatchet) against targets such as a collarbone, horizontally from behind the shoulder (like a baseball bat) onto the base of the jaw, backward on a horizontal plane (the reverse of the former, think tennis backhand), onto the same targets, and backward into the groin of someone attempting to grab you from behind.

Elbows

The elbow is a powerful strike that's incredibly versatile. It can be swung forward and backward horizontally, downward and backward on a vertical plane and upward and downward at a forty-five-degree angle. It can be used to block strikes and apply locks. The portion of the arm we use is the last two inches of the ulna right where it gets to the elbow joint. The elbow is a technique I've never failed to get a knockout with. It's also particularly effective as a pre-emptive strike.

I've heard some so-called experts claim it can't be used in a fight which means they haven't watched very much Muy Thai or studied boxing at all. Most boxers who get cut during fights are hit by elbows that are snuck in under the guise of being hook punches and Muy Thai fighters never have a problem using elbows.

Fingers And Thumbs

The fingers and thumbs can be used into the eyes and various cavity pressure points when grappling. They can also be used for grabbing and twisting things such as hair, testicles, and fingers.

Slap

When I was seventeen years old, I discovered I could knock people out by slapping them hard and fast across the side of the jaw. It was much more effective in security work because it didn't break the skin or bone like a punch often would and there was no risk of injuring my hands. I picked up the technique by watching an old bouncer who went by the name of "Cyclone" who used to drop everyone with it.

Recently, it's come to everyone's attention after articles began appearing in martial arts magazines labeling it the "power slap." There are several methods of delivery, but the most effective is undoubtedly the version whereby you drop the palm into the target a split second before the whole hand would have made contact. That multiplies the effect of the technique fivefold and provides a kinetic energy dump that has to be felt to be believed.

Other versions include; opening the hand as wide as possible which is designed to cover so many of the facial nerves at once that the pain overwhelms the nervous system and causes you to blackout, and cupping the hand, which is supposed to utilize a cushion of air to do damage. The latter doesn't bear up under any sort of scrutiny, but does provide an effective means of slapping the ear and cupping it which will ram air down the ear canal and rupture the external and internal ear drums.

Eye Strikes

One of the beauties of an eye strike is that it doesn't matter who your opponent is, or how big they might be, there isn't an exercise in the world that can toughen up your eyes. A single grain of sand can be excruciating and bring a grown man to his knees. You don't have to get fancy with it either, nor do you need to toughen up your fingers like you see some martial art styles advocate.

Simply extend and relax your fingers and jab them towards the eyes of the opponent. You have a lot of chances to land this as only one of four fingers has to make it into one of two eyes. Your reach is longer than any other tool in your box which can make the difference between being able to hit the enemy or not.

Another advantage to the eye strike is that I only have to catch one eye to cause both eyes to water up which can blur their vision. Fighting with impaired vision is a nightmare. Also, consider that one of the techniques that regularly stops both MMA matches and MMA fighters in their tracks, is an accidental strike to the eye.

Knees

Kelly McCann, one of the top Combatives instructors in the world, who runs the renowned "Crucible," calls knee strikes *"violent walking."* If you've ever walked up stairs two at a time, hiked up bleachers or waded into the ocean stepping over waves, you've practiced knee strikes. They can be done into the groin, the body, or the face of an attacker. You generate far more power if you grab hold of the person you're going to knee and reef the knee into him that way. By not being able to travel backwards he can't absorb any of the shock. Don't stop at one either. You can either alternate them or continue pumping the same knee in again and again.

Stomps

Stomping on someone may sound brutal at first, but picture a scenario where a slight female victim has 'surprised' her attacker and managed to knock him to the ground, but has not taken him out of the fight. He's about to get up and the element of surprise is now gone. In that situation she's justified in stomping on his ankle to break it and incapacitate him so he can't chase her.

It can also be used in a multiple fight situation. Imagine five armed attackers going after someone. Again, if our 'victim' is lucky enough to get one down, he needs to ensure he's going to stay down, otherwise he runs the risk of the attacker getting back up and re-entering the fray. Of course, this second time around our attacker is potentially going to be even more angry and more intent on wreaking havoc due to his being humiliated.

Stomps can also be used on someone's instep whether they're in front of you or grabbing you from behind. The bones in the top of the foot are not that strong, especially under the heel of a stout shoe. You don't even have to look. By slamming the side of your foot on the attacker's shin and simply ramming your foot downwards using the shinbone as a guide, you'll automatically hit the top of his foot. The pain this creates will cause a distraction and usually loosens up the grip of whatever hold you've been placed in.

Groin Kicks

For a lot of people the groin kick is the magic technique. They assume, wrongly as it turns out, that all you have to do is kick someone between the legs with one of these and the fight is all but won. In reality it's not that effective. If you catch someone unawares with a 'kick in the balls', it will work like a charm. If you catch someone who is sexually aroused you'll get the same results. Unfortunately, in a fight, your aggressor will not be unprepared, or (one hopes), sexually aroused and instead will be charged with adrenalin. Your kick therefore will probably not be the *coup de grace* you expected it to be. Now, some people will drop when you

249

kick them there, but don't assume, never assume, that it will work as advertised.

The other thing that bears mentioning, is that it is an extremely hard target to hit, because everyone is aware of its vulnerability and tend to protect it more so than any other target, other than, perhaps, the eyes.

To deliver the kick you must not retract it first as in the popular football kick. Instead you fling it from where it is and point the toe like a ballerina. The goal is to land the top of the foot, right where it joins the ankle, into the groin and hitting the testes from underneath, then retracting the foot twice as fast as you threw it which causes a whipping effect and makes catching the foot difficult.

Side Stamp Kick

This technique is well known to aficionados of WWII Combatives and involves leaning backwards at an angle, drawing your knee to your chest and stomping the opponent's lead leg just above the knee. To help you visualize the technique imagine you're camping and you want to break a branch for the fire. You'd put it on a tree trunk at a forty-five-degree angle and stamp on the center of it in the manner I described above. Just substitute the enemy's leg for the branch and you have the right idea. The stamping motion is no different than what you'd use if you were attempting to crush a can underfoot.

Incidentally, a Bulgarian policeman did his thesis on martial arts, and in particular, on the efficacy of the various strikes taking into account the time it takes to teach someone how to do it versus the result if it lands effectively. His study determined that this technique was number one out of every strike in all the martial arts.

31

TARGETS

There are weak spots on the human body that you must target if you want to get the most bang for your buck. Some people will not appear to be effected (gun shots do not effect some people either!!), but you still stand a better chance of injuring someone hitting them in a naturally weak area than you do hitting them in a strong one. Once again, too many theoreticians allege that there are pressure points that can be struck with little more than a poke and it will drop the biggest attacker in his tracks. Would that it were so. Sadly, as I mentioned earlier, some people have been shot and stabbed multiple times and kept coming. There are absolutely no guarantees. The problem with pressure points is (and even the experts will agree), not everyone is susceptible to them, some are in different locations on different people (though in the same vicinity), and under the influence of a cocktail of drugs and alcohol, they may not have any effect on the person being struck at all.

Stick with the basic ones, that also happen to be fairly large and accessible, and you'll stand the best chance of creating the maximum damage.

Primary Targets

Primary targets are so named because they're the ones that will have cause the most damage to someone you're fighting. In a serious situation therefore these are the first ones you should be going for. Don't forget, due to the fact that they are so vital, the human organism strives to protect them at all costs. Sometimes it's easier to hit a tertiary or secondary target instead to wear the person down before gaining access to a primary slot.

Eyes

Very effective when hit. When cats fight dogs they don't try for the groin or the knee, they go for the eyes. Even a glancing blow can cause intense pain and/or watering of the eyes which makes it difficult for the attacker to see. They can be flicked, gouged, pushed, or have foreign substances such as sand or drinks flung into them. If the eye strike doesn't land it will be because the person you were targeting pulled their head out of the way or blinked reflexively which can, in itself, set them up for a different follow up shot.

Throat

If you can shut down the windpipe you shut down oxygen to the system. I'm going to repeat myself and mention the results are what you get in an ideal world when the strike makes good solid contact and actually works like it says on the tin. In reality, it's a hard target to access with a strike because the person, if he knows anything about fighting, will have his chin tucked in. As a pre-emptive strike, however, it comes into its own and as a grab while grappling it's also effective.

Groin

Only good if the attacker is sexually aroused or not in fight mode, but if you do land a solid shot, and he's not a Viking berserker, it will definitely diminish his ability. I can tell you from personal experience it makes you feel nauseous and weakens you somewhat if it doesn't drop you. The groin can be slapped, kicked, punched, yanked, crushed, or any combination of the above.

Head

It's what you must hit to get knock outs. One way of knocking someone out is caused by what we call *"brain splash."* The brain is surrounded by fluids in the cranium, and if we hit the skull fast and hard enough, we cause the brain to slosh round inside the head and bounce off the inside of the cranial cavity which gives us our knockout. It's easier to cause more movement by hitting lower down on the head than up high so this is where you should be focusing your shots.

There are targets on the head such as the point of the chin or the jaw. The jaw is on a hinge point and there are nerves that run along it and there's also a nerve ganglion inside the skull called the *Medulla Oblongata* which can be overloaded by shock or pain. Despite all of those, the best chance for someone not interested in devoting years to studying various methods of delivery, is just to bang away as fast and as hard as possible on the skull and try for brain splash. If you're accuracy is not all there, use the palm heel strikes as this will prevent the hands from being damaged hitting the head (which can resemble a bowling ball in some cases).

Secondary Targets

Ears

The ears can be slapped with either one hand at a time or both hands at once. The theory behind the strike is to force jets of air down the ear canals which will cause the membrane called the ear drums to rupture. The sensation is incredibly painful and affects the balance of the person being hit. One of my top black belts was testing for his second dan – an intense grading which consists of thirty 3 minute rounds of fighting with a fresh black belt every single round – and he was caught with one of these which ruptured his ear. His balance was very obviously affected and it was testimony to his internal fortitude that he was able to continue.

Collar Bone

The collar bone or clavicle is reportedly the easiest bone in the body to break. If it breaks, it tends to render that side of the body completely inoperable. It can be hit with either a hammer fist or the blade hand

Solar Plexus

The solar plexus is one of the best places to hit someone if you can pull it off. There's a slight delayed reaction normally, but if you do catch someone properly, it renders them completely out of action. They'll be curled up in a fetal position, sucking wind, and praying for salvation. The problem is you have to have a good solid shot and you have to be accurate enough to hit it. Knees work well and so do uppercut punches with a closed fist. To find it, tap along the sternum from the center of the chest downwards towards the belly. When the bone of the sternum can no longer be felt you'll possibly feel a small notch of bone seemingly on its own. That's the xyphoid process and the solar plexus is just below it. Go any lower than that and you'll run the risk of hitting the abdominal wall, and if your opponent has any sort of sports background, his abs will probably be strong enough to withstand your shots there.

A tip from my old days on the door is that the solar plexus is almost always just behind the third shirt button on the average dress shirt.

Kidneys

The kidneys can be located on each side of the lower back muscles and about two inches above the average person's belt line. Hitting them hard, typically from behind with a punch or a bladed hand can cause shock, intense pain and unconsciousness

Thigh

Most people remember this one from school and generally not with fond memories. On the outside of the thigh is a nerve running down the outside of the femur. If hit hard enough it can cause loss of motor skills with the leg and intense pain. The beauty of this technique is, that even if the person is numbed up due to drug or alcohol consumption, while they may not feel any pain, their leg will not support them. The best weapon to use on this target is a knee driven in to it.

Knees

If you've been around the myths of martial arts long enough you've heard the one about it only taking forty-five pounds of pressure to break someone's leg at the knee. Those tests are done on cadavers that don't have muscle tone, aren't surging with adrenalin and aren't bouncing around trying to hit you. On a live human being, who's amped up and intent on hurting you, it's a lot harder to hit and do damage than the theorists would have us believe. If you're standing, the strike must be delivered just above the knee.

Instep

The small bones of the foot are not that hard to damage with the heel of a stout shoe. While not a debilitating shot compared to knocking someone out, it is still painful enough to cause someone to let you go who's attempted any sort of grab; and that can be a grab from behind, the front, or the side. An added freebie is to rake the side of the shoe down the shin bone en route to the top of the foot which can often assist you in locating the target in the dark.

Incidental Targets

Incidentals include things such as pulling hair, breaking fingers, and biting, etc.

Hair

Hair can be an incredibly effective handle used to control people and drag them from one location to another. The key is not just to pull, but to pull against the direction of growth. For example, if I'm in front of someone and I want to pull them towards me to knee them in the face I must grab the hair on the back of the head. Conversely, if I'm behind my subject trying to separate them from someone else, for example, I would reach over and grab the hair on the front of their head and yank backwards.

Fingers

The fingers can be snapped backwards to the point where they break. That alone may not be enough to cause someone sufficient pain to affect a release. What you must do next to ensure that you gain a release is to rotate the finger around in its joint as if trying to pry lose a drumstick from the body of a turkey. It's this rotation that causes sufficient damage to the nerve endings, etc., to put the person in shock.

Biting

Biting is another technique that can be incredibly effective in gaining a release. Again, a lot of so called experts, usually people who've never bitten anyone for real, denigrate the technique saying it doesn't cause enough pain to stop someone. To begin with, I don't have to stop someone with it, but I may need it to cause them to let me go. My second point is, that like the finger break, it's not a simple matter of snapping the finger and leaving it. To bite properly, you must lock the incisors together and then drop the entire body weight as you affect a tearing motion with the head. Visualize someone trying to eat a raw steak and tear a piece loose, or a tiger or lion using their bodyweight to drag down a gazelle or other four-legged prey.

(Caveat: I wish someone had told me that you had to floss afterwards. It's very disconcerting the first time it happens.)

Fish Hooking

Fishhooks are a technique that have been round for hundreds of years in the fight game but have come to the forefront in recent years due to being outlawed in MMA competitions. The technique is done by catching the corner of the mouth with the finger and pulling while being careful not to put the finger so far in the mouth the bad guy bites it off. It's incredibly painful and again, can be used as pain compliance or to affect a release, but not as a fight stopper.

Nostril Tear

Nostril rip is an old unarmed combat technique, and once again, while not a fight stopper, is good enough to get someone to let you go or rethink their game plan. If someone is running in to tackle you for example, you stick out your two fingers as if a reverse of Churchill's V for victory and ram them into the nostril cavity and rip and tear. On the average person, not some coked up monster, the pain is intense enough for them not to want to play anymore.

Joint Locks

There are a slew of techniques that fit under this category and yet most of them are useless in the field of self-protection. The reason is that originally they were joint breaking techniques and not joint locking. Why would anyone, on a battlefield, use two arms to tie up one arm of an opponent and hold him compliant by use of pain?

They were practiced by taking the joint to the point where damage would be done and while doing this it was discovered that they could be used to gain compliance from someone due to the pain and threat of damage to the joint.

They're very common in police defensive tactics programs used as pain compliance to make an unwilling subject move from one location to another or to control someone until a more effective restraint (typically hand cuffs) can be applied. For a civilian, however, we run into several problems. Let's say you're accosted at an ATM somewhere and you grab the guy in some sort of an arm lock...what next? Are you going to then administer a lecture on why what he was doing was wrong and make him promise to behave if you let him go? Are you going to stay there and hold him until someone else arrives who can give you a hand transporting the bad guy to the authorities? Perhaps you're going to take the technique through to its logical conclusion and break the joint. Here's the problem with the latter. Let's assume the scenario is in a bar fight. Someone gets irritated at your looking at their girl and comes over and shoves you in the chest. You grab him in an arm bar again and take it through to its logical conclusion and break his arm. Now, you've just crippled/maimed or seriously injured someone who was in a pushing contest with you. In the eyes of the law that is excessive force, because, as you'll remember in the "Use of Force Continuum", you can only use enough force to stop someone from hurting you and it must be acceptable under the "reasonable man" doctrine. No reasonable man is going to agree with you in a court of law after you've broken someone's arm for grabbing your shirt.

What about the versions of these we see in MMA competition that take place on the ground? Same problem. While it looks cool on TV to make the bad guy tap out here's the bad news. In the street most people, unless they've had training, don't know what tapping out is. So what are you going to do? Hold him on the ground again and hope he cries *"Uncle"*? Administer a lecture again and make him promise to behave after you let him up? Or, break his arm and face the same legal woes mentioned earlier?

Bottom line is they have a limited application for security guards and police officers. In their line of work, when it might be necessary to temporarily restrain someone until hand cuffs can be applied, and that's about the extent of it.

If you're in a life and death struggle however, and deadly force is justified, then by all means, use them to break the joint which will hopefully render the assailant unable to continue his attack.

32

WEAPONS

We can split weapons into two main camps…those designed specifically for the purpose such as firearms and knives etc., and improvised weapons such as grabbing a rock or an ashtray and using it during a fight.

Those weapons, whether improvised or specific, can be divided into several sub-categories such as impact weapons, bladed weapons, and projectile weapons. We can further split those into two more sub-categories and they are "Effective" and "Ineffective."

The first rule of weapons though is never carry or buy one if you're not prepared to use it. Too many people buy weapons as deterrents only and are killed by the bad guys they point them at when the bad guys call their bluff. There are many cases of weapons being produced as a deterrent that have worked, but the consequences are so dire if the bluff is called, that it's just not worth the risk. Keep in mind also that 68% of all police officers who are shot in the line of duty are shot with their own weapons. So, not only do you have to be willing to use your weapon, you'd better be sufficiently well trained with it that the bad guy can't wrest if from you and use it against you.

The next thing to be aware of is that they are not a magic wand when it comes to fighting. To begin with, they must be in your hand to use them, and as has been previously mentioned, most professional criminals will ambush you so you may have no chance to fumble about and get your weapon. For far too many people they are a panacea when it comes to self-defense. They think if they buy the weapon and put it in their purse or bedside drawer everything will be fine.

Another point to consider is, even if it's in your hand, if you haven't practiced with the weapon under stress you probably won't be able to operate it under stress either. Almost every cop in the world has sprayed himself with his tear gas/OC the first time he's pulled it on the job.

Let's begin then with projectile weapons that are specifically designed for the purpose. Before we do let me just say that I'm not going into too much detail here. There are a plethora of books on the subject of shooting that will go into chapter long discussions over which caliber is best for stopping someone in their tracks, and cover, far better than I could, all the other minutia that are firearms.

Firearms

Firearms can be broken down into several categories. They are; handguns which include pistols and revolvers, and long guns which include rifles and shotguns. Each of those categories can be further broken down. In handguns we have revolvers and semi-automatics. The former typically hold 5-6 shots in a drum that revolves every time you pull the trigger. Most people will have seen these if they've watched a cowboy movie. The latter will have eight to fifteen rounds in a magazine that fits inside the handle. Their forte, and the reason all the pros use them, is that they hold more rounds than a revolver and they can be reloaded faster. Both revolvers and automatics come in various calibers ranging from .22 all the way to .50. Most experts agree that you will need a lot of luck on your side to stop someone with anything smaller than a .380.

There is a myth in the shooting world that revolvers are somehow foolproof and automatics can go wrong. The truth is that any weapon, if it's neglected and not well maintained, can malfunction.

Long Guns

In the long gun category, we have bolt action rifles, semi-automatic and automatic rifles, and shotguns. Just as is the case with handguns they come in various calibers from the BB gun all the way to the .50 caliber sniper's rifle by Barrett. A bolt action rifle is typically used by hunters as time between shots is generally slower than with a semi-automatic. That's because, between every shot, you must grab a lever and pull it back which extracts the empty shell after you've just fired a round, and slide it back forward to push the next round inside. Sometimes you even have to load another round yourself as the rifle won't come with a magazine. A semi-automatic on the other hand will fire one round every time you pull the trigger and the rifle itself will do the extraction and loading of the rounds. The military version of these will usually fire full auto, which means when you depress the trigger and hold it, the gun will empty itself in less than two seconds.

Shotguns

A shotgun may be a two-barreled hunting weapon or a pump action (or auto loader) that will hold two shells – in the case of the former – or up to eight shells in the case of the latter. The size of shotgun ammunition is referred to as the "gauge". The gauge would equate to the "caliber" in another type of firearm. The range of the most commonly used gauges goes from a .410 (lady's shotgun) to a 12 gauge. There are other gauges outside of that range which are not commonly used.

There are some common myths when it comes to shotguns. The first is that you don't have to aim them – that if you point them in the general direction and pull the trigger everything will be taken care of. Not so. While they will spread at greater distances, up close (as in a home defense scenario) the pellets that make up the cartridge tend to stay close together.

The other big myth is that a shot gun is the ultimate home defense weapon. Again, not in my humble opinion. To begin with, you must use two hands to hold it, so keeping someone at bay and trying to use a cell phone or cordless to call the cops becomes a delicate juggling act. Next, walking through your house with one, in a manner that doesn't present the barrel for the bad guy, hiding behind a corner, to grab, is difficult unless you're specifically trained in the sort of maneuvers a SWAT team will use to clear a house.

Third problem with them is they kick like a mule and even some big guys will flinch when shooting them. One of my girlfriends was convinced that she should be left with the shotgun when I was out of town once. I took her down the back yard and had her fire one round through it which was enough to convince her she wanted the pistol instead.

Handguns

Handguns are probably the most popular for self-protection due to their being able to be concealed so easily. The trade-off for that concealability factor is they lack power and accuracy compared to their longer brethren. Also, if you miss you may hit an innocent, there are many places where you are not allowed to take them, and you must have them in your hand at the time of the attack. The Tueller drill proves that if someone has a knife in their hand and you have a gun holstered and they are 21 feet away, they'll get to you before you can pull the gun and engage. That drill, sometimes called the twenty-one-foot rule, came about as a result of a law enforcement officer trying to figure out just how far away someone had to be before he could safely draw his weapon and use it. The twenty-one feet it took surprised a lot of people.

Lastly, you must practice combat hand gunning. Shooting paper targets that don't shoot back at a well-lit range has very little bearing on what a real gun fight will be like. The best way to practice, after you've learned the mechanics of shooting on a range, is to buy some air soft guns, (guns that shoot plastic pellets), and construct some scenarios of your own then go get trained at a reputable shooting school.

With regards to which one to choose, the easiest way is to go to the local range and rent several different models and see which one you're comfortable firing, which one fits your hand, and most important, which one you shoot best with. It's not as obvious as it would seem because sometimes, just because the gun fits your hand well, doesn't automatically mean you will shoot well with it. Don't let well-meaning friends try and talk you into a particular model and don't be swayed by slick looking ads. You're the one who should be comfortable both toting the weapon and firing it.

Sprays And Gasses

Sprays come in several varieties. There is the older tear gas which was a chemical irritant and the newer OC (or pepper spray) so called because it is made up of oleoresin capsicum (essentially, the stuff that makes peppers hot) which does a much better job of stopping someone. Amongst these types are versions that spray a fine mist, a stream, or foam and some that even come with a dye that will stain the bad guy.

The problems are the same as with guns. It works only if you have it in your hand when it's needed. You must practice under stress, (and very few do), and you must ensure that it's not very windy and you're pointing it the right direction. You can't use it in a car as it will, in all likelihood, blow back on you, and it doesn't work on some people. There's also the very real risk, under stress, that you'll end up spraying yourself which is something rookie cops are fairly notorious for.

By the way, change your canister every year as it has a shelf life.

After projectile weapons come bladed weapons which is any weapon with an edge to it. Common bladed weapons include knives, swords, and hatchets.

Knives

Knives can be generally broken down into three categories and they are fixed blades, folding knives and utility knives (such as found in a kitchen). Fixed blades and folders are most typically used for combat purposes. A bayonet issued to a soldier for combat is considered a fixed blade knife. Tactical folders such as those made by Benchmade™ and Cold Steel™ are more concealable versions of their fixed bladed cousins and they do that by being hinged where the blade meets the handle. The problems with knives for self-defense are the following...

Juries frown on them. They have a stigma attached that they are used by bad guys such as the Indians in all the westerns, the terrorists on 9/11 and the maniacs in the middle east who have such a fondness for beheading their enemies on live T.V.

A lot of people don't see them so their deterrent effect is negligible.

Just because you've stabbed someone repeatedly doesn't mean you've stopped him, especially if he's not aware you're stabbing him. (Most people won't be aware as it feels like being punched).

There are other problems as well. Most of the ones allegedly designed for self-protection come with macho war like names. As my mate Hock Hockheim is fond of pointing out, if you go into court for using a "ninja death fang jihad 2000", you're going to be slaughtered by the prosecuting attorney and painted as some sort of a blood thirsty lunatic. In one case that I'm aware of, told to me by Hock, a guy was charged with murder initially by the DA's office simply because the knife he accidentally stuck his mate with was a K-Bar, a knife that used to be issued to the US Marines and Navy Special Warfare (SEALs). The DA's attitude was that he must have been planning to kill someone when he bought such a knife. If he'd used a simple fishing knife instead he would have been exonerated.

Finally, there's no real control with a knife. Either you stab someone and run the risk of killing them or you don't. Unlike something like a club, where one has some level of control over how hard they hit someone, you can't cut or stab someone softly (yes, I'm very aware that you can use the pommel of the knife to hit someone, and in some instances that's the first thing you SHOULD hit them with, but then why not just use your hammerfist?)

After projectile weapons and bladed weapons come impact weapons which is any weapon designed to do damage through the use of blunt force trauma. The most common of these is undoubtedly the baton or "billy club" as twirled by police officers the world over.

Batons

Prior to the advent of the extendable baton, carrying a stick or club just wasn't practical for anyone except perhaps a cop on the beat, due to their length and difficulty in concealing. After ASPs™ (ASP™ is a manufacturer of equipment primarily for law enforcement, including extendable batons) came on the market, it became slightly more viable, However, the light weight of the extendable batons caused them to lose favor fairly rapidly amongst police officers who were restricted to what targets (on the body) they could hit.

Once again the problems are, do you have it at hand when you need it and have you been trained with it both in combat and under stress? If not, there's a very good chance the bad guy will take it from you and use it on you.

There are viable models out there that have the heft and structural integrity to do damage and one such company that used to produce those is Winchester. It's my understanding they're no longer in production, but have been replaced by the "Peacekeeper Baton." Keep in mind, that unlike the police, who are severely limited as to what targets they can hit, you can hit anywhere on the body should the situation warrant it.

Finally, there are weapons that don't really fit into any of the above categories. They are:

Stun Guns

Stun guns, despite what you see in Hollywood, are pretty much a joke. I've had students in seminars hold them on one another during stress inoculation drills with the instruction they weren't to be turned off until the recipient removed his knife from his pocket etc. Stories of memory loss, nerve damage and paralysis etc., are nothing but marketing hype. The big problem, unless you're using a Taser, is that you have to get into bad breath range with someone who's involuntary flinch, when hit, will more than likely either hit you or knock your stun gun flying.

Tasers can be an effective alternative providing once again, it's in your hand, you've been trained to use it under combat conditions and there's only one attacker. You also need to check your local jurisdiction as some places have restricted them to sworn law enforcement officers only.

Kubotans

This is the name given to the small six-inch-long piece of plastic or tubular steel that you see attached to people's key rings. Basically they're junk unless you're a law enforcement officer trying to use a pain compliance wrist lock on a subject. If you try that then you face the same problem we talked about with pain compliance, i.e. are you going to hold someone until help comes? A cop can because he's got back up. Do you?

As for striking with it, if you can't knock someone out with your hand, the addition of something as light as the kubotan won't help. Using them into pressure points can be marginally effective but so can your finger tip. The last option, flailing with the keys like you see advertised on some products, is absolute stupidity and the manufacturers should be ashamed of themselves using such misleading, and potentially dangerous, advertising.

Gadgets

This includes all the so called self-defense weapons that naïve people buy believing once again they have the magic wand when it comes to self-defense. These include keys in the fist, alarms that debilitate by virtue of being so loud, plastic knuckle dusters, kubotans with spikes sticking out et al. The essential point is they are not worth the money and will not stop a determined amped up aggressor.

It works like this...if you can't knock someone out with your own unaided fist, then sticking a piece of plastic in it, no matter what its configuration, isn't going to help you one whit. The only thing that would is picking up something sufficiently heavy to do damage such as half a house brick or a hammer. Put that in someone's hand, even a child or frail octogenarian, and they'll wreak havoc with it. In other words, it's the weight of the weapon doing the damage and not the configuration.

33

IMPROVISED WEAPONS

There is a history, in both unarmed combat and escape and evasion courses, of studying things that can be used as improvised weapons. The reason for learning them is obvious as your primary weapons system is defunct or, as in the case of being captured, taken from you, you're expected to fight back with whatever comes to hand.

Almost anything can be used as a weapon, including such things as a can of vegetables, a beer glass, an ashtray, or a pool cue. The problem is that some are better than others while others will only work if you are already capable of knocking someone out with your bare hand anyway.

I'll go over them in this section so as to make you aware of some of the ones you might not have originally thought of and discuss their pros and cons. Keep in mind, to do damage a weapon must (normally) have sufficient heft, i.e. it must be heavy enough to do damage. Most of the gimmicky self-defense tools on the market miss that point. Take for example the old staple of a bunch of keys held between the fingers and raked across the face. It's supposed to cause so much pain that your attacker will break down screaming and run from you. Would that it were so. Remember that there are criminals out there on cocktails of drugs and alcohol that have kept coming after being shot multiple times, having night sticks broken over their heads, being Tazed, being gassed, and being punched and kicked by piles of people. Admittedly you might gain an element of surprise on some inexperienced juvenile and buy yourself time to hit him with a decent shot or scare him off because you're prepared to fight, but one should never train with the easy end of the spectrum in mind. Train as if you have to deal with the Terminator and you'll prepare yourself for every eventuality. The keys, on such an individual, will do nothing but make him mad…it's certainly not going to stop someone in their tracks and that should be the goal of any weapon improvised or not.

Before we cover such weapons, keep in mind that there are viable alternatives to weapons heavy enough to do damage and those would be liquids of various types covered in this section.

Keys

Forget it. They're too light to do damage other than superficially scratching your attacker which means all you're going to do is make him mad. It doesn't matter if you have them on your Gucci keychain and use them as a flail or stuck between your fingers and used to rake the attackers face. The only exception to this might be if you got lucky enough to drive one of them into his eye(s) which begs the question why not just use your fingers?

The best application for keys is going to be using them to drive away, throwing them away from your vehicle to buy yourself time to get your kid(s) out of the car in the event of a car-jacking, or locking your doors whenever you leave or arrive anywhere.

Watch

The advice here was to slip a heavy diver's watch down over the first three fingers of the hand, (which is the same diameter as your wrist), and then punch with it as an improvised knuckle duster. This is another dubious use of a watch. If granny can't knock the bad guy out with her punch, slipping a watch over her knuckles isn't going to make any difference…except she'll probably hurt her hand punching with it if she lands against anything halfway solid.

268

Pen

Anyone who's seen the original Bourne movie with Matt Damon no doubt remembers the scene in the Paris apartment where he sticks his assailant in the fist with his pen. All the un-initiated audience members oohed and aahed at the hero's deft use of tools to hand. He'd have been better off picking up the desk. What happens next in the film is indicative of what would happen in real life…the bad guy looked at it and then pulled it out of himself and kept on fighting.

What about sticking it in his neck or eyeball? Again, great in theory but remember, it's hard enough to hit someone in the head with your fist, let alone trying to get something as small as the nib of a pen in something as small as the eye. You're also assuming you'll have no qualms about actually ramming a ball point pen into someone's eyeball. Most people won't have the callous disregard for a fellow human's eyesight to be able to pull off such a stunt. I've even met people who've gone green at the gills at the very thought of such a move.

Now, if you are capable of pulling that move off by all means grab hold of a tactical pen. You'll see the one I recommend under the resource page at H2BG.com

Comb

There are two versions of this technique, one involves using a rat tail comb and sticking it in the attacker's eye and the other involves using the teeth and raking them across the face to slice the person open. Regarding the eye strike, see above under pens, and with regards to the scraping/slicing, it will be nothing but a minor nuisance to someone determined to do you harm.

Compact

This is another stand by in most self-defense books which utilize the contents of a woman's purse to show how everything can be used as a weapon. Again, if you don't have the force in your palm heel to do damage to someone, the addition of the compact isn't going to make any difference at all.

Shoes & Belts

Sorry, once again these fall into the above categories as "nigh on useless." A belt with a really heavy buckle whipped violently fast can be used to keep someone with a knife at bay providing you: a) have a belt with a heavy enough buckle; b) can whip it violently fast enough; and, c) know how to bring it back on target after he ducks the first swipe. Most people don't. You also have to have the time to get it into play and it better not be needed to keep your trousers up.

As for shoes, I've seen books that advocate slipping your high heels on your fists and jabbing away. Once again we're back to "if you don't have the force to do it with your empty hand the shoe isn't going to help at all."

Credit Cards

Shades of the CIA super assassin. Two versions exist of this one; a) sand one edge down till you can cut with it; or b) break it in two so you have a jagged edge. The former shows pre-meditation which will get you in trouble with the law and the latter assumes you have time to break your card in half (ever tried that by the way?). Even if you pulled off either, all you've got is something that's going to give a wound a tad worse than a paper cut.

(A far better use of your credit card is to buy multiple copies of this book and give them to your friends and family – shameless plug.)

Heavy Hitters

This generic category is going to cover anything that is heavy enough that if you hit someone with it, or put it in your hand and hit someone with it, that it will do damage regardless of whether the swinger is a 300 pounder or your grandmother. There's too many to list them all, but think of things like rocks, half bricks, lumps of wood, baseball bats, golf clubs, fire extinguishers, pool cues, bar stools, hammers, monkey wrenches, telephones (rotary dials not cell phones), irons, cans of vegetables, full bottles, etc.

One of my student's friends was bouncing to pay his way through college in a small town. A guy he'd thrown out earlier turned up at his house at 0400 in the morning with five mates intending to seek revenge. He heard them in time to make it to the front door as they crashed through, and fortunately for him, his girlfriend had been doing some ironing earlier, and he was able to snatch up the iron. He hit the first one in the head and dropped him, did the same with the 2nd and the rest got smart and legged it before he could smooth them out as well. Great example of an improvised weapon that works.

Liquids

Liquids require no weight at all and very little accuracy if they're the right kind. My older brother came out of dubious diner with me one night on the way home from working a door and a vagrant went for him with a broken bottle. My brother threw his scalding hot coffee and its Styrofoam container in his face before kicking him. The guy went down clawing at his eyes screaming like a banshee. Hot liquids are brilliant.

Other viable liquids include OC spray, bleach, acids, and alcohol. I've had liquor in my face on more than one occasion during large scale brawls and extractions and it hurts like hell. A mate of mine got gassed in a bar in Marseille one night and was jumped by two Arabs. He had to spend the fight holding one eye open enough to see what they were doing and attempt to fight them off with the hand not holding the eye. It's premeditated, but another Legionnaire I knew would carry chlorine bleach in a nasal spray bottle. Given sufficient time he could have it to hand and squirt a stream into someone's face/eye area. It worked on two occasions that I'm aware of, but again, it's premeditated as far as the law is concerned, so, if you get caught with something like that, good luck.

A fire extinguisher, something I've seen used 3 times in my career on the door, is a viable option during a large attack, at least as far as causing panic and confusion for a second or two.

Pointy Things

Think of broken bottles, beer glasses, beer jugs, screwdrivers, chisels, knitting needles, chopsticks, fiberglass aerials, forks, garden forks, broken pool cues, scissors, and garden shears, et al.

The first question is going to be can you bring yourself to stab someone? It's not as easy as it looks. Some people pull it off, during the heat of the moment when their survival mechanism kicks in, but most would have a real problem with actually plunging something into someone. That brings us to the second part of the problem. Where can you stab someone so that they are immediately incapacitated? You might pull it off if you rammed something into the brain and wriggled it around but how do you gain access? The heart and the femoral artery are other viable targets I guess but again, does the situation warrant killing someone? And do you have the time to sit around and wait while they bleed out? What if they don't know they've even been stabbed? Trust me, most of the time you don't and it feels like you've been punched. I was in a fight in Australia where I was stabbed three times and even had one of my lungs collapse. I was unaware I'd been knifed and thought I'd just cracked a rib, and went afterwards looking for some of my mates to go and get even. Approx. 2 hours later one of my friends noticed the bleeding and the wound, at which point we went to the hospital where I found out about my lung. Good luck if you'd been counting on some self-defense gadget with a blade to stop me that night.

I'm aware of a film from a corrections facility where one prisoner is stabbed over 200 times. He is seen to be fighting back right up until about the 184th stab. Still want to count on stabbing someone or poking them to get them to stop in their tracks?

Coins

Coins are the only improvised weapon I've had repeated success with. You could lump sand or gravel in to this category as well. I used to keep a handful in my pocket when working the door so that if, and again, this assumes I have enough advanced warning, someone was brandishing a weapon I could throw them in his face before making my move. It automatically causes a flinch reflex, the hands to go up, the eyes to close and the head to turn which buys you the time to get in and hit them hard.

Miscellaneous

This is everything else that doesn't fit into the above category. We run into these in the military a lot. Things like a cake of soap tied into the end of sock and used as a cosh (bludgeon). The use of a motor cycle or military helmet, the folding shovel, or a roll of coins held in a fist as an improvised knuckle duster. Like all the above, they're not bad provided you have the mental wherewithal to actually hit someone with them and the time to prepare them in advance. Finally, and this is the most important piece of all, you must have them to hand when you need them. The sock in the drawer and the soap in the bathroom aren't going to be much good when the home invaders kick the door in at 3 a.m.

If you want to come up with more of these, I suggest a study of any books about the prison system and the stuff that they have come up with out of sheer necessity. I've seen knuckledusters made with torn sheets, vomit, and rats teeth, knives made with cellophane and toothbrushes, and a slew of other criminally genius items of mayhem. Ask any corrections officer to tell you about them as they get courses on what to look for.

RESOURCES

All the resources for the book can be found on the website located at www.H2BG.com under the resource page.

By putting it all on the website I can remove and add the latest information saving you, the reader, from wasting time chasing defunct links and companies that are no longer operational. If I didn't do it this way, 12 months after going to print, half the sites/links would be out of order.

For information on bodyguard training, security driving, tactical shooting, self-defense, government websites related to travel safety et al log in there and you'll find it all.

As mentioned in the "Now That You've Finished" section if, when logging in, you find a link that is out of date, or if there's a training company you know of that's not mentioned, please let me know and we'll take care of it immediately.

HOME SECURITY CHECKLIST

- ☐ Are you aware of the crime statistics of your neighborhood and sub-division?
- ☐ Do you have a neighborhood watch? Are you concerned enough to be part of it?
- ☐ Do you know your neighbors?
- ☐ Do you have motion detector lights around the house?
- ☐ Have you trimmed back any shrubbery that a criminal could hide in?
- ☐ Are your locks good quality?
- ☐ Do you have a peep-hole?
- ☐ Do you have deadbolts and do you use them?
- ☐ Do you have an alarm system?
- ☐ Do you have several panic buttons strategically located in the house?
- ☐ Do you have a dog? Does he live inside? (2 points) Outside (1 point)
- ☐ Do you have a list of emergency numbers programmed in your phone?
- ☐ Do you have the same list in the safe room?
- ☐ Do you have a safe room?
- ☐ Do you have it properly stocked?
- ☐ Do you know where your nearest hospital is?
- ☐ Do you know where the nearest police station is?
- ☐ Have you looked at your house as a criminal would and figured out the weak spots?
- ☐ Do you have a good fence?
- ☐ Are your doors solid?
- ☐ Do you have smoke detectors?
- ☐ Do you have carbon monoxide detectors?
- ☐ Does your home look lived in when you're away on vacation/business?

- ☐ Have you bought timers to turn lights on and off to create the illusion of occupancy?
- ☐ Is your garage as secure as the other entry points?
- ☐ Is the attic alarmed?
- ☐ Do you lock your tools away so criminals don't have access to them?
- ☐ Do you have a good first aid kit?
- ☐ Do you know how to use your first aid kit? Have you checked the contents lately?
- ☐ Have you practiced a fire drill for your house with your kids? (They do it at school)
- ☐ Have you practiced gathering up the family members and getting to the safe room?
- ☐ Do you have a rendezvous point outside in the event of a house fire?
- ☐ Do you have a rendezvous point away from home in the event of a disaster?
- ☐ Do you know where flashlights and candles are in the event of an outage?
- ☐ Do they have fresh batteries?
- ☐ If your house is storied do you have a fire ladder?

FOR THOSE WHO OWN WEAPONS

- ☐ Have you got a practical, functioning, personal weapon near your bed?
- ☐ Do you practice with it on a regular basis?
- ☐ Does it have an additional light or do you have a flashlight to use with it?
- ☐ Do you know your arcs of fire? (most homes are made of sheet rock will not stop rounds)
- ☐ Is it secure from children or visitors to your house?

276

NOW THAT YOU'VE FINISHED

If you liked the book please take ten minutes to log into Amazon, Good Reads, or Smashwords and leave a review. Your opinion really helps someone decide as to whether to buy a copy (and then if enough people do I can afford a proof reader) and it helps me see where I'm going wrong. It's also critical for self-published authors who don't have the backing of a big publishing house and we love you for it.

If you didn't like it please let me know that as well. Also, if you have any suggestions for it such as more information in certain sections, or tips and tricks that I've omitted, let me know that as well. I'll do updated versions at some point and give you full credit for your suggestions.

Also, if you're on Facebook or Twitter, etc., please let your friends know about it and what you thought. It's my hope that you thought the information was valuable enough to get it out to people you care about.

You can reach me on NickHughesDefense.com which is a central location for all the other places on the web that I can be found.

Also check out KravMagaLKN.com which is my Krav Maga club website

Thanks a million.
Peace.

279

281

F

G

H

287

P

R

S

294

295

T

X

Y

Z

ACKNOWLEDGMENTS

Where to begin? Anyone who's ever written a book, or attempted to write one, knows it's never a solitary process. You ask friends for advice on cover designs and possible titles. You get others to read drafts and offer constructive criticism. In other words, it is simply impossible to thank everyone who contributed to this humble effort, by name.

With regards to the effort of the writing itself, thanks to everyone who offered support, criticism and advice.

As far as the material is concerned…despite Marcus Wynne's glowing foreword…I stand firmly on the shoulders of giants. To all the martial artists and warriors throughout history who developed and codified the techniques I've used over the years to save my bacon, I thank you.

They're the men who put their lives on the line so that we know what works and what doesn't; they're the men who are ultimately responsible for this book. Again, they are far too numerous to thank individually and many are no longer with us.

On an individual basis – and if I forget anyone forgive me – I'd have to say thanks to my uncle Jeff who ignited the flame all those years ago when he showed my brother and me what he was learning before shipping out to Vietnam; to my brother Anthony (RIP) who kept me going when I wanted to quit, and who toughened me up by ensuring I didn't get a free ride from his fellow instructors. To my fellow students and instructors who I've met on this long and incredible journey all the way from Doug Tritton and the guys at the school Judo club to the guys I train with today. Thank you all.

Special thanks also to my two models John and Christine who appear in the book and Alexandra and Blake who appear on the cover. Also, a special mention to Heather for the pics and Bud Adams for the editing.

ABOUT THE AUTHOR

ABOUT THE AUTHOR

Nick Hughes started his martial arts training in 1969 with the school **Judo and Jujutsu** club. During this time he also cross trained with members of the school's **boxing and wrestling** teams and undertook **Tae Kwan Do** when a club was formed at the school in 1973. In 1975, looking for something more practical, he began studying **Zen Do Kai** under instructors Jones and Anderson. **Zen Do Kai** was developed by Jones for bodyguards and bouncers. Based 80% on traditional **Goju karate**, Zen Do Kai borrowed heavily from every other fighting system with the principle of *"if it works use it."* Nearly all black belts in the system had hands on experience in the real world which meant teachers in the style knew what worked and what didn't. Nick began his own "practical" training by working on night club doors at the age of sixteen, (being 6'3" and 200lbs at that age certainly helped) and stayed with ZDK until 1984.

Wishing to further his security career as a bodyguard Nick arrived in London where he quickly discovered the agencies that hired such minders only used ex-military special force's personnel. He promptly went to France and joined the **French Foreign Legion's famous 2nd REP** (parachute regiment) where he served as a para-commando recon diver before relocating to Africa as a frogman and signals operator. On his return to mainland France he finished out his contract with the HQ regiment's Military Police Unit as both an officer and unarmed combat defensive tactics trainer.

Arriving in the UK in 89 he began his bodyguard career, and when not working, began studying Judo with the **British Judo Association** and **Kali and Filipino martial arts** with England's top instructor **Mr. Bob Breen**. He also became a member of the teaching staff for **CQB Services** and began writing articles on practical martial arts for Europe's leading martial arts magazine **"Fighting Arts International."**

During his career as a bodyguard he protected various members of the Saudi Arabian Royal Family, numerous rock and roll stars, diplomats, politicians and businessmen and movie stars all over the world including Russia and Germany.

In 1994 he quit the personal security field to pursue other interests and moved to the Unites States of America. He continued his martial arts studies there and obtained a **4th dan in Ju-jutsu**, a **3rd degree in Yoshinkan Aikido**, a **1st degree in Judo** in conjunction with his **6th degree in Combat Karate** and his **5th dan in Zen Do Kai**. He also obtained his certification in **Violent Patient Management, Spontaneous Knife Defense** and **Sexual Harassment and Rape Prevention** under PPCT Management Systems and trains in Filipino arts under both Ray Dianaldo (FCS) and Brian Corey of Balintawak.

He has conducted seminars all over the US most notably with **The Karate College** with **Bill Wallace and Joe Lewis**.

After 9/11 he was approached by people interested in learning self-protection without the need to devote five years to the study of traditional arts. Reverting to his antecedents in unarmed combat training he came up with a civilian friendly version called **F.I.S.T. – Fight Survival Training** – and released a series of DVDs with **Hock Hockheim** of the **Scientific Fighting Congress**.

In 2010 he began teaching **Krav Maga**, the Israeli Defense Force's version of unarmed combat under the auspices of **Ernie Kirk** of Krav Maga PA. Later, he spun this off into **Warriors Krav Maga** which includes more soft skills and legally friendly techniques than the original version does and he continues to teach this in NC at Warriors Krav Maga's headquarters.

In 2010 he was contacted by the producers of **Spike TV's hit series "Deadliest Warrior"** to represent the French Foreign Legion in a showdown against the Nepalese Gurkhas. The episode was season 3s penultimate episode and aired on Spike TV on the 14th of September, 2011.

He has trained local SWAT teams in Dignitary Protection, appeared on radio and TV and continues to write books and articles related to self-protection.

He popped up on **Kelly McCann's** radar who recommended Paladin Press take a look and soon thereafter a series on French Foreign Legion Combatives was released. He is also a certified personal trainer with the **N.A.S.M.** (National Academy of Sport's Medicine.)

Along with Joe Hinkle he has most recently released an app for smartphones to be used in conjunction with this book and is working on an online university for Warriors Krav Maga.™